ReFocus: The Films of Nuri Bilge Ceylan

ReFocus: The International Directors Series

Series Editors: Robert Singer, Gary D. Rhodes and Stefanie Van de Peer

Board of advisors:
Lizelle Bisschoff (Glasgow University)
Stephanie Hemelryck Donald (University of Lincoln)
Anna Misiak (Falmouth University)
Des O'Rawe (Queen's University Belfast)

ReFocus is a series of contemporary methodological and theoretical approaches to the interdisciplinary analyses and interpretations of international film directors, from the celebrated to the ignored, in direct relationship to their respective culture – its myths, values, and historical precepts – and the broader parameters of international film history and theory.

Titles in the series include:
ReFocus: The Films of Susanne Bier Edited by Missy Molloy, Mimi Nielsen and Meryl Shriver-Rice
ReFocus: The Films of Francis Veber Keith Corson
ReFocus: The Films of Xavier Dolan Edited by Andrée Lafontaine
ReFocus: The Films of Pedro Costa: Producing and Consuming Contemporary Art Cinema Nuno Barradas Jorge
ReFocus: The Films of Sohrab Shahid Saless: Exile, Displacement and the Stateless Moving Image Edited by Azadeh Fatehrad
ReFocus: The Films of Pablo Larraín Edited by Laura Hatry
ReFocus: The Films of Michel Gondry Edited by Marcelline Block and Jennifer Kirby
ReFocus: The Films of Rachid Bouchareb Edited by Michael Gott and Leslie Kealhofer-Kemp
ReFocus: The Films of Andrei Tarkovsky Edited by Sergey Toymentsev
ReFocus: The Films of Paul Leni Edited by Erica Tortolani and Martin F. Norden
ReFocus: The Films of Rakhshan Banietemad Edited by Maryam Ghorbankarimi
ReFocus: The Films of Jocelyn Saab: Films, Artworks and Cultural Events for the Arab World Edited by Mathilde Rouxel and Stefanie Van de Peer
ReFocus: The Films of François Ozon Edited by Loïc Bourdeau
ReFocus: The Films of Teuvo Tulio Henry Bacon, Kimmo Laine and Jaakko Seppälä
ReFocus: The Films of João Pedro Rodrigues and João Rui Guerra da Mata Edited by José Duarte and Filipa Rosário
ReFocus: The Films of Lucrecia Martel Edited by Natalia Christofoletti Barrenha, Julia Kratje and Paul Merchant
ReFocus: The Films of Shyam Benegal Edited by Sneha Kar Chaudhuri and Ramit Samaddar
ReFocus: The Films of Denis Villeneuve Edited by Jeri English and Marie Pascal
ReFocus: The Films of Antoinetta Angelidi Edited by Penny Bouska and Sotiris Petridis
ReFocus: The Films of Ken Russell Edited by Matthew Melia
ReFocus: The Films of Kim Ki-young Edited by Chung-kang Kim
ReFocus: The Films of Jane Campion Edited by Alexia L. Bowler and Adele Jones
ReFocus: The Films of Alejandro Jodorowsky Edited by Michael Newell Witte
ReFocus: The Films of Nuri Bilge Ceylan Edited by Gönül Dönmez-Colin

edinburghuniversitypress.com/series/refocint

ReFocus:
The Films of Nuri Bilge Ceylan

Gönül Dönmez-Colin

EDINBURGH
University Press

Edinburgh University Press is one of the leading university presses in the UK. We publish academic books and journals in our selected subject areas across the humanities and social sciences, combining cutting-edge scholarship with high editorial and production values to produce academic works of lasting importance. For more information visit our website: edinburghuniversitypress.com

© editorial matter and organisation Gönül Dönmez-Colin, 2023, 2025
© the chapters their several authors 2023, 2025

Grateful acknowledgement is made to the sources listed in the List of Illustrations for permission to reproduce material previously published elsewhere. Every effort has been made to trace the copyright holders, but if any have been inadvertently overlooked, the publisher will be pleased to make the necessary arrangements at the first opportunity.

Edinburgh University Press Ltd
13 Infirmary Street
Edinburgh EH1 1LT

First published in hardback by Edinburgh University Press 2023

Typeset in 11/13 Ehrhardt MT by
IDSUK (DataConnection) Ltd

A CIP record for this book is available from the British Library

ISBN 978 1 3995 0297 9 (hardback)
ISBN 978 1 3995 0298 (paperback)
ISBN 978 1 3995 0299 3 (webready PDF)
ISBN 978 1 3995 0300 6 (epub)

The right of Gönül Dönmez-Colin to be identified as the editor of this work has been asserted in accordance with the Copyright, Designs and Patents Act 1988, and the Copyright and Related Rights Regulations 2003 (SI No. 2498).

Contents

List of Illustrations vii
Notes on Contributors viii
Acknowledgements xii

Introduction 1
    Gönül Dönmez-Colin

1. **Portrait of the Provincial Artist as an Urban Intellectual** 19
    Gönül Dönmez-Colin
2. **Vanishing Image of History:** *Uzak/Distant* (2002) 37
    Mahmut Mutman
3. **Portraits and Landscape:** *İklimler/Climates* (2006) 51
    Cecília Mello
4. **Aesthetic Silences and the Political Bind:** *Üç Maymun/ Three Monkeys* (2008) 68
    Vuslat D. Katsanis
5. **The Aesthetics of Space and Absence:** *Üç Maymun/ Three Monkeys* (2008) and *Bir Zamanlar Anadolu'da/ Once Upon a Time in Anatolia* (2011) 84
    Adam Ochonicky
6. **Transnational Indistinctions:** *Bir Zamanlar Anadolu'da/ Once Upon a Time in Anatolia* (2011) and *Kış Uykusu/ Winter Sleep* (2014) 103
    Ebru Thwaites Diken
7. **The Politics of Dialogue and Ethics of Engagement:** *Kış Uykusu/Winter Sleep* (2014) 119
    Emre Çağlayan

8. Staying in the Primary Home, Relationships, Desires to Go and Roots: *Kış Uykusu/Winter Sleep* (2014) and *Ahlat Ağacı/The Wild Pear Tree* (2018) 135
Hasan Akbulut

9. Of Fathers, Sons and 'Solitary, Misshapen' Trees: *Ahlat Ağacı/The Wild Pear Tree* (2018) 152
Coşkun Liktor

10. 'Gender Trouble' and the Crises of Masculinities in the Films of Nuri Bilge Ceylan 168
Gönül Dönmez-Colin

11. Auteurism, Recognition and Reception: Ceylan as a Global Auteur 186
Özgür Yaren

Index 203

Illustrations

Figures

1.1	Men Left Out of Dominant Narratives.	22
1.2	The wheel turns, nothing changes.	26
3.1	Bahar's opening close-up.	58
3.2	The ruins of the Temple of Artemis in Sardis.	58
3.3	Bahar's final, disappearing close-up.	65
4.1	İsmail during a prison visit, looking back at his father.	75
4.2	Exterior of the family home.	77
4.3	Hacer during a car ride with Servet.	79
5.1	The bedroom door frame, frosted glass door and mirror (which reflects Hacer sitting by a window) produce depth and portals within the crowded apartment.	91
5.2	The absent Anatolian countryside is both a pre-diegetic and post-diegetic space.	93
5.3	The Anatolian landscape is framed as a ripple of time in which past, present, and future locations are simultaneously visible.	96
8.1	Doctor looking at himself in the mirror.	137
8.2	Aydın with his sorrowful stance at the end of the film.	143
8.3	The well that brings father and son together.	145
10.1	Yusuf harassing women on the tram.	171
10.2	Yusuf in a 'conventional Yeşilçam narrative trope' pose to attract the females.	173

Tables

11.1	Admissions in France & Turkey	199

Notes on Contributors

Hasan Akbulut is a professor in the Department of Radio-Television and Cinema, the Faculty of Communication, Istanbul University teaching film analysis, cinema and cultural identity and spectatorship. He graduated from the Ankara University with an MFA (1999). His PhD thesis was on the representation of women in Turkish melodramas (2003). He is the author of *Nuri Bilge Ceylan Sinemasını Okumak: Anlatı, Zaman, Mekan* (2005); *Kadına Melodram Yakışır: Türk Melodram Sinemasında Kadın İmgesi* (2008); *Yumurta: Ruha Yolculuk* (with S. Büker, 2009); *Yeşilçamdan Yeni Türk Sinemasına Melodramatik İmgelem* (2014) and *Perdeyi Aralamak: Filmlerde Anlatı ve Eleştiri* (2018). He is one of the founding members and the current editor of *sinecine: Journal of Film Studies*. He has published numerous articles on art cinema, Turkish cinema, melodrama and cinema spectatorship and has also done research on cinema-going practices in Turkey. Between 2019 and 2020, he conducted research on transnational film reception as a visiting researcher at the Moving Image Research Centre (MIRC) of the University of East London and the Department of Film Studies at King's College London.

Emre Çağlayan is the author of *Poetics of Slow Cinema: Nostalgia, Absurdism, Boredom* (2018) and Assistant Professor of Film Studies at the American University of Paris. His research explores the intersections between film theory and global art cinema, with a focus on the ways in which moving images shape our lived experience.

Gönül Dönmez-Colin is the author of *Women in the Cinemas of Iran* and *Turkey: As Images and As Image-makers* (2019); *The Routledge Dictionary of Turkish Cinema* (2014); *Turkish Cinema: Identity, Distance and Belonging* (2008);

Cinema of North Africa and the Middle East (ed.) (2007); *Cinemas of the Other: A Personal Journey with Filmmakers from the Middle East and Central Asia* (2006/2012), *Women, Islam and Cinema* (2004) and *Paylaşılan Tutku Sinema* (1998) among other works. She has contributed extensively to numerous anthologies and journals since the 1990s (most recently *The Routledge Handbook on Contemporary Turkey* ed. Joost Jongerden, 2021) as well as other international publications including *Le Monde Diplomatique* (France). She has studied at the American College in Istanbul, the Faculty of English Philology of Istanbul University and Concordia and McGill Universities in Montreal, Canada, where she lectured for two decades in addition to a year in Hong Kong as a visiting lecturer. She has curated panoramas and retrospectives on Turkish, Iranian and Central Asian cinemas, worked as consultant for several major film festivals, participated in international symposiums and served on numerous film festival juries, from Montreal, Mumbai, New Delhi, Thiruvananthapuram, Istanbul, Ankara, Antalya, Karlovy Vary and Vesoul to Almaty. Her research interests are the cinemas of Iran, Turkey and Central Asia, transnational Kurdish cinema, intersectionality and gender. Her work has been translated into several languages.

Coşkun Liktor is an independent scholar and film critic. He holds an MA degree in American Culture and Literature and a PhD in Cinema and Media Research. He worked as Assistant Professor in the Department of American Culture and Literature at Haliç University in Istanbul for several years teaching courses on film studies, popular culture and American literature. He has published academic articles in international peer-reviewed journals analysing films through the lens of psychoanalytic, feminist and poststructuralist theories. His research interests include critical theories, New Cinema of Turkey, Gothic fiction and horror film. He writes regularly for Turkey's prominent film journal *Altyazı* and he is a member of the Film Critics Association (SIYAD), the Turkish branch of FIPRESCI.

Vuslat D. Katsanis is an Associate Professor of Literary Arts and Studies at The Evergreen State College in Olympia, WA and co-founder of the MinEastry of Postcollapse Art and Culture in Portland, OR. As a scholar of comparative literature, film, and visual culture, her work focuses on post-1989 Turkish and global migrant cultural productions and critical theory. She has published essays on the films of Nuri Bilge Ceylan and Fatih Akın and has translated several works of short fiction and poetry between Turkish and English. An additional area of interest is inclusive writing pedagogy. Katsanis is the co-editor of *A Socially Just Classroom: Transdisciplinary Approaches to Teaching Writing Across the Humanities* (2022). She holds a PhD in Comparative Literature from the University of California, Irvine with a certificate of emphasis in Critical Theory and an MA in Visual Studies.

Cecília Mello is a Professor of Film at the Department of Film, Radio and Television, University of São Paulo, Brazil. Her research interests include audio-visual realism, cinema and urban spaces and intermediality with an emphasis on Chinese and British cinemas. She is the author of *The Cinema of Jia Zhangke: Realism and Memory in Chinese Film* (2019), which garnered Honourable Mention – Best Monograph 2020 from the British Association of Film, Television and Screen Studies, and *Realism and the Audiovisual Media* (with Lúcia Nagib, 2009) among other works.

Mahmut Mutman is a senior researcher at the Institute for Advanced Studies at Tampere University, Finland. Previously he worked at the Middle East Technical University, Tufts University, Bilkent University and Istanbul Şehir University. He specialises in the fields of critical theory, postcolonial studies and film and media studies. He is the author of *The Politics of Writing Islam: Voicing Difference* (2014); co-editor of a special issue of *Inscriptions* (1992) titled *Orientalism and Cultural Differences* and a collection on *Orientalism, Hegemony and Cultural Difference* (1996) (in Turkish). He has published several articles on orientalism, nationalism, Islamism, postmodernism and film and media in *Cultural Critique, Postmodern Culture, New Formations, Rethinking Marxism, Anthropological Theory, Radical Philosophy, Third Text, Toplum ve Bilim* and *sinecine: Journal of Film Studies*.

Adam Ochonicky is the author of *The American Midwest in Film and Literature: Nostalgia, Violence, and Regionalism* (2020). His work has appeared in *Mediapolis: A Journal of Cities and Culture, Adaptation, Horror Studies, Screening the Past, Nineteenth-Century Literature, Quarterly Review of Film and Video* and the *Television Finales* anthology (2018). He completed his PhD at the University of Wisconsin-Milwaukee. He is an Assistant Professor of English at the University of Wisconsin Oshkosh and the Media Review Editor for *Middle West Review*.

Ebru Thwaites Diken is an assistant professor in the Department of Film and Television at the Istanbul Bilgi University. She holds a BA in Economics from the Boğaziçi University, Turkey and a PhD in Sociology from Lancaster University, UK. Her current research interests include female subjectivity in film and television, film and social theory, Scandinavian cinema, director's ethics and digital visual cultures. She is the author of *The Spectacle of Politics and Religion in Contemporary Turkish Cinema* (2018) and co-editor (with Diğdem Sezen, Feride Çiçekoğlu and Aslı Tunç) of *Female Agencies and Subjectivities in Film and Television* (2020). She has also contributed to several international peer-reviewed journals.

Özgür Yaren is a film scholar and professor at the Ankara University lecturing on film and photography. He received his PhD from the Ankara University with a thesis titled 'European Migrant Cinema' (2008). He was a post-doc researcher at UC Berkeley, California twice in 2011 and 2014-15. He has published several articles in prominent journals such as *Camera Obscura*, *The Journal of Popular Culture* and *European Journal of Cultural Studies*. His latest work, 'The Quest for Cultural Power: Islamism, Culture, and Art in Turkey' is included in *The Routledge Handbook on Contemporary Turkey* (Joost Jongerden, ed. 2021). Yaren's research interests include film history, aesthetics and sociology of art with a recent focus on exploitation films, cultural legitimacy and conservative taste in the fields of art. He has been leading comprehensive research funded by The Scientific and Technological Research Council of Turkey titled 'The Transformation of the Fields of Art in Turkey: Cultural Distinction and Conservative Taste' with a focus on the Islamic-conservative art taste and aesthetic criterion of conservative elites. He has translated several books and articles from English to Turkish, including *Story and Discourse* by Seymour Chatman. He is a board member of SANART Association of Aesthetics and Visual Culture and a member of the European Sociological Association.

Acknowledgements

I would like to thank all contributing authors for devoting their time to this project with dedication, openness and generosity. Bringing together diverse professionals on a subject which we are all passionate about has been a stimulating experience of new discoveries, of sharing, exchanging and expanding. I would like to thank Nuri Bilge Ceylan for his kind permission to reproduce the cover image. Special thanks go to the EUP team who were supportive at every stage of the project.

I am grateful to Phyllis Katrapani, film professor and filmmaker, for reading my three chapters and sharing her valuable observations and comments as a professional in the field, and scholar Maya Lamothe-Katrapani for assisting me with my research and for her insightful remarks and suggestions. I would like to acknowledge with gratitude the daily intellectual and emotional support of André Colin who stood by my side with patience and love during the long journey of this book.

In memoriam, I would like to remember three exceptional actors who are no longer with us but live on through their memorable performances: Mehmet Emin Toprak (1974–2002), Mehmet Emin Ceylan (1922–2012) and Ayberk Pekcan (1970–2022).

Introduction

Gönül Dönmez-Colin

Nuri Bilge Ceylan is one of the most distinguished filmmakers in contemporary global cinema and the most influential filmmaker of Turkey. He has won several awards at prestigious film festivals, including the Grand Prix twice (2003 and 2011), the Best Director (2008) and Palme d'Or (2014) at the Cannes Film Festival. Although his self-reflexive, small budget and slow-paced films initially distanced home audiences weaned on Hollywood fare and its local equivalents, Ceylan soon gained mentor status among film students and young filmmakers, and public endorsement followed as he enlarged his crew and cast popular actors.

Ceylan is part of a small group of pioneer filmmakers, including Zeki Demirkubuz, Derviş Zaim and Yeşim Ustaoğlu that appeared in the late 1990s during a stagnant period in film production. The movement, which came to be identified by the critics as the New Turkish Cinema, focused on transnational approaches to narrative forms and modes of production searching novel economic, aesthetic and thematic models while exploring national, global and individual identities.[1] Not a nouvelle vague in the French sense, these filmmakers followed individual paths that merged in certain thematic and artistic points– the dominance of the auteur and the mise-en-scène, self-reflexive counter-cinema practices, distanciation, subversion of the genres, counterpoint and elliptic editing and a tendency to use non-professional actors (Dönmez-Colin 2008, 2014).[2]

Ceylan is Turkey's greatest living filmmaker, in the sense Pedro Almodóvar describes Luis García Berlanga and Luis Buñuel 'as the two masters from whom all Spanish films derive'.[3] His workmanship might be quite different from those mentioned by Almodóvar but what makes him the greatest is similar: the way he 'links the universal and the local in his films' (Villena 2021, as quoted by Graham 2021). Like Berlanga, who had roots in Valencia but lived in Madrid, whose 'cinema and personality were impregnated with the character and sociology of Valencia' (Ibid), Ceylan, a long-time resident of Istanbul has returned to the Yenice of his childhood and adolescence film after film with an oxymoronic detachment and nostalgia, meshed with the ambivalence of a *transfuge de classe* (a class-over, or class defector, or someone who has been compelled by class humiliation to transcend their social identity) like the protagonists of the French *auto-fiction* novelists, Annie Ernaux, Didier Eribon and Édouard Louis, and their mentor, the late sociologist Pierre Bourdieu (1984).[4] As the son of a bureaucrat with a graduate degree from the US (father Emin's diploma visible on the wall in *Mayıs Sıkıntısı/Clouds of May*,1999), Ceylan's crossover might not have involved radical economic advancements, but growing up in the province, the periphery, having been identified as *taşralı*, that derisive word of scorn from the bourgeois social class of the metropolis, and having been accepted into the urban intellectual milieu through education (an engineering degree from the prestigious Boğaziçi University) and a profession as an artist is a path similar to the one followed by the French *transfuges*. As in their works, a certain self-reflexivity marks Ceylan's films, acutely perceptible through characters like Muzaffer in *Clouds of May*, Mahmut and Yusuf in *Uzak/Distant* (2002), İsa in *İklimler/Climates* (2006), Aydın in *Kış Uykusu/Winter Sleep* (2014) and Sinan in *Ahlat Ağacı/The Wild Pear Tree* (2018), the nature of whose ambitions for transcendence of class from the snubbed provincial identity to the more acceptable urban bourgeois includes betrayal for conveying an implied approval of bourgeois life.

Throughout his career, which includes photography, Ceylan has presented a society at the threshold of modernity, suffering from the erosion of traditional cultural values, while transforming local stories into transnational narratives. The archaic system of education (Muzaffer: 'What do they teach you at school?' 'Nothing', responds little Ali), nationalist indoctrination ('How happy it is to say I am a Turk!' chant the children every morning before starting school), ecological concerns ('Cranes don't come anymore because of the pesticides'; 'walnuts don't ripen on time'), inflation ('50 liras to fix the hem of the trousers!'), the closure of factories, unemployment, precariat youth seeking escape through migration to the metropolises or through marriage, disdained rural relatives, the urban/rural and intellectual (artist)/ordinary citizen divide, absurd echelons of hierarchy, slimy politicians, pompous bureaucrats, self-absorbed intellectuals, despised tenants, stone-throwing children, internal exiles, women caged inside their gender, collective amnesia and the unbearable sense of perpetually missing the boat are all part of the world Ceylan mirrors, a world that is instantly identifiable to the viewer irrespective of geographical distances.[5] In *Bir Zamanlar Anadolu'da/Once Upon a Time in Anatolia* (2011) a corpse is buried somewhere, but the culprits do not remember where. The darkness that blankets the first part of the film evokes the shroud over centuries of crimes committed on the Anatolian land. The imagery and the narrative are pervaded by a sense of collective guilt that evokes the celebrated author Yaşar Kemal's novel *Fırat Suyu Kan Akıyor Baksana/Look, the Euphrates is Flowing with Blood* (1997) which underscores the mass graves of the disappeared, the ethnic cleansings and the genocide of the Armenians, the spectre of which appears on an illuminated rock that resembles a human face (Dönmez-Colin 2014: 75–8). Another spectre, in the form of a boy dripping water, challenges the conscience of the guilt-ridden men in *Üç Maymun/Three Monkeys* (2008), the title of which implies 'See No Evil, Hear No Evil, Speak No Evil'. In *Winter Sleep*, appropriately defined as a metaphor for the country by the local critics, the fairy chimneys of Cappadocia tower over the characters, threatening in their verticality. They are permanent in the transient life of the humans, looking over serenely as they destroy each other with envy, avarice or indifference while turning a heritage site dating back several centuries B.C. into a future Disneyland with hotels named 'Othello' and wild horses captured to boost tourism. The Trojan Horse towers over the town square in *The Wild Pear Tree*, a false *lieux de mémoire* (memory site, Nora 1984/1992), an artifice left from a Hollywood movie,[6] a simulacrum (Baudrillard 1988). It is also a spectacle just like the 'Othello' Hotel, abstracted from its context and devoid of any power to connect the inhabitants slumbering in collective amnesia to the centuries-old histories of the land. Spectacles are both 'the outcome and the goal of the dominant mode of production' Debord claims, as the spectacle 'is not something *added* to the real world – not a decorative element . . . On the contrary, it is the very heart of society's real unreality. In all its specific manifestations – news or propaganda, advertising or the actual consumption of entertainment – the spectacle epitomises the prevailing model of social life . . . In form as in content the spectacle serves as total justification for the conditions and aims of the existing system. It further ensures the *permanent presence* of that justification' (1995: 13). All the world is a stage, and the actors play characters who role-play depending on circumstances as Aydın's sidekick, Hidayet (Ayberk Pekcan) reminds the alcoholic tenant, 'Don't try to play the actor with me, İsmail'. It is not accidental that the locus of *Winter Sleep* is a hotel named after a Shakespeare play and the protagonist is a retired actor contemplating to write the history of the Turkish theatre.

ORDINARY TALES OF ORDINARY PEOPLE[7]

Ceylan's directorial debut was *Koza/Cocoon* (1995), an 18-minute black-and-white film without dialogue. Starring his parents, Fatma and Mehmet Emin Ceylan, as an estranged elderly couple, the film competed at the 48th

Cannes Film Festival, initiating Ceylan's long relationship with the prestigious film event. Invitations to seventeen international film festivals followed, along with the Turkish Ministry of Culture's Achievement Award. He cast his family and friends in his first feature *Kasaba/The Small Town* (1997), the second, *Clouds of May* and partially, the third, *Distant* and took charge of most technical credits. All except *Distant* were shot in Yenice, the provincial town of his childhood near Çanakkale in the Gallipoli region. All focused on the different levels of alienation experienced by liminal characters oscillating between their rural and urban identities, hybrids of their own cultural identity as provincial, *taşralı*, and the cultural identity of the urban, the coloniser that overpowers them (Bhabha 1994). With *Climates* (2006), a multi-layered film on the disintegration of a relationship, Ceylan began to collaborate with a producer (Zeynep Özbatur/Atakan) and a cinematographer (Gökhan Tiryaki), but the main cast constituted Ceylan and his wife, Ebru, with his parents appearing in secondary roles. *Three Monkeys*, his first digital film, featured a cast familiar to local audiences while focusing on a dysfunctional family to re-address integrity, honesty, truth and personal defence mechanisms, the underlying themes of his previous films. *Once Upon a Time in Anatolia*, widening the screen to cinemascope through a murder story without suspense, widened its scope to include the country and its historical and socio-political landscape, sculpturing characters from the Anatolian soil as metonyms for the country much like the exiled national poet Nazım Hikmet's epic-in-verse *Memleketimden İnsan Manzaraları/Human Landscapes from My Country* (1939) (Dönmez-Colin 2014). With *Winter Sleep* Ceylan revived his interest in the primary unit, a husband and wife (plus a sister re-appearing after *The Small Town* and *Distant*) enclosed in the foreboding atmosphere of the Cappadocian landscape buried under the snow just like Istanbul in *Distant*. *The Wild Pear Tree* returned to the father-son preoccupation of some of his earlier films through anti-heroes in provincial settings, Ceylan's preferred space.

Ceylan's work involves universal allegories of ordinary people trying to survive in a hierarchical and unjust society, although he avoids the moral clarity of a political filmmaker. Everyone is compromised in his films, everyone is conniving, including the young. Ephemeral politics do not interest Ceylan as he has underlined in numerous interviews,[8] yet a close reading of his films charts the social and political transformation of Turkey from the post-1980 coup d'état years to the 2020s pertaining 'to a performativity, tracing multiplicity of the self across time, nations and exile' to quote Hatty Nestor on the work of another artist, the Cuban Ana Mendieta, whose work, Nestor claims, inspires her to encounter 'a dwelling that falls between absence and presence, memories folded into one another, fragments scattered across time and history' (2021), an appropriate trope for Ceylan's oeuvre.

The family and its dissolution is one of Ceylan's dominant thematic concerns. Most of his films show the family as fragile and open to fractures, evoking comparisons with Yasujirō Ozu's 'home dramas', a genre Richie points out 'is cultivated in Asia where the family remain the social unit' although Ozu's 'home drama' is of a special sort as 'he neither affirms the family nor condemns it' creating 'a world that is the family in its varied aspects and his focus is on its dissolution' (1974: 1–2). In *Cocoon*, the couple never talk to each other, hardly appearing within the same frame. In *The Small Town*, one son is gone forever; another has returned, but never found his actual place, while their father, who pontificates on his contentment in the security of the small town, repeatedly recounts his past serving the Ottoman army when he travelled as far as India. Women shed silent tears for their loss and children are seen but not heard. The unemployed, unskilled young man dreams of escaping his stifling circumstances. In *Distant*, the divorced protagonist, a liminal *transfuge*, stalks his ex-wife on her way to Canada with her new husband but words fail him when he tries to speak to her. *Climates* is about the disintegration of a relationship triggered by the non-committal disposition of the male protagonist to the confines of a family life. *Three Monkeys* is about deceit and infidelity in a marriage and the individuals' moral struggle to hold the family together against all odds. In *Anatolia*, the village woman's infidelity results in the murder of her husband; the doctor has been separated; the judge's wife committed suicide following his infidelity, while the commissar and his wife bear the burden of a sick child. The couple in *Winter Sleep* are alienated; the sister is divorced; the schoolteacher and the imam are too poor to get married; İsmail, the tenant with a wife and a child, is an abusive alcoholic, and the old neighbour is a widower. *The Wild Pear Tree* is about a family in which the father has lost his honour, and hence the respect of his family. The dissolution of the family may not be a tragedy in modern Turkey as in Ozu's Japan, but Ceylan's characters are still 'casualties' in the way Richie describes the Ozu characters who suffer social wrongs in the early films, and in the later ones, by being human and consequently aspiring to a state impossible to attain (Ibid: 5).

Loss of innocence and experience of shame and guilt appear as motifs early on in Ceylan's films. Little Ali in *The Small Town* turns the turtle upside down despite his sister's warning that this would result in the turtle's death. The feeling of guilt gives him bad dreams.[9] Ali's patronising older sister Asiye, a child ill at ease in her skin (the collar of her uniform always askew), experiences shame in the idyllic atmosphere of the classroom when the teacher identifies her lunchbox as the source of the stale odour. Shame takes more adult forms as we watch Mahmut trying to eliminate semen stains from the sheets after loveless sex or hiding his interest in pornographic films from his younger cousin.[10]

Deceit and dishonesty are prominent motifs in Ceylan's work, which could also be interpreted as a self-reflexive trope for the art (and artifice) of cinema: in

Clouds, the filmmaker/protagonist conceals from his parents that he is recording their personal life and exploits his cousin Saffet with a false promise to help him find a job in the city. Little Ali, promised a musical watch if he carries an egg in his pocket for forty days intact, resorts to stealing to replace the broken egg." In *Distant*, Yusuf phones his mother long distance without asking Mahmut's permission but tells her he is whispering not to wake him. Mahmut accuses Yusuf of stealing an old watch and does not inform him when he finds it in a drawer. In *Three Monkeys*, justice is thwarted when an innocent man confesses to a crime, and a chain of deceitful events follow. In *Anatolia*, the doctor who tries to keep his distance by maintaining the outsider's gaze, omits an important detail in his report about the cadaver, signing the papers without further interrogating the presence of dust in the victim's lungs, hence joining the majority who live in blissful ignorance, the central theme of Ceylan's previous work, *Three Monkeys* – see no evil, hear no evil, speak no evil. In *The Wild Pear Tree*, someone steals Sinan's money and Sinan steals his grandfather's old books and his father's dog to publish his book.

Connected with deceit and dishonesty, adultery is also a common thread in the narrative. In *Distant*, Mahmut's lover is married; in *Climates* (2006) infidelity and the subsequent lies determine the future of İsa and Bahar's relationship; in *Three Monkeys* (2008), adultery complicates further the already complicated lives of the characters, resulting in tragedy, and in *Anatolia*, two deaths are related to adultery: Kenan kills the husband of his lover while a tormented prosecutor keeps denying the connection between his infidelity and the sudden death of his wife.

Although television is on most of the time (a standard prop in most contemporary films from Turkey, reflecting a certain reality for the average Turkish household), no one pays attention to news about local politics. Father Ceylan is seen sleeping during the early episodes of *Clouds of May* as the speaker announces the difficulties of the government to form a coalition. On the other hand, melodramas of Yeşilçam, the commercial cinema that was popular from the 1950s to the early 1980s, are favoured, particularly by women. In *Three Monkeys*, they are the evening diversion of Hacer after work, while her husband sits in prison. In fact, from the narrative that involves love, passion, betrayal, infidelity, a suspicious husband and the repeated use of pathetic fallacy – the thunder and lightning – *Three Monkeys* proceeds like a typical Yeşilçam melodrama, starting with a private driver as one of the protagonists. The plot line resembles *Baba/The Father* by Yılmaz Güney (1971) about a poor employee who takes the blame for a crime committed by his boss's son for a large amount of money and goes to jail, only to find his family fractured and damaged on his release. In *The Wild Pear Tree*, Sinan's mother and sister spend most evenings in front of the television. In addition to the popular series, they are seen watching Güney's *Umutsuzlar/The Hopeless Ones* (1971). During a masterclass in Vienna, Ceylan praised Yılmaz Güney's cinema, but also admitted his fondness for Yeşilçam, citing as his motivation for the script of *Three Monkeys* a desire to tell a typical Yeşilçam story using his own style of filmmaking.[12]

Apart from the twenty-first century aesthetics and Ceylan's particular vision as a filmmaker, a crucial difference between Yeşilçam and Ceylan's films is the existential nature of Ceylan's characters, who have only themselves to blame as opposed to the fate-dominated narratives of Yeşilçam. In *Three Monkeys*, the contrast and the desaturation of the colours, with a particular concentration on red, the mouth-level shots, the awkward silences, the avoidance of eye contact and the absence of significant connections with other human beings accentuate the aloneness of the members of the family occupying a dwelling abstracted from reality. The industrial dystopia, the wretched railroad tracks, the featureless station, the house soon to be demolished and the ships in the sea (a reference to a half-sunk ship in the snow in *Distant* as observed by Yusuf, who ironically hopes to become a seaman) draw a picture of transience in a waste land although Kesal and Gedik argue that also '. . . hidden in the story is the understanding of a failed democracy and the inner-party politics, at best embodied in the story of Servet, a representative of political corruption and social decay; at worst, in the story of Eyüp, a representative of patience and perseverance' (2019).[13]

CEYLAN FROM LOCAL TO GLOBAL: INSPIRATIONS, DIALOGUES, TRANSMEDIATIONS

Ceylan could easily be identified as the national filmmaker of Turkey even at a time when 'nation-state' cinemas have given way to alternative forms of filmmaking. He carries the banner in the most prestigious film festivals. As Yılmaz Güney's name has been synonymous with Turkish cinema for decades, Ceylan's is the first to come to mind when contemplating the contemporary cinema of Turkey. If we follow Crofts' theorising about what constitutes national cinema –'"production", "audiences", "discourses", "textuality", "national-cultural specificity", "the cultural specificity of genres and nation-state movements", "the role of the state" and "the global range of nation-state cinemas"' (1998: 387–9 as quoted in Hjort and Mackenzie 2000), Ceylan's films qualify in most of these categories. Ceylan has also been identified as a transnational filmmaker, a filmmaker of global cinema, or world cinema, terms that identify 'related or competing phenomena, depending on the specificity of the theoretical account in question' (Hjort and Mackenzie 2000) and as Stam argues, do not necessarily 'name hostile camps or ideological enemies and at times are substitutable for each other', the word 'transnational' suggesting 'a wide variety of movements and interdependencies – the regional, the diasporic, the exilic – that can be figured as alongside, underneath, and beyond the national', 'world' being more 'honorific' while 'transnational' and 'global' being used 'usually more analytical than evaluative in tone' (2019: 231–3).[14]

There is something essentially 'Turkish' about Ceylan's films that focus on culture-specific characters navigating culture-specific narratives.[15] But he presents them through the prism of the aesthetics of the East and the West. His content is local, his form is universal. His earlier work in particular displays an affinity with Yasujirō Ozu as mentioned earlier, as well as Andrei Tarkovsky (Deleuzian time-image and recollection-images of Bergson) and Abbas Kiarostami, among others.[16] Eleftheriotis and Needham underline that the spatial composition, the ellipses in the narrative, the 'intermediate spaces' and 'still lives' highlighting the paradox of humanity's presence by its absence in Ceylan's cinema, all evoke Ozu (2006: 20–1). Reliance on characters rather than plot development is another aspect of Ceylan's approach that resembles Ozu's style, alongside a firm sense of reality that they share, despite the backgrounds gradually becoming prettier. Like Ozu, in his earlier films, Ceylan follows a basic theme, preserving continuity by using the same actors, the same characters, the same problems and similar storylines. The monotony of the provinces – the same fountains, same hills, same steppes – is in all his films, starting with *Cocoon* (Dönmez-Colin 2014). Nostalgia for a once-visited place is an overriding motif, particularly in *The Small Town*, *Distant* and *Anatolia*. Photographs often appear as tools to evoke this nostalgia, but as Richie comments about Ozu, 'Nostalgia lies not in later reflections, but in the very effort to preserve the image' (Richie 1974: 15) as the wedding picture of Mahmut and his ex-wife in his mother's house in *Distant* and the pictures of another ex-wife in the doctor's drawer in *Anatolia* indicate.

Ceylan's employment of sound and silence also evokes Ozu as well as Tarkovsky, another major influence on his work whose films *Zerkalo/Mirror* (1975) and *Stalker* (1979) appear diegetically in *Distant*. Sound and music were never just an 'acoustic carpet' or decorative addition to Tarkovsky's images, they were always an integral part of the film's auratic structure (Tarkovsky, Schlegel and Schirmer 2019: 15). As he wrote in *Sculpting in Time: Reflections on the Cinema*:

> It may be that in order to make the cinematic image sound authentically, in its full diapason, music has to be abandoned. For strictly speaking the world as transformed by cinema and the world as transformed by music are parallel, and [in] conflict with each other. Properly organized in a film, the resonant world is musical in its essence . . . Above all, I feel that sounds of this world are so beautiful in themselves that if only we could learn to listen to them properly, cinema would have no need for music at all (1986: 159–62).

The passion of Tarkovsky for 'authentic, unstaged sounds' is discernible in Ceylan's cinema starting with *Cocoon*, which relies on the sounds of nature except the occasional unobtrusive melodies of Bach. In *Distant*, the sounds of the ship horns, the seagulls, the waves, or the chime on the balcony embellish the narrative. In *The Wild Pear Tree*, during the fountain episode between the soon-to-be-married village beauty Hatice and the protagonist Sinan with a precarious future, the rustling of the leaves in the soft breeze replaces dialogue, increases the sexual tension and accentuates incommunicability.

Several favourite motifs of Kiarostami – the winding paths, the turtle, the perched villages appearing from nowhere, rolling objects, women doing laundry, laundry swaying in the wind – appear regularly in Ceylan's films. The artistic choices of both filmmakers include ellipses, dead moments and repetitions that are, in the Deleuzian sense, not the reoccurrence of the same thing, but the beginning of a new one and a refusal to remain the same (Dönmez-Colin 2019). Drawing parallels between Kiarostami's *Bad Mara Khahad Bord/The Wind Will Carry Us* (1999) and Ceylan's *Clouds of May*, US critic A. O. Scott underlines 'a painterly regard for rural landscape, an unsentimental interest in children and an unobtrusive curiosity about the ways movie reality parallels and intersects with ordinary life' (2007). The 'daughter of the mukhtar serving tea with a kerosene lamp' episode in *Anatolia* has been compared to the 'seduction of the milkmaid in the cellar' episode in *The Wind Will Carry Us* receiving similar criticism of exoticism (Dönmez-Colin 2019). The quest on the hillside in *Anatolia* evokes the relentlessly circular driving of the protagonist on arid landscape in Abbas Kiarostami's *Zendegi va digar Hich/Life and Nothing More* (1992) and *Ta'm-e Gilas/Taste of Cherry* (1996). Although the style of Kiarostami is minimalist pseudo-documentary compared to the pseudo-western, neo-noir hybridity of *Anatolia*, the thematic presence of death/burial pervades the narrative in all three films. During an interview with Geoff Andrew, Ceylan remarked that Kiarostami was one of his favourite filmmakers: '. . . with Kiarostami's films, I really felt as if seeing my own country. Iran and Turkey are similar in appearance, at least in terms of the people and countryside . . . And he [Kiarostami] has great compassion for his characters' (2004). A strong motif in Kiarostami's work, the distant gaze of the urban intellectual alien to the rural or provincial landscape of his country is focal in several of Ceylan's films, particularly in *Clouds of May*, *Distant*, *Anatolia* and *The Wild Pear Tree*. This aspect also bridges Ceylan's work with his national filmic heritage, notably the works of Ömer Kavur, Erden Kıral and Yılmaz Güney. *Kuru Otlar Üstüne/About Dry Grasses* (2023) in production while this work was in preparation revives this theme through the story of a schoolteacher appointed to a job in a remote corner of Turkey, Adıyaman in the southeast, near Mount Nemrut, as announced in the local press.

The intertextuality of Ceylan's work, both the horizontal (connecting the author and the reader, or the filmmaker and the viewer in this case) and vertical axis (the text to other texts, or other films) (Kristeva 1980; Fiske 1987: 108, 117) forming shared codes when united and depended on prior codes and 'specific textual and intertextual slippages' (Fiske: Ibid) can be decoded variously by different viewers. İsa's neck problem in *Climates* (he sleeps with his head in a drawer) reminds me of Tsai Ming-liang's *He Liu/The River* (Taiwan, 1997), whose protagonist, an introverted young man with issues about his family and his sexuality, experiences severe neck pains after playing the role of a corpse floating down a polluted river. Both films reveal the sadness of modern existence, particularly in traditional societies that experience the trauma of liminality. The aerial shot of the rooftops divided by the straight line of a street in *Anatolia* evoke the courtyard shots of Zhang Yimou's *Da hong deng long gao gua/Raise the Red Lantern* (PRC, 1991), a film that shares some of the same claustrophobic elements – rural stillness and the suffocating ritual and monotony, existential human conditions that defy time or geography (Dönmez-Colin 2014). The best buffalo yoghurt discussion in the same film, between the commissar and his inferior, oddly trapped with the accused inside a small car while searching for a cadaver, has been linked to the best hamburger discussion before a massacre in Quentin Tarantino's *Pulp Fiction* (1994), a *clin d'oeil* to one of Ceylan's favourite filmmakers while highlighting the absurdity of the situation. The rolling of the apple, impromptu according to Ceylan, conjures Parajanov's *Sayat Nova/The Colour of Pomegranates* (1968) and Tarkovsky's *Ivanovo detstvo/Ivan's Childhood* (1962) (the episode of the truck spilling apples on the beach). The title itself is an homage to Sergio Leone as Ceylan has specified.

Ceylan's films also interact with each other (a distinguishing mark of Kiarostami's work) from atmosphere to character and images that define characters (such as the image of the grandfather lying still on the earth in *The Small Town* and the father in *The Wild Pear Tree*), but also through the employment of banal props, physical objects that gather semiotic value through the narrative such as the lighter with the tune of *lambada* in *Clouds of May* that fascinates the little Ali. In terms of defining character, the theme song of *Love Story* on the commissar's mobile phone in *Anatolia* connects with the ring on Hacer's in *Three Monkeys*, an arabesque song of lament that identifies her as belonging to the lower-class, uneducated masses in the eyes of her husband's boss Servet, and as one of the 'weaker sex' open to exploitation from a higher power (i.e., man), as well as the lyrics serving as a premonition (to the viewer) of her eventual abandonment. The commissar's tune, meanwhile, challenges his authority by flashing a softer side of his macho façade to his inferiors. Two other props also serve as character definers: Yusuf's wind-up soldier in *Distant* and İdris's shock producing chewing-gum confiscated from a student, both connected with a puerile laugh that follows, insinuating immature personalities.[17]

Ceylan's affinity with the Russian classics, a common fascination of the Turkish intelligentsia, is manifest in the freely borrowed Chekhovian narratives and extensive dialogues in his films (particularly *Winter Sleep*) but also noticeable in the widespread use of essential Dostoyevsky themes – crime and punishment, innocence and conscience and guilt. The sense of imprisonment, a recurring Dostoyevskian motif privileged by Ceylan's local contemporaries as well (Demirkubuz is one example) hovers over the atmosphere in several films, from the narrow corridors in *Distant* to the confined space the family occupy in *Three Monkeys*, culminating in İsmail's prison visits when both the father and the son are shown behind bars. *Winter Sleep* featuring the Cappadocian caves, one of the most visually mesmerising landscapes in Turkey, is shot mostly indoors, evoking a sense of being buried alive for most characters, especially the women who never step outside.

History repeats itself, Ceylan reminds us, and its spectres appear in various forms. At times history is a metaphor as a circular phenomenon through the repetition of the character traits or destinies as in the case of the two protagonists of *The Wild Pear Tree*, İdris and Sinan, the father and the son resembling one another and sharing the same destiny despite the son's resistance. *The Wild Pear Tree* and the Colombian classic, *Cien años de soledad/One Hundred Years of Solitude* (Gabriel García Márquez 1967) share thematic overlaps regarding the inescapability of the past, the spectres of which visit the protagonists, and the solitude of the individual as a metonym for the solitude of a nation.[18] Leaving out important events and details to encourage spectator/reader participation (Servet's car accident, his affair with Hacer, his eventual murder, and Eyüp's life in prison in *Three Monkeys*; murder in *Anatolia*), a narrative device that goes back to the tragedies of Sophocles, is a preferred style for both Márquez and Ceylan, confirming the perpetual dialogue between great arts regardless of the borders of geography, time or medium.[19]

THE FILMS OF NURI BILGE CEYLAN

The Films of Nuri Bilge Ceylan provides contextual analysis of the cinema of Nuri Bilge Ceylan through thematic readings of his films by internationally acclaimed scholars who respond to his cinema from their unique perspective and expertise within the context of the present aesthetic, social and political concerns, globally and locally. Contributing authors come from diverse backgrounds and experiences, maintaining a borderless approach to support Ceylan's global vision. All except two originate from Turkey, which provides an insider's insight into the history, geopolitics, culture, tradition and language in interpreting the cinema of a filmmaker whose films are global by being local. The two 'outsiders' – though not 'outsiders' to Ceylan's oeuvre – Cecília Mello and Adam Ochonicky, from Brazil and the United States, respectively, provide remarkable counterpoints.

The aim of the volume is to present Ceylan's cinema at an academic level through its aesthetics, style and thematic concerns. The chapters cross-reference Ceylan's complete oeuvre while reflecting on individual films to seek a thread that usually runs through works of influential artists (Kiarostami, Truffaut, to name but two). The authors seek to highlight the intertextuality between Ceylan's own films and the films of his main influences – Kiarostami, Tarkovsky, Ozu, Antonioni – and his contemporaries – Lucrecia Martel, Lav Diaz and Hong Sang-Soo, among others – as well as the intermediality (photography, painting, music, literature) while pursuing cross-cultural references. Although the chapters follow a chronological order according to the production dates, they also overlap while maintaining an intertextual relationship between films matching Ceylan's style of filmmaking.

The first chapter, **Portrait of the Provincial Artist as an Urban Intellectual** by Gönül Dönmez-Colin introduces Ceylan's earlier feature films, *Kasaba/ The Small Town* (1997), *Mayıs Sıkıntısı/Clouds of May* (1999) and *Uzak/ Distant* (2002) leading to *İklimler/Climates* (2006) emphasising the conflicting identities of the main characters. Mahmut Mutman in **Vanishing Image of History:** *Uzak/Distant* (2002) 'focuses on Ceylan's filmic image as tracking and tracing spatial/class difference', Yusuf, the young rural cousin coming 'to embody the vanishing image of history'. Cecília Mello in **Portraits and Landscape:** *İklimler/Climates* (2006) gives a close analysis of Ceylan's next film from the point of view of its intermedial relationship with photography and painting. Acknowledging the significant role of photography in Ceylan's career, she discusses the film's 'intermedial relationship with the art of painting and with the art of photography, noticeable in two opposing but complementary types of shots: the close-up "moving portraits" of faces and the establishing shots of landscape'. In **Aesthetic Silences and the Political Bind:** *Üç Maymun/ Three Monkeys* (2008), Vuslat D. Katsanis argues for the 'political reach of slow film aesthetics and narrative silences' through *Three Monkeys*, reading the film's slowness within the 'context of Turkey's national politics, focusing on the characters' experiences of rupture on political, sociological and individual registers and arguing that the slowness of the image and the silences of the characters contrast sharply with the experience of living in a rapidly shifting political landscape'. In **The Aesthetics of Space and Absence:** *Üç Maymun/Three Monkeys* (2008) **and** *Bir Zamanlar Anadolu'da/Once Upon a Time in Anatolia* (2011), Adam Ochonicky analyses aesthetic elements in the two titular films with a focus on 'Ceylan's treatment of space and absence within the film frame', demonstrating how Ceylan projects 'ruminations on time, death and history into the very landscapes and environments upon which the narratives unfold'. Examining Ceylan's 'spatialisation of absence', the chapter further situates the filmmaker within 'a tradition of art cinema, from his own noted influences such as Michelangelo Antonioni to contemporary peers like Lucrecia Martel'. In **Transnational Indistinctions:** *Bir Zamanlar Anadolu'da/Once Upon a Time in Anatolia* (2011) **and** *Kış Uykusu/Winter Sleep* (2014) Ebru Thwaites Diken discusses Ceylan's cinema in terms of its 'transnational intimations, contemplative dimension, subtractive aesthetics and its approach to modernity through indistinctions rather than distinctions'. Demonstrating how Ceylan's films 'move from the local singularities to the universal by producing decisive differences in their seemingly loyal repetition of Chekhovian, Dostoyevskian and Shakespearean themes', she concludes that 'Ceylan explores the universal within the singular. The stories take place in local historical and social contexts; yet the focus on universal affects such as envy, spite, resentment (which are, as Nietzsche, Girard and others have shown, constitutive of sociality) pushes Ceylan's cinema beyond national borders, blurring, effectively, the distinctions between good and evil, between the urban and the rural and between the traditional and the modern'. In **The Politics of Dialogue and Ethics of Engagement:** *Kış Uykusu/Winter Sleep* (2014), Emre Çağlayan explores 'the politics and ethics of Ceylan's films against a cultural background in which the very concept of a political film, and the whole notion of what counts as moral behaviour, are in crisis'. He demonstrates this point of view 'through a close analysis of how *Winter Sleep* engages with our emotions and makes ethical propositions, which contrast with the decline of mutual understanding and tolerance (and the rise of political conservatism) in contemporary Turkish society'. In **Staying in the Primary Home, Relationships, Desires to Go and Roots:** *Kış Uykusu/Winter Sleep* (2014) **and** *Ahlat Ağacı/The Wild Pear Tree* (2018), Hasan Akbulut investigates 'relationships between characters as performance with a dramaturgical approach' and discusses 'the dynamics behind their desires to go, their search for roots and belonging and the provinciality they carry within themselves'. He interrogates the meaning of the primary home for the characters and argues that 'such ties have a contradictory nature that both prompts the characters to desire to go and immobilises them by anchoring them where they are'. In **Of Fathers, Sons And 'Solitary, Misshapen' Trees:** *Ahlat Ağacı/The Wild Pear Tree* (2018), Coşkun Liktor argues that fathers in Ceylan's films are generally depicted as 'ineffectual or humiliated figures stripped of paternal authority' and focuses on the father/son relationship in the film, which 'carries socio-political implications, thus opening room for the interpretation of Ceylan's films as allegorical takes on Turkish national identity and the political situation in Turkey'. In **'Gender Trouble' and the Crises of Masculinities in the Films of Nuri Bilge Ceylan**, borrowing from Judith Butler (1999) for the title, Gönül Dönmez-Colin examines the representations of women and the crises of masculinities in Ceylan's films in a transition period in modern Turkish society where dominant narratives are collapsing. To conclude the volume, in **Auteurism, Recognition and Reception:**

Ceylan as a Global Auteur, Özgür Yaren, underscoring 'the tension between different modes of artistic recognition in global and national contexts' explores the manner in which Ceylan has 'secured his position in the complex and precarious map of artistic recognition'. Yaren focuses on 'spectatorship and reception of Ceylan's films both in Turkey and around the globe' demonstrating 'the issue of reception, and an account of the development of Ceylan's career within national film culture, global film networks and a pan-European eco-system of cinema'.[20] Nine voices from different backgrounds converge on several points, particularly the trajectory of Ceylan's work from the local to the global and its embedded politics, two central themes that run through the volume, while presenting distinctive interpretations on how Ceylan proceeds along this trajectory.

Laura Marks calls 'the dialogical process of the cinematic experience', that which takes place between the spectator and the film, the 'intercorporeal relationship' when the film body and the spectator's body 'touch' each other (2002: xx). My 'intercorporeal relationship' with the cinema of Ceylan began with *Distant*, although this was a gradual process. My first viewing of *Distant* was during the International Istanbul Film Festival at the anachronic Beyoğlu Sinema (one of the locales where Yusuf's stalking ends in the film) where the projection was of mediocre quality. One sees so many films during a festival. I decided to give it another chance during the Rotterdam International Film Festival several months later. The large amphitheatre was packed after *Distant* won the Grand Prix and the Best Actor Awards (ex-aequo Muzaffer Özdemir and Mehmet Emin Toprak) at Cannes. Having taken the last available seat on the first row close to the engulfing concave screen, I felt the snowflakes fall on my face as Yusuf walked the familiar venues of a sad city buried under the snow. The present merged into the past. I was carrying Yusuf's melancholy mixed with nostalgia for my hometown, my *hüzün*, as Orhan Pamuk would name it. I was Mahmut, the disillusioned artist/intellectual on a bench by the Bosphorus reflecting on the centuries of history buried under the turbulent waters of the strait while the salty smell of the waves blurred my memories. I have watched *Distant* over a dozen times since. Each time I encounter something new, a different affective level or a different cinematographic interpretation and I experience a different 'intercorporeal relationship' although none of these would cancel my feelings of that afternoon with a spellbound crowd behind me.

Eventually, I met Ceylan in Istanbul. We have had several informal conversations over the years and I found him a modest and approachable artist. In 2014, I was invited to curate a program of the New Cinema of Turkey for the Kerala International Film Festival (IFFK) and to conduct a masterclass with Nuri Bilge Ceylan. The Kerala experience gave me the chance to know him personally as I witnessed his respect and sensitivity towards colleagues whose screenings he attended diligently even though he had seen the films before. He would not leave the theatre before the end credits rolled, not to offend them (*ayıp olur*, he would say, 'it would be shameful'). A meticulous artist who never surrenders until he is totally satisfied and, even then, keeps interrogating himself; a filmmaker with an exceptional talent to see through the human soul with all its glory and blemishes, its quirks and foibles; in addition to his immense creative talent Ceylan's success lies in his modesty, self-reflexivity, curiosity and respect for fellow human beings.

With this volume, I am excited to have the opportunity to present Ceylan's work as a guiding light to scholars, filmmakers and amateurs of cinema to accompany them on their journey through the film world of Nuri Bilge Ceylan.

Gönül Dönmez-Colin
Lourmarin 2022

NOTES

1. 'Cinema of Turkey' is the widely accepted attribution today to recognise the contributions of the diverse nations and minorities of the country.
2. As I have discussed elsewhere, Ceylan's approach has been self-reflexive from the start; Demirkubuz and Zaim have maintained a social and political locus in focusing on the lives of ordinary characters, whereas Ustaoğlu (the only woman) has evolved from an intensely political perspective towards the social and psychological repercussions of the political on the individual, particularly the woman, as her work has matured. These pioneers were soon joined by Semih Kaplanoğlu, Tayfun Pirselimoğlu, Barış Pirhasan and Reha Erdem, among others (Dönmez-Colin 2008, 2014, 2021).
3. Pedro Almodóvar on filmmaker Luis García Berlanga in *The Executioner*, Criterion Collection, released in Oct 2016. https://www.criterion.com/current/posts/4270-pedro-almod-var-on-luis-garc-a-berlanga (last accessed 21 September 2021)
4. For further on *transfuge*, see Bourdieu's work on social distinctions and class identity (1984), which informed Édouard Louis' *The End of Eddy* (2017), a story of social alienation in which Louis describes his 'folie social' (social madness) after moving to Paris when he starts to obsessively pursue entry into the capital's most selective milieu to erase his modest social origins, and his memoir, *Who Killed My Father* (2020); Didier Eribon's *Returning to Reims* (2009) interrogating the desire to transcend working class identity and Annie Ernaux's *The Years* (2018) in which she narrates sixty years of history that 'shifts subtly from rural working-class to an urban, left-wing, bohemian bourgeoisie'. All these writers question the possibility of writing about the transcendence of working-class condition in a way that is not effectively betrayal, or an implicit praise of bourgeois life (Court 2019).
5. During an interview, when asked whether the identity crisis of the Turkish intellectual stemmed from being caught between the East and the West, Ceylan responded: 'Imperialism has succeeded in making the underdeveloped countries feel slightly ashamed of their culture and traditions . . . Those who assimilate the point of view of the *other* see their own customs and traditions as extremities created by ignorance' (Dönmez-Colin 2008).
6. It was built for *Troy* (Peterson, 2004), a historical war epic that was a box-office hit.
7. During an interview after his first film, *Kasaba/The Small Town* (1997), Ceylan said, 'I do not like marginal stories. I also do not like extraordinary stories which happen to ordinary people. I like ordinary stories of ordinary people (Shrikent 1999).

8. During the masterclass in Kerala in 2014, Ceylan's response to my question regarding the political aspect of his films was 'It is not necessary for cinema to chase current news. A filmmaker need not be a journalist. Cinema, or art in general can inject the feelings of pride, or shame, for instance, infiltrate to the souls of the people, make them face the weaker points of their characters, which is not customary in the Eastern societies. Making a film by social reflexes does not interest me. Trying to understand the human soul is more interesting'.
9. Dreams play a significant role in other films of Ceylan as well – *Distant*, *Climates*. See Suner (2010) and Diken, Gilloch and Hammond (2018).
10. Pajaczowska and Ward refer to British psychoanalyst Phil Mollon's hypothesis that sexuality, with its biological imperative, threatens to dissolve the symbolic boundaries of culture and disturbs the order of social structure rendering sex as 'intrinsically shameful' and compare this with the 'theory of the shamefulness of sex being derived from its infantile origins' and deduce that whether 'biological or infantile, each source, nevertheless, insults the ego with its insistence on "another story" which the ego is impotent to influence or control. We are, as Freud contended, no longer masters in our own house (Freud 1917: 143)' (2008: 12).
11. Children entering the adult world and learning about cheating and shame is a recurring motif in the earlier films of Kiarostami.
12. I have discussed Yeşilçam extensively elsewhere (Dönmez-Colin 2004, 2008, 2014, 2019).
13. Ercan Kesal plays Servet in the film and, along with Nuri Bilge Ceylan and Ebru Ceylan, is its screenwriter.
14. For more on this, see 'Transnational Indistinctions: *Bir Zamanlar Anadolu'da/Once Upon a Time in Anatolia* (2011) and *Kış Uykusu/Winter Sleep* (2014)' by Ebru Thwaites Diken and 'Auteurism, Recognition and Reception: Ceylan as a Global Auteur' by 'Özgür Yaren.
15. Asked about the poster of *Distant* that displays the figure of a man seemingly suffering from an existential angst while a mosque appears in the background – an image not included in the film – Ceylan commented that he 'wanted to underline, particularly for the international film festival circuit that the story was taking place in the East, in a Muslim country' as a counter-narrative 'to Western prejudgments that assume such sentiments are characteristic of the Western world and unlikely for a Muslim country, which is no longer the case' (Köstepen, Yücel, Okur, Türk 2003).
16. For a comparison between Ceylan's work and Antonioni's 'incommunicability trilogy' – *L'avventura* (1960), *La notte* (1961) and *L'eclisse* (1962) – see Adam Ochonicky's chapter, 'The Aesthetics of Space and Absence: *Üç Maymun/Three Monkeys* (2008) and *Bir Zamanlar Anadolu'da/Once Upon a Time in Anatolia* (2011).
17. To my knowledge, the pioneer of modern Turkish cinema, Lutfi Ö. Akad was the first to use props, with the wind-up-duck in *Kanun Namına/In the Name of Law* (1952) marking transitions and serving as premonition.
18. Receiving the Best Director prize for *Three Monkeys* at the Cannes Film Festival (2008), Ceylan dedicated the award to his 'beautiful and lonely' country; the title of the Nobel Prize (1982) acceptance speech of Márquez was 'Solitude of Latin America', a major theme in the oeuvre of both.
19. In *One Hundred Years of Solitude*, Ursula tells her husband José Arcadio Buendia, 'Children inherit their parents' madness' (Márquez 1970:46). One may go further and find certain similarities between İdris and José Arcadio Buendia, two obstinate family heads, who set their hearts on unattainable projects, much to the dismay of their spouses and the mockery of the townspeople. Father Ceylan in *Clouds of May* is another impractical obstinate dreamer.
20. All quotations in this paragraph are taken from the individual author's presentations of their chapters.

WORKS CITED

Baudrillard, Jean (1988), 'Simulacra and Simulations' in *Jean Baudrillard: Selected Writings*, ed. Mark Poster. Stanford: Stanford University Press, 166–84.
Bourdieu, Pierre (1984), *Distinction: A Social Critique of the Judgment of Taste*, trans. Richard Nice. Cambridge: Harvard University Press.
Court, Elsa (2019), 'Postcards From Peripheral France', *The White Review*, April. https://www.thewhitereview.org/reviews/postcards-peripheral-france/ (last accessed May 1, 2022).
Debord, Guy (1995), *The Society of the Spectacle* (originally published as *La société du spectacle* in 1967), trans. Donald Nickerson-Smith. New York: Zone Books.
Dönmez-Colin, Gönül (2021), 'Contemporary Cinema of Turkey: Being and Becoming' in Joost Jongerden (ed.) *The Routledge Handbook on Contemporary Turkey*. London and New York: Routledge.
_____ (2019), *Women in the Cinemas of Iran and Turkey: as Images and as Image-makers*. London and New York: Routledge.
_____ (2014), *The Routledge Dictionary of Turkish Cinema*. London and New York: Routledge.
_____ (2008), *Turkish Cinema: Identity, Distance and Belonging*. London: Reaktion Books.
_____ (2004), *Women, Islam and Cinema*. London: Reaktion Books.
Eleftheriotis, D., G. Needham, (2006), *Asian Cinemas: A Reader and Guide*, Honolulu: University of Hawai'i Press.
Fanon, F. (2008), *Black skin, white masks*, trans. C. L. Markmann. London: Pluto Press.
Fiske, John (1987), *Television Culture*. New York: Methuen.
Freud, S. (1917), 'A Difficulty in the Path of Psychoanalysis' in S.E. of the *Complete Psychological Works of Sigmund Freud*. Published in 1955. London: Hogarth Press and The Institute of Psycho-Analysis.
Graham, Thomas (2021), 'Why Berlanga is Spain's greatest film director' https://www.bbc.com/culture/article/20210903-why-berlanga-is-spains-greatest-film-director (last accessed 21 Sept 2021)
Hjort, Mette and Scott Mackensie (eds.) (2000), *Cinema and* Nation. London and New York: Routledge.
Kesal E. and Hande Birkalan Gedik (2019), '3 Monkeys: Understanding Change in Turkey Through a Film'. http://www.ercankesal.com/3-monkeys-understanding-change-in-turkey-through-a-film/ (last accessed 13 June 2022)
Köstepen, Enis and Fırat Yücel, Yamaç Okur and İbrahim Türk (2003), *Altyazı*. Feb.
Kristeva, Julia (1980), *Desire in Language: A Semiotic Approach to Literature and* Art, edited by Leon S. Roudiez and translated by Thomas Gora, Alice Jardine and Leon S. Roudiez. New York: Columbia University Press.
Marks, Laura (2002), *Touch: Sensuous Theory and Multisensory Media*. Minneapolis: University of Minnesota Press.
Márquez, Gabriel García (1970), *One Hundred Years of Solitude* (originally published in Spanish in 1967 as *Cien años de soledad*), trans. Gregory Rabassa, New York: Avon Books.
Nestor, Hatty (2021), 'Tracing Mendieta, Mendieta's Trace: *The Silueta Series* (1973–1980) https://maifeminism.com/tracing-mendieta-mendietas-trace-the-silueta-series/ (last accessed 23 December 2021)
Nora, Pierre (1984–92), (ed.) *Les lieux de mémoire*, Gallimard: Paris. Translated into English as *Realms of Memory: The Construction of the French Past* (1996–1998), edited by Lawrence D. Kritzman, translated by Arthur Goldhammer under the direction of Pierre Nora. New York: Columbia University Press.
Pajaczkowska, Claire and Ivan Ward (eds) (2008), *Shame and Sexuality: Psychoanalysis and Visual Culture*. London and New York: Routledge.

Shrikent, Indu (1999), 'Ordinary Stories of Ordinary People: An Interview with Nuri Bilge Ceylan'. *Cinemaya: The Asian Film Quarterly*, 43, Spring, pp. 22–3. See also interview with the French critic Michel Ciment, 'Nuri Bilge Ceylan: les variations sur un theme me plaisent . . .' *Positif*, CDLXXXII (April 2001) during which he repeats the same response.

Stam, Robert (2019), *World Literature, Transnational Cinema, and Global Media*. London and New York: Routledge.

Tarkovsky, Andrey (1986), *Sculpting in Time: Reflections on the Cinema*, trans. Kitty Hunter-Blair. London: Bodley Head.

Tarkovsky, A, Hans-Joachim Schlegel and Lothar Schirmer (ed.) (2019), *Tarkovsky: Films, Stills, Polaroids & Writings*. London: Thames and Hudson.

Villena, Miguel Ángel, 'Berlanga was irreverent and a hooligan'. https://www.archyworldys.com/interview-miguel-angel-villena-berlanga-was-irreverent-and-a-hooligan/ (last accessed 21 September 2021)

CHAPTER ONE

Portrait of the Provincial Artist as an Urban Intellectual

Gönül Dönmez-Colin

A long-time photographer, Nuri Bilge Ceylan was thirty-six years old when he shot his first film, the 18-minute *Koza/Cocoon* (1995), the only short film of his career. A gallery of slowly moving images conveying the alienation of an elderly couple, played by Ceylan's parents, Fatma and Mehmet Emin Ceylan, the film circumvents dialogue or background music (except the occasional piece of Johann Sebastian Bach) in favour of the sounds of nature, setting the tone for Ceylan's feature films to follow. *Kasaba/The Small Town* (1997), his first feature, evokes Ceylan's childhood in Yenice, neither a village nor a town, an in-between space that defines the identity of its inhabitants. *Mayıs Sıkıntısı/Clouds of May* (1999), a mock 'making-of' of *The Small Town* introduces the motif of the man with the camera in the character of Muzaffer (Muzaffer Özdemir) arriving from the metropolis and manipulating his family and friends to participate in his film project. Muzaffer appears as Mahmut in *Uzak/Distant* (2002), a divorced photographer with provincial roots who has lost his artistic ambitions in the whirl of the metropolis succumbing to commercial work (a former occupation of Ceylan) and has distanced himself not only from his ideals but also from his family, his women and his soul.

The first three features have been grouped by critics and scholars as 'Province Trilogy' justified by their spatio-temporal continuity and the reliance on common tropes, although Ceylan has asserted in interviews that he does not think he makes films about provincialism and cosmopolitanism. As he and his immediate environment have provincial roots, the province appears by itself. 'I write about people I know well, and they have provincial characteristics. Turkey is the province of the world. The feeling of provincialism has infiltrated our blood. No matter what we do, it appears from somewhere' (Özyurt 2007).[1]

Province is a strong definer in all films of Ceylan, but more as a vehicle to explore the complexities hidden inside liminal characters, the *transfuges* I have mentioned in the Introduction, who carry the province within them, like the turtle tied to its home, no matter where they go. The province inside appears at times as nostalgia for innocence lost or the security that its womb-like insularity offers, but mostly as shame, or even a sense of culpability as the ambition for transcendence of economic, social or cultural class involves betrayal of the roots.

The pathos and solitude of small-town existence Ceylan captures on screen resembles the images on the canvasses of the American painter Charles E. Burchfield (1893–1967), displaying a certain 'sympathy with the particular' to quote Edward Hopper (1882—1967), another distinguished painter, and creating something 'epic and universal'. As modern life accelerates with progress and expansion, people from small towns feel isolated, left behind. The forms of isolation and impersonality that appear in Ceylan's films are comparable to Burchfield's observations of small town America a century ago, about which Hopper claims, 'No mood has been so mean as to seem unworthy of interpretation' (Marker 1990: 43).

The alienation of the provincial characters in a country facing rapid social and economic growth that has liminalised those unable or unwilling to follow the status quo is the central theme in Ceylan's two first features, which develops into the theme of the abandoned dreams of the urbanised provincial artist/intellectual in *Distant* to reappear in his latest films to date, in *Kış Uykusu/Winter Sleep* (2014) through Aydın, a retired theatre actor struggling to write the history of the Turkish theatre, and in *Ahlat Ağacı/The Wild Pear Tree* (2018), as Sinan, a young aspiring author precaritised by dominant narratives of society and politics (Rancière 1977: 28).

The documentary genre has never featured in Ceylan's work, though his earlier films follow a particularly realistic program using realist devices – bountiful use of long takes, location shooting, non-professional acting and a focus on current issues, exposing living conditions in small towns he had experienced first-hand, from ecological concerns to unemployment and migration and the plight of the young generation with limited prospects. Ceylan has returned to some of his earlier concerns in his later work through well-crafted scripts enacted by professional actors in staged settings.

This chapter explores *The Small Town*, *Clouds of May* and *Distant* in terms of the ways the characters negotiate multiple identities – provincial/artist/urban/intellectual/son/lover/citizen – and personal and collective memory and temporality in a rapidly changing environment of social, political and economic uncertainties.

SMALL TOWN MELANCHOLY

Ceylan began to investigate identity, memory and temporality with his first feature *The Small Town*, a film that evokes *Zerkalo/Mirror* (1975) by Andrei Tarkovsky, one of his acknowledged influences. Based on a story called *Cornfields* by his sister, Emine Ceylan, the film delves into the personal histories of four male characters belonging to different generations – Grandfather Nuri (Mehmet Emin Ceylan) who reflects on the passage of time while reminiscing his adventures in faraway lands as a young soldier and a prisoner, Father Emin (Sercihan Alevoğlu), who had studied engineering abroad but returned home to dispense his knowledge to the uninterested, Cousin Saffet (Mehmet Emin Toprak) dreaming of going as far away from his small town as possible, and little Ali (Cihat Bütün) suffering the pains of growing up as a provincial child. Each of these males, who are left out of the dominant fiction, evokes one part of Ceylan's life: Ceylan who spent his childhood in the province but studied engineering at the prestigious Boğaziçi University in Istanbul; who worked in menial jobs in London for survival; who escaped to the Himalayas to stay as far away from home as possible but stood in front of the snowy caps one day and realised how much he missed home.[2] A form of self-reflexivity from a filmmaker at risk of boring his audience with languid time-images is discernible in the presentation of the characters of the 'educated father', who tires everyone with his impractical knowledge and the grandfather who repeats the same stories night after night as if to refresh his own memory. The village fool Ahmet, the outcast who appears briefly at one corner of the frame becomes significant when the same face resurfaces as the filmmaker shooting *The Small Town*, in the next film, *Clouds of May*.

Following the solemn image of an early morning on an empty square with a stray dog, *The Small Town* cuts to children playing happily in the falling snow, a re-constructed memory as observed through the gaze of the village fool Ahmet (Muzaffer Özdemir). Özdemir appears as the prodigal son in the next film, *Clouds of May* as mentioned above, returning to his small town as a filmmaker to observe life through his camera lens without being part of it, and as the disillusioned provincial artist at the threshold as an urban intellectual (like the kitchen-mouse bound to get stuck on the trap band if it dares to cross the line) in *Distant*. The 'man with the camera' character is taken over by the filmmaker in *Climates*, Ceylan as İsa stumbling among the ruins with his dangling camera (a clin d'oeil to the stumbling village fool in *The Small Town*) while his girlfriend watches from above with mixed feelings of sympathy and disdain.[3]

The rural classroom episode is significant in exhibiting an ethereal quality, 'pure recollection images', summoned from the depths of memory (Deleuze 2005: 51–2 as quoted in Dönmez-Colin 2014: 204), selectively. One child reads, 'Solidarity means believing in one another as regards to feelings, interests and thoughts. People cannot live alone' as the camera shifts to the profile of

Figure 1.1 Men Left Out of Dominant Narratives:

1.1.1 The Outcast. (Source: screenshot from *Kasaba/The Small Town* 1997.)
1.1.2 The Outsider.
1.1.3 The Old.
1.1.4 The Provincial Child in a Double Bind.

a young man, precaritised by the same society, gazing nowhere. The window, the glass blurred with the frozen temperature of the exterior divides this world of tolerance and calm of childhood with the world outside, covered with snow, uninhabited except by Ahmet, the outcast and Saffet, the outsider.[4] Intangible objects (a flying feather) and sounds – drops of water from wet socks hissing on the stove (a Tarkovsky motif), a squeaky door, chirping birds and the familiar refrain of incomprehensible textbooks – perpetuate calm and compassion of the past before the loss of innocence. Even a late arrival is welcomed with tolerance and kindness in this subjective recollection of images. Then, the teacher, a somewhat lost young man, probably assigned from the metropolis to do his compulsory service, reprimands Asiye for the stale odour coming from her lunchbox and shame sets in.

The sudden shift to idyllic outdoor scenes of spring echoes the re-birth of nature with the plum trees offering juicy fruit, albeit in a graveyard. Ali (evoking the unidentified boy in *Cocoon* who kicks over a hive of bees, or the little girl in Béla Tarr's *Sátántangó* (1994) who takes her frustration on the cat when locked out of the house while her mother does sexual favours) overturns the turtle despite warnings from his sister that the reptile may die consequently. Shame, fear and punishment begin to disturb Ali's dreams. The ancient tombs with Arabic inscriptions are reminders of the inescapable presence of the past in a country trapped between its pull and the uncertainties of the future, or death itself, which also haunts the family gathering in the cornfields as the mother reminiscences her dead son much to the indifference of the others. Mundane issues of inflation or unemployment merge with the questions of faith and 'god's inexplicable ways' in the secluded space of one ordinary family which is at 'the core of the homeland, retrieved in the archaic backlands, where political issues are resolved in the private sphere and social drama turns into family melodrama' evoking 'point zero' of Italian neo-realism, the Brazilian Cinema Novo and New German Cinema (Nagib 2007), which I will return to later in the chapter. 'I wanted the children to see the different stages of adulthood, the darkness of it, the complexities of it', Ceylan explains during an interview with *Cinemaya* regarding the family gathering episode. 'They do not understand what adults are talking about at that moment, but they soon learn as it registers in their subconscious' (Shrikent 1999).

Belonging to a home or homeland and the (im)possibility of return, which Ceylan explores further in *Clouds of May* and *Distant* are the essential themes of this gathering, along with the impossibility of communication. Saffet, always on the edge of the frame declares: 'I don't want to stay here for the rest of my life' foreshadowing the statement of Sinan in *The Wild Pear Tree*, who does not want to waste his life among 'small-minded, bigoted people who look like "peas in a pod"'. What follows here is more like an interior monologue of coming to terms with the joys and pains of leaving home:

Saffet: Trees on the right, trees on the left.
Grandfather: Why do you speak so distant? One says, 'my tree, my earth'.
Saffet: What's the difference if you're buried under your own earth when you're dead? The earth is the same earth.

The home motif is periodically extended to nature as well in the film: the turtle carries its home on its back; the stork flies away but returns to the same spot. To leave or not to leave is the perpetual question that keeps haunting most Ceylan characters.[5] In *Distant*, the protagonist decorates his living space in modern urban style but keeps a back room with a floor mattress (a *döşek*) and a kilim; in *Winter Sleep*, Aydın raves about leaving, but never does. Suspended between two contrary spaces, these characters live transitory lives. Mahmut in *Distant* sleeps in a sleeping bag on his own bed; İsa and Bahar in *Climates* sleep in impersonal hotel rooms; in *Winter Sleep*, they live in a hotel.[6]

The film interweaves three diverse levels of temporality within the actual timeframe of the late 1990s: the grandfather's 'past' during the World War I depression years; the father's 'past' during the post-World War II period of poverty and underdevelopment, and the children Asiye and Ali's 'present', the 1970s. Just as in the Italian neo-realist movement and the French *nouvelle vague*, the image becomes time-image in the film, the screen as 'the cerebral membrane where immediate and direct confrontations take place between the past and the future, the inside and the outside' (Deleuze 2005: 121 as quoted in Dönmez-Colin 2014: 203) while the fluidity of thought-images (thought-waves) circulates in the time-memory universe of Ceylan's imaginary. Like Tarkovsky, who says the rhythm is the dominant, all-powerful factor of the film-image (1987: 114–16), Ceylan is not interested in the specific sequences progressing in time, but the rhythm itself. Within the general framework of day followed by night, the narrative merges the four seasons. Gently falling snow seen through the classroom windows slides into the images of the plum trees in the spring as the children wander in the fields, and to summer by the time they join their family in the corn fields, then to autumn, when they are back indoors, completing the cycle of seasons–life.

The change of seasons trope, the wheel of life, which reappears in *Climates* and *The Wild Pear Tree*, is established during the family gathering through the rotation of the soliloquies but also through the earlier image of the turning chairs in the amusement park. The second conjures Emir Kusturica's first film, *Sjećaš li se Doli Bell? / Do You Remember Dolly Bell?* (1981). Adolescent Dino and the unemployed unskilled Saffet both stay on the side of the frame as outsiders, observing but never being part of the picture. The wheel turns, but nothing changes. While Dino tries to escape his limited existence by learning to practise hypnosis, which could give him power over others, Saffet wants to cross borders to have a more promising future elsewhere. Kusturica allows his protagonist an emotional outlet through sexual experience and first love, whereas Ceylan does not consider any romantic release for Saffet. Both males are dreamers although

Figure 1.2 The wheel turns, nothing changes. (Source: screenshot from *Kasaba/The Small Town* 1997.)

the village boy Dino is more innocent, whereas the older Saffet from the small town has become cynical after several disappointments including abandonment by his adventurous father and failure to pass the university entrance examinations. Kusturica's village is more primitive than Ceylan's 'small town' and in Tito's Yugoslavia, people experience a different level of isolation, but at the end, the malaise is loneliness, whether for Ceylan, Kusturica or Márquez as I mention in the Introduction, missing the boat as a so-called 'Third World' nation trying to catch up with the West; at the threshold of modernity bogged down by tradition; belonging neither here nor there, and in an Asian country with a quarter of its land in Europe in the case of Turkey. As Ceylan has defined during an interview, '*The Small Town* is a film like an island' (Aliçavuşoğlu 1997: 10).

CLOUDS OF BOREDOM

Clouds of May (meaning boredom, or troubles, of May in Turkish), also filmed in Yenice, underscores, just like *The Small Town*, the strains faced by four males of different generations: Muzaffer (Muzaffer Özdemir), an aspiring filmmaker settled in the metropolis returns home to use his family for a film project to the dismay of his provincial parents ('What kind of a film?' the father asks, 'evidently, not something that would bring money'); Father Emin (Mehmet Emin Ceylan) fights a losing battle against the government to save the trees he has tended for many years; cousin Saffet (Mehmet Emin Toprak) who has failed the university entrance examinations, dreams of leaving the small town for a better life, and little Ali (Muhammed Zimbaoğlu) struggles to carry an egg intact in his pocket for forty days to receive the musical watch promised by his aunt.

The opening sequences establish the tone of the film. Before the credits roll, we are introduced to cousin Saffet who gazes at the emptied main street captured within a window frame, waiting for the postman to bring his entrance exam results. The long shot of the street through the glass is followed by the close-ups of Saffet's weary face, which reflect 'the pain and sting of absence from the centre, the metropolis' felt by a young man trapped inside the 'normalcy' and family-centred complacency of the small town with its 'squabbling couples and marital dramas, of petit bourgeois shopkeepers, neighbourhoods, and afternoons in front of the television', the 'source of claustrophobia and anxiety' (Jameson 1991: 280–1). The announcer from the invisible television reads about the skirmishes between the political parties and the failure of the Bülent Ecevit government to form a coalition while Father Emin takes his afternoon nap. The sudden arrival of Muzaffer, annoyed by the dysfunctional bell (a subtle trope for the lack of communication that Ceylan returns to in *Distant* as Saffet/Yusuf tries to ring the bell of Muzaffer/Mahmut) disrupts the routine of the family.

The classroom episode revives the one in *The Small Town* as children recite every morning, 'How happy it is to say I am a Turk' and read paragraphs about how to be a good citizen without understanding a word, exposing the futility of such systems of education. Ali's response, 'Nothing' to Muzaffer's question of what they teach at school is apt. (The nationalist indoctrination foregrounded in these two films is ironically revived in the gaze of Yusuf in *Distant* as he stares at youth waving flags in the metropolis while he is dreaming of escaping.)

The episode in the children's park showing Muzaffer brooding on a swing suggests a momentary return to his childhood as the image of Ali's back appears in the next shot to complement the earlier comment of Muzaffer to his mother about seeing himself in Ali. Nostalgia for what is lost is the dilemma of an individual cut off from his roots, who knows there is no going back 'home'. The image of the turtle, traditionally perceived as a nomad travelling with its home, repeated in both films, provokes the question of whether the turtle is also a prisoner in its home. For a man privileged with the anonymity of the city, the insular small-town life, neither a town nor a village, but forever condemned to liminality, where family members support each other to the point of suffocation and everyone knows everyone else's story, could be confining. This sense of claustrophobia is accentuated through minor details such as the itching feet of the mother, supposedly a hereditary condition. One is condemned to wait in an obscure corner with real or imaginary illnesses until death arrives (Dönmez-Colin 2014: 230).

The loss of innocence, Ali stealing an egg to replace the broken one, and what is lost in nature are reminders of the passage of time along with the episode of watching *Cocoon*, Ceylan's short film in the presence of the two protagonists, Ceylan's parents. Mother Fatma (Fatma Ceylan), distressed to see herself look old asks, 'Does this tool make one look older?' Muzaffer, too involved with his own project to be tactful to the elderly parent responds, 'Not at all'. 'Time flies', she sighs. 'We have grown old' (Dönmez-Colin 2008: 195).

For Anastopoulos, this episode is one of the highlights of the film, an episode that could be compared to painting or music, 'variations on the same theme and concurrently, a change of perspective'. Although Ceylan returns to the same themes as a painter who paints the same portrait or the landscape repeatedly, *Clouds of May*, a film which 'springs from the entrails of the previous one (*The Small Town*), is neither its copy nor its mirror, it is rather its echo, its reflection, its correction through a different perspective.

> This time Ceylan concentrates not only on small details
> of everyday life, but also on what is usually carefully hidden
> while permeating the surface of the world. The film plunges
> into the substance of things, people and circumstances. The
> family is not only the subject but also a necessary condition of
> this work, and the relationship between its members, the need for
> communication and the difficulty of intimacy predominate,
> under the relentless passage of time and the indifferent gaze
> of nature (2006: 27).

Ceylan's relationship with nature carries a feeling of nostalgia for innocence lost. In that sense, the musical lighter that fascinates Ali 'unites the traditional world with the modern one, creating a new mythology with humor' (Ibid.). The threat of the contemporary world coming to destroy the traditional is further stressed by the arrival of the officials of the Ministry of Agriculture to cut the trees Father Emin has tended for years. One of the most moving scenes in the film features Emin, stepping out of his role in Muzaffer's film to try to catch up with the officials' car pedalling his old bicycle, evoking another meta-film, Jafar Panahi's, *Ayneh/The Mirror* (1997) made two years earlier, in which little Mina, frustrated with the film crew, decides to step out of the frame of the camera lens and follow her own course, 'breaking the fourth wall' separating fiction from real life in the Brechtian sense (Dönmez-Colin 2008: 195; 2014).

A similar device that Ceylan adapts to his shooting agenda is the autonomous camera, a favourite of Iranian filmmakers, particularly Abbas Kiarostami and Jafar Panahi with concerns about the gaze of the censorship in their country.[7] In *Clouds of May*, Muzaffer arranges his camera to record intimate moments between his parents and eventually others that he tries to test for casting without informing them or by telling them the camera is not on. Highlighting this technique in the films of Abbas Kiarostami (*Dah/Ten*, 2004; *Ta'm e guilass/ The Taste of Cherry*, 1997; *Panj/Five*, 2003) and Jafar Panahi (*In film nist/ This is not a Film*, co-directed by Mojtaba Mirtahmasb, 2011; *Pardeh/Closed Curtain*, co-directed by Kambuzia Partovi, 2013; *Taxi/Taxi Tehran*, 2015 and

Se rokh/Three Faces, 2018), Nagib refers to the 'indexical power of this radical attempt at capturing life as it happens without the intervention of a human being' (2020: 75). Removed from 'engaged politics', this 'method is 'nonetheless political in that it brings into filmmaking the uncinematic statis praised by Adorno as contrary to the aims of the cultural industry' according to Nagib. 'It is also in tune with Bazin's realist tenet of the prevalence of the objective over the subjective world as enabled by the camera's automatic objectivity'(Ibid.). However, as Nagib points out, quoting Chéroux and Frodon, this type of set up brings both the documentary and fiction genres 'into a crisis through an interrogation of the truths and lies of representation (2016: 13).

The feelings of obligation and guilt while working with non-professional actors in real circumstances – and particularly with family members – surface subtly in the film through self-reflexive episodes of Muzaffer's inconsiderate and insincere behaviour that disturbs the routine of his family. Muzaffer is an outsider, not interested in their issues. While his father cuts wood, he idles around listening to classical music from his car. Even when he offers help to ease his conscience, he does not have a clue how to hold the axe and split the wood. He lures Saffet to act as his assistant with a cursory promise of helping him secure a job in the city, but distances himself once the work is done (Saffet as Yusuf arrives at the door of Muzaffer/Mahmut in *Distant*). Occupied with his concerns about casting, he ignores the grief of his uncle who has just lost his wife. On the other hand, his family show the same indifference towards him and his film project. Each character has their own problems, evoking the family gathering in *The Small Town* and the discernible lack of communication between the characters. Young or old, no one listens to each other because each one is occupied with their own obsession.

Clouds of May 'is a hymn to descent' claims Anastopoulos. The lines on the face of the ageing father and the knots on the trees speak about the passage of time and the inevitability of losing people and things we love one day. At the same time nature reflected in the water, the whistling of the wind and the sparks of the fire at night convey the fullness of life, 'imparting an almost religious sense of the eternal'. 'Life and death coexist in Ceylan's films and his heroes flow between them like water in a brook . . . *Clouds of May* is, for Nuri Bilge Ceylan, what *Andrei Rublev* was for Tarkovsky, the film through which he crystallises his artistic beliefs . . . The film that determines his relationship with Man, Nature, Time and Creation . . . the path from which he does not stray, walking it again and again in successive variations towards a deep understanding of himself and of the world' (2006: 27).

DISTANT

Considered by Nuri Bilge Ceylan his most autobiographical work, *Distant* with its polysemic title continues the central themes of the two previous films:

home, identity and belonging. The protagonist Mahmut (Muzaffer Özdemir) is distant to the women in his life – his ex-wife, his mistress, his mother and his sister; distant to his country cousin, a reminder of the roots he had severed while trying to build a new identity; distant to his work, having succumbed to material gain rather than pursuing artistic dreams, and distant to commitment, coercing his wife to have an abortion. He is also distant to his immediate environment; in a spacious flat, the bed is in the living room, where he sleeps in a sleeping bag like a transient traveller, as mentioned earlier.

For Diken, Gilloch and Hammond, the title itself is 'eminently spatiotemporal' and 'typically suggestive and ambiguous'. While it 'identifies' the estrangement of the two characters, it also 'refers to the aesthetic space of observation and reflection, the gap between subjects and objects of the gaze, between the camera and what it captures'. In that sense, the 'notion of "distance"' that Ceylan 'opens up and out on screen is at once optical, physical, emotional and memorial' (2018: 61).

The predicaments of an artist of Ceylan's generation, a person with provincial ties, is foregrounded through Mahmut, who photographs tiles for a ceramic company, having given up his artistic aspirations. The transformation of the intellectual after the 1980 coup d'état, during the apolitical atmosphere of the Turgut Özal years (prime minister and president, 1983–93), parallel to the global social and economic changes and the increased hegemony of the neo-liberal perspective have distanced engaged artists like Mahmut from their ideals. Several once-idealist filmmakers work on lucrative television series or make commercials, although *Distant* was the first film to foreground critically the neo-liberal lifestyles of the 'new intellectual' (Dönmez-Colin 2008).

The opening sequences display an early morning country landscape buried in snow, with a tiny figure slowly approaching the camera. A bus stops in the distance and a male figure hops on. Cut to a blurred image of a woman removing her black stockings while a man watches her, then takes off his shoes and approaches with a weary sigh. The image is still blurred. Next, the man is seen trying to wipe off the semen stains as the telephone rings and a woman's annoyed voice is heard reproaching her son for ignoring her messages.[8]

Yusuf (Mehmet Emin Toprak), the country cousin Saffet of the two earlier films, enters the narrative through another rural man, the doorkeeper, the 'outsider-within', the migrant/peasant incorporated into middle-class domestic sphere with the creation of middle-class housing as a response to the expansion of the urban middle class, creating a powerful common physical and symbolic space for encounters between the urban and rural classes (Özyeğin 2002: 47). Responsible for ensuring the sanctity of the dwelling, privy to the secrets of the inhabitants, but perpetually positioned on the threshold where the lights switch on and off reducing his existence to almost invisible, the Anatolian man watches Mahmut's mistress with a judgmental gaze mixed with a city-acquired resilience to any behaviour contrary to his family-centred morals. His exchange with the middle-aged gay tenant with a young lover is more accommodating, but he literally closes the door on Yusuf.[9] The provincial 'other' is not welcome, not even by other provincials.

Mahmut's form of hybridisation, linguistic, cultural and even political is contradictory and ambivalent in the context of Bhabha's theory of 'Third Space of enunciation' (1994: 37). What he had experienced when he arrived in Istanbul with just a few pennies in his pocket is re-enacted with the roles reversed when his country cousin arrives at his door; the coloniser and the colonised (the urban and the rural) engaging in imbalanced and unequal power relations.[10]

The relationship between Mahmut and Yusuf reflects the tension between the two poles of Turkish society. Yusuf goes to cafes where strangers share tables whereas in Mahmut's regular hangouts, the tables are arranged for privacy. Mahmut is 'distant', Yusuf is 'distanced'. The provincials are permitted to exist in the metropolis if they are invisible like the doorkeeper families, confined to dingy basements or isolated in squatter settlements. Yusuf is the 'ghost on board' (Şen 2019) and his actions confirm urban prejudices. He harasses women, smokes cheap cigarettes, leaves his smelly shoes around and does not flush the toilet. He has never heard of Bach or Tarkovsky. He likes the pop singer Sezen Aksu and the television sit-coms. He walks into a book shop or a movie theatre only while stalking a woman. Earning money is his only aim. He carries the claustrophobic proximity of the small-town living with him (like the turtle that carries its home on its back) to the isolating but liberating anonymity of the urban life that the city cousin Mahmut has chosen.

Mahmut pushes Yusuf to the back room at the end of a long corridor (his suppressed provincial past – the kilim and the traditional *döşek* laid on the floor). Yusuf leaves the lights on and Mahmut switches them off just like the doors that Mahmut keeps closing, as if to protect his home territory and chosen identity by leaving the 'other' outside, not realising that by locking the other out, one also locks oneself in. In this sense, the trope of the mouse trapped in the kitchen applies to both characters, although the method of each to discard the animal is quite different.

Despite their obvious differences, Mahmut and Yusuf, as Ali and Muzaffer in *The Clouds of May* and most of the characters in *The Small Town*, are the same character. The unidentified tiny dot in the distance in the opening sequence, which gradually takes the shape of Yusuf, could be Mahmut, Mahmut's recollection of leaving home, alone one early morning, without the customary goodbye rituals, or it could be Ceylan himself. During Mahmut's absence, Yusuf occupies his space, settling at his desk and littering the house with his cigarette butts. On Mahmut's return, during a confrontation in the corridor while the two men are positioned at the thresholds of the two doors (the in-between space), the camera is on Mahmut reprimanding Yusuf for playing with the wind-up soldier toy he bought for his nephew. Yusuf's image is repeatedly mirrored on the glass behind Mahmut, but the image is blurred, reflecting Mahmut's youth in Yusuf's image in the fusing of the two images.

In the final episode, Mahmut, the disillusioned urban artist/intellectual sitting on a bench facing the Anatolian coast, decides to smoke his cousin's cheap cigarettes that he had spurned earlier. Perhaps now he is prepared to face his suppressed 'other' when the 'other' is already gone. Whether Yusuf, who leaves Mahmut's place without warning, will free himself from the fixations of typology and stereotyping *(taşralı)* with his action or choose mimicry (Bhabha 1994: 86) like Mahmut, is left to the audience imagination. Ceylan leaves the door open regarding the future of Yusuf, the new colonised other.

Acclaimed critic Tony Rayns, who believes Ceylan 'practices filmmaking as a cottage industry' using his family and friends as cast and collaborators, employing a 'committedly sparse' style, preferring 'musicality' of natural sounds over scores, 'formalist rather than dramatic considerations' governing the framing and composition of both static and panning shots, suggests that 'Ceylan, in fact, looks more and more like a subscriber to the screenwriting method recommended by his fellow Dostoyevsky fan Paul Schrader: identify a personal problem or issue, create a protagonist who embodies it and then devise a fiction in which the problem is tested to its limit' (2004: 72). Does this method work in *Distant*, asks Rayns? 'Mahmut is a much less compulsive character than, say, Travis Bickle or Mishima, and his middle-aged hang ups are undoubtedly as "ordinary" as they come. And Ceylan spends more time pondering the many implications of "distance" than he does getting to grips with the root causes of Mahmut's detachment from the world. In so far as the film has a "story arc" at all, it centres on Mahmut's growing apprehension of his own problems; he ends up much more self-aware than he was when Yusuf arrived, albeit no closer to sorting himself out. The viewer of course is shown both Mahmut and Yusuf (sometimes together, more often alone) and invited to draw broader conclusions about "distance" from their behaviour. But the real focus is on Mahmut's retreat into solipsism, and it's a matter of individual taste whether the result seems poignant or wilfully defeatist' (Ibid). Rayns' final judgment on Ceylan at this stage of his career is: 'He hasn't yet achieved the poetry of Ozu's film language, or the intensity of Tarkovsky's, but he is recognisably working towards what Paul Schrader once called a "transcendental style". It could be that the only thing holding him back is his insistence on the ordinary' (Ibid). In retrospective, Rayns' final comment seems like a premonition that has been fulfilled.[11]

THE 'POINT ZERO'

I would like to return to the trope of the empty space that binds the three films. The almost static shot of an empty square introduces *The Small Town*; the empty street sets the tone of *Clouds of May*, and the snow-covered country road in the opening sequences linked to the images of parks and shipyards dormant under the heavy snow stands as the major trope in *Distant*, which is eventually juxtaposed with the equally alienating images of bustling Beyoğlu with shops, cafes and cinemas. These images evoke two Brazilian films, made shortly after *The Small Town*, *Central do Brasil/Central Station* (Salles, 1998) and *O primeiro dia/Midnight*, (Salles and Thomas, 1999) that Nagib claims 'evolve around the idea of an overcrowded or empty centre in a country trapped between past and future, in which the zero stands for both the announcement and the negation of utopia. In their drive for novelty, both refer to previous cinematic "zeroes", ranging from Rossellini's foundational neo-realist films to European and Brazilian new wave outputs' (2006: 223). Nagib underlines that these films which were made in a period of 'the reconstruction of a national utopian imaginary, during the film revival from the mid 1990s onwards, included the geographical exploration of the country with renewed curiosity about the human element and its regional peculiarities', the search for a 'centre' and a 'point zero' becoming a recurrent motif (Ibid). The period roughly corresponds to the emergence of a new film movement in Turkey, following a stagnant time of production, Ceylan as one of the pioneers, which eventually has led to more explorations of the countryside with variations on the thematic approaches – from boredom to nostalgia.[12]

One may also claim that the path Ceylan has chosen was born out of absence. Commercial Yeşilçam cinema, which was dominant from the 1950s until the early 1980s, maintained a folkloric attitude towards rural life, banking on village stories of love, revenge, honour killings and blood-feuds. These films were made by urban filmmakers who cast stars that tilled the soil in impeccable costumes flashing false eyelashes. As Daldal underlines, the social realist movement was concerned mostly with the problems of the urban workers (2003). A few filmmakers like Yılmaz Güney tried to focus on genuine issues combining the content with artistic form. Migration was always an attractive subject but hardly anyone turned the camera to the people of the small towns, the liminals, or the life of a provincial who arrives in the metropolis, not to fill his pockets with cash, but to become an artist, a writer, or a filmmaker, an intellectual who carries the province with him, not in his appearance or mannerism (the fodder for Yeşilçam comedies), but deep inside, as a definer of his actions and life decisions. It became performative for Ceylan to make such films, as a fight against invisibility.

The 'point zero', as Nagib rightly points out, may also refer to 'nation, history and film history'. As in the cases of the previous new waves, 'the return to zero was not meant to turn film history into a "tabula rasa" . . . Rejecting postmodern deconstruction, they make a step forward which, in fact, implies a return to certain conventions of genres such as melodrama' (2006: 223). While breaking away from the narratives of the 'fathers' in his earlier work, Ceylan has also revived certain conventions of the Yeşilçam melodramas, diegetically, thematically and stylistically as his work matured, citing as his motivation the challenge to tell a typical Yeşilçam story using his own style of filmmaking, as mentioned in the Introduction.[13]

Finally, the rhythm of the films examined in this chapter evokes Béla Tarr's approach to creating 'geographies of indifference' through techniques of slow cinema. Just like Tarr's interiors that provide claustrophobic environments in which human relationships flourish with difficulty while his exteriors become landscapes of endless wandering for his characters (Orban 2021), Ceylan's cinema hardly releases the character from the burden of existence. Men out of tune with dominant narratives remains a strong motive in all films of Ceylan to date.

NOTES

1. Although I agree with Ceylan's reflections of a national reality, his comment also evokes the 'mimic man' that perpetuates the prejudices and injustices it purports to combat (Fanon 2008).
2. According to Rancière, a society's ideological 'reality' is its 'dominant fiction', which represents a category for theorising hegemony, 'the privileged mode of representation by which the image of the social consensus is offered to the members of a social formation and within which they are asked to identify themselves' (Jacques Rancière 1977: 28).
3. *İklimler/Climates* (2006), featuring İsa, a university professor photographing the Roman ruins while on vacation with his younger partner Bahar, could be a prequel to *Distant*, if we consider the soon-to-be separated İsa and Bahar as the past of the already divorced Nazan and Mahmut. Mahmut and İsa are both identified with a still camera and both men are involved in a clandestine affair with a woman played by the same actor, Nazan Kırılmış/Kesal. I reflect on these four films, *The Small Town*, *Clouds of May*, *Distant* and *Climates*, as a tetralogy that I have named elsewhere Portrait of the Provincial Artist as an Urban Intellectual (Dönmez-Colin 2014).
4. The window, the fascination of many painters including Magritte and Hopper, literary names such as the poet Cavafy and filmmakers like Hitchcock (*Rear Window*, 1954) or Ivory (*A Room with a View*, 1985), is a significant motif in the films of Ceylan. In *The Small Town*, it separates the warmth of the classroom from the cold and cruel world outside, both physically and symbolically and in *Clouds of May* during the opening sequence, it has a narrative significance by displaying the desolate isolation of the small town. *Anatolia* is bookended with the blurred image of men drinking behind a foggy glass before one of them is murdered (a trope for the blurred vision of the spectator regarding the motif of the murder) and the doctor gazing at the victim's wife and child through the morgue window after omitting a crucial detail from his report. *Winter Sleep*'s final and perhaps most crucial episode depicts Nihal gazing at her husband behind the glass of her bedroom window while Aydın recites, Romeo fashion, his monologue/love letter to her, words she cannot hear but perhaps run over in her memory. *The Wild Pear Tree*'s opening scene focuses on Sinan observed through a semi-opaque glass, reflecting his state of mind when he returns home after his studies.
5. For more on this, see Hasan Akbulut's chapter, 'Staying in The Primary Home, Relationships, Desires to Go and Roots: *Kış Uykusu/Winter Sleep* (2018) and *Ahlat Ağacı/ The Wild Pear Tree* (2018)'.

6. During my masterclass with Ceylan in Kerala in 2014, he dismissed the idea that the sleeping bag could signify the absence of a feeling of belonging somewhere or having roots. 'I like sleeping in sleeping bags', he declared. At the same time, he has been repeating during interviews that he can be at home anywhere, but nowhere.
7. For the use of the autonomous camera by Jafar Panahi and Abbas Kiarostami, see Nagib 2020: 70–6.
8. For more on *Distant*, see my chapter in this volume, '"Gender Trouble"' and the Crises of Masculinities'.
9. Ceylan has mentioned during interviews that he had a gay neighbour in the building where he shot *Distant* and where he lived, who used to bring young men home and was eventually killed by one of them. Originally, he planned to include the murder in the film and did some shooting but then decided that the murder would take centre stage and eclipse the real subject, which for him is 'existential issues'.
10. Ceylan revives the trope of the urban as the coloniser and the rural as the colonised in *Three Monkeys*. Eyüp, the private driver is an uprooted migrant, whose fragile home is shaken by Servet, the boss with urban appearance and mannerism, who tempts him with a hefty sum of money to sacrifice his freedom and seduces his wife with the same disposition.
11. *Distant* won the Grand Prix and the Best Male Actor awards (shared between Mehmet Emin Toprak and Muzaffer Özdemir) at the Cannes Film Festival (2003). A few months earlier, Toprak died in a traffic accident.
12. See Suner 2010; Dönmez-Colin 2008, 2014.
13. It is worth noting here that, in terms of finding a balance between art house and box office success, the New Cinema of Turkey has never gained the popularity of Cinema da Retomada, except for the later works of Ceylan, which, like their Brazilian counterparts have resorted to using famous names from popular television series (such as Melisa Sözen as Nihal, Ayberk Pekcan as Hidayet, Serhat Kılıç as Hamdi in *Winter Sleep*; Murat Cemcir as İdris, Hazar Ergüçlü as Hatice, Bennu Yıldırımlar as Asuman in *The Wild Pear Tree*, or a popular folk singer like Yavuz Bingöl as Eyüp in *Three Monkeys*.)

CITED WORKS

Aliçavuşoğlu, Esra (1997), Interview, '*Kasaba Tıpkı Ada Gibi Bir Film*' *Cumhuriyet Kültür*, December.
Anastopoulos, Thanos (2006), 'The Craft of Descent' (Trans. Tina Sideris), in Dimitris Kerkinos (ed) *Nuri Bilge Ceylan*, Thessaloniki International Film Festival Balkan Survey Tribute to Nuri Bilge Ceylan. Athens: Hellenic Ministry of Culture.
Bhabha, Homi K. (1994), *The Location of Culture*. London and New York: Routledge.
Chéroux, Clément and Jean-Marie Frodon (2016), *Jafar Panahi: Images/Nuages*. Paris: Filigranes éditions/Centre Pompidou.
Daldal, Aslı (2003), *Art, Politics and Society: Social Realism in Italian and Turkish Cinemas*. Istanbul: The Isis Press.
Diken, Bülent, Graeme Gilloch and Craig Hammond (2018), *The Cinema of Nuri Bilge Ceylan: The Global Vision of a Turkish Filmmaker*. London and New York: I.B. Tauris.
Dönmez-Colin, Gönül (2014), *The Routledge Dictionary of Turkish Cinema*. London and New York: Routledge.
____ (2008), *Turkish Cinema: Identity, Distance and Belonging*, Reaktion Books: London.

Jameson, Fredric (1991), *Postmodernism, or The Cultural Logic of Late Capitalism*. London and New York: Verso.

Kesal E. and Hande Birkalan Gedik (2019), '3 Monkeys: Understanding Change in Turkey Through a Film'. http://www.ercankesal.com/3-monkeys-understanding-change-in-turkey-through-a-film/ (last accessed 13 June 2022)

Marker, Sherry (1990), *Edward Hopper*. New York: Crescent.

Nagib, Lúcia (2020) *Realist Cinema as World Cinema: Non-cinema, Intermedial Passages, Total Cinema*. Amsterdam: Amsterdam University Press.

____ (2007), 'The Zero, the Centre and the Empty Utopia; From Rossellini to Walter Salles' in *Studies in European Cinema*, 3/3, pp. 223–33.

Orban, Clara (2021, *Slow Places in Béla Tarr's Films: The Intersection of Geography, Ecology, and Slow Cinema*. Washington, D.C: Rowman & Littlefield.

Özyurt, Olkan (2007), 'Fotoğraf Çekmek Benim İçin Terapi Gibi'. Interview. *Radikal: Kültür/Sanat*. 8 April, 23.

Rancière, Jacques (1977), 'Interview: The Image of Brotherhood", trans. Kari Hanet, *Edinburgh Magazine*, 2, 28.

Shrikent, Indu (1999), 'Ordinary Stories of Ordinary People: An Interview with Nuri Bilge Ceylan'. *Cinemaya: The Asian Film Quarterly*, 43, Spring, 22–3.

Suner, Asuman (2010), *The New Turkish Cinema: Belonging, Identity and Memory*, London and New York: I.B. Tauris.

Rayns, Tony (2004), '*Uzak*' in *Sight & Sound*, 14/6, London: BFI.

Tarkovsky, Andrey (1987), *Sculpting in Time*, New York: Alfred A Knopf.

CHAPTER TWO

Vanishing Image of History: *Uzak/Distant* (2002)

Mahmut Mutman

Nuri Bilge Ceylan's *Uzak/Distant* (2002) is often described as the climax of what has come to be called his 'trilogy' following *Kasaba/The Small Town* (1997) and *Mayıs Sıkıntısı/Clouds of May* (1999). The filmmaker's use of his friends and family members in these early works is usually explained in terms of being a budget-friendly choice, but Ceylan turns it into an astonishing cinematographic search for origins and memory. Before moving on to an analysis of *Distant*, I would like to present a general discussion of this early period in Ceylan's work.

DISCIPLINARY REFLECTIONS

The discipline of film studies celebrated Ceylan's early trilogy as 'self-reflexive' and 'autobiographical': the *auteur* filmmaker reflecting on the emergence of his own process of filmmaking by making a film on it. In a stimulating essay in which she frames *Distant* in a thematic of home and exile, which is to say, a problematic of geographical *displacement*, Asuman Suner finds 'frequent employment of self-reflexivity' as well as 'self-inscription' (2006: 364, 374). By the neologism 'self-inscription', she means a kind of discourse that combines self-reflexive and autobiographical elements, as she also finds a 'highly autobiographical tone' in Ceylan's cinema (Suner 2004: 307). Similarly, James Harvey-Davitt refers to 'a hypercritical form of self-reflexivity' in *Distant* and *İklimler/Climates* (2016: 10). A major film platform, MUBI, advertises *Distant* as 'a self-reflexive film from Nuri Bilge Ceylan, on cinema, the artistic process, and the notion of home' (MUBI 2020).

Elaborating on Hamid Naficy's highly acclaimed *An Accented Cinema* (2001), Suner aims to think of a problematic of geographical-cultural 'displacement' together with the concept of 'self-reflexivity' coded as synonymous with a critical attitude. The core of her argument is that there should be no essential difference between a displacement from the 'Third World' to the West, and one from the country to the city within the same (third-world) country. Since both involve cultural difference, they must be treated in the same theoretical framework to enrich Naficy's concept of 'accented cinema', which is limited to the postcolonial filmmakers located in the West (Suner 2006).[1] This geographically based concept of displacement is considered as the natural basis for critical agency understood as self-reflexivity. A rich but circular theoretical discourse is thus created around the notions of self, home, exile, diaspora, journey, displacement, reflexivity and return. While the thematic of home vs. exile (or diaspora), i.e., the problematic of displacement, gives such an approach its apparent critical edge, it is already closed by the concept of self-reflexivity, or *self-consciousness*, which implies a return to self and a unifying presupposition. For Suner for instance, it is obvious that all three films unfold a single story – accordingly, a single and unified self (the filmmaker returning home, returning to his practice, returning to himself: the identity of the filming and the filmed): in *The Small Town*, the filmmaker turns to his origins and tells the story of his family; in *Clouds of May*, the filmmaker appears as a character in order to tell the story of how he made the previous film, and in *Distant* a major character in the first two films, his cousin (whose name is now changed to Yusuf) comes to visit the filmmaker (photographer in the story) in Istanbul (Suner 2004: 311–12, 319). This reading gives a strong narrative continuity and consistency to a series of disparate stories and discontinuous images, as the explicit change of names, places or professions in the three films plainly shows.[2] Surely, there is an undeniable autobiographical element in these stories. The answer Ceylan gives when asked by the BBC, however, is not as assured as these descriptions convey:

- Would you describe *Uzak* as an autobiographical film?
- Maybe about fifty percent autobiographical, but I couldn't say what is and what isn't. All my films are in some sense based on my own experiences, but once you start making the film you begin to forget which [parts are autobiographical], because you change everything.[3]

A question demands an answer. But even under this imposing condition, the filmmaker is not sure about the process of creating: remembering or thinking *and* changing experience, such that one becomes incapable of remembering what is remembered and what is changed. I am reminded of Freud's concept of primal scene, which follows a similar movement. Ceylan's description of his experience of filmmaking is akin to Freud's complex account of this controversial concept (Freud 2002).[4] In his most developed thoughts on the subject, the founder of psychoanalysis argued that the primal scene is indeed a retroactive fantasy construction; nevertheless this does not lead him to completely give up on its interruptive and event-like nature in favour of a merely conscious construction.⁵

MEMORY WITHOUT RECOLLECTION

Accordingly, my criticism above does not suggest that we discard the concept of origin, but instead that we should pose the question of essence or origin anew, i.e., to displace the question itself (rather than replacing it with a geographically grounded concept of displacement). How do we construct this question in the context of memory? Although remembering is ordinarily seen as our ability to recollect past experiences, this received wisdom assumes that I had full knowledge of the remembered experience as I was going through it. This is the customary assumption (shared by the concept of self-reflexivity) that memory is conscious and voluntary. Walter Benjamin found another kind of memory in Proust's work: 'involuntary memory', which Proust replaced with Bergson's concept of pure memory (Benjamin 1968: 158–9). For Proust involuntary memory was a chance occurrence, emerging out of a contingent encounter with an object, which is associated with an affect, and suddenly revived a past event or place. Attending to the non-conscious implications of Proust's discovery, and working it through Freud's notion of memory trace, Benjamin argued that 'only what has *not* been *experienced explicitly and consciously*, what has not happened to the subject as an experience, can become a component of involuntary memory' (Benjamin 1968: 160–1 – my emphasis).

Therefore, rather than simply leaving essentialism aside; a genuine critique of its homogenising force must insist on the complexity and heterogeneity of what counts as essence. Let us follow then the trope of return and go back to the beginning *before* beginning, Ceylan's first movie, his beautiful experimental short, titled or framed by a rich metaphor of essence: *Koza/Cocoon* (egg, envelope, membrane, film) (1995). *Cocoon* is a short, black-and-white, non-narrative film about a couple (husband and wife). The film opens with pictures of the couple in their youth and then moves to various images of them in old age, together or alone, sleeping, walking, sitting or doing housework in and around what looks like a farmhouse. We also have images of a male child of about eleven years old, though occupying less space than the couple. The images of natural environment around the house, the trees, the grass, the leaves also take part in this flow. All images have a definitive photographic quality, even when they involve a short sequence or just some camera movement. Involving no speech or dialogue, the silent parade of images is accompanied by musical pieces from Bach, Peter Gabriel and Vyacheslav Artyomov. On first impression, it seems as if the abandonment of the narrative strategy gives these images their *discontinuous* character. However, it is also, more importantly, the filmmaker's singular photographic talent of playing with light and dark as if the whole film is traversed by finitude: a Caravaggio-like, dim light allegorising the passing of time. While these ghostly images allude to the internal relationship between the cut of the image and the discontinuous time of death (which returns *into* the frame with the image of a dead cat), they are also marked by intense affectivity and tactility, which signifies the filmmaker's passion for the image, for what it is capable of saying without saying, as much as his love of the people and the places he shoots. What do we see, or what is it that *touches* us in this veritable de-spectacularising of the image? It is what Michel Foucault called 'memory without recollection [*la mémoir sans souvenir*] . . . a memory utterly purged of all recollection' (Foucault 2008: 158).[6] It is a particular kind of memory work, which cancels recollection, but keeps the affects and the percepts.[7] The removal of recollection from memory is what turns the image into an apparition or ghost, while giving it a uniquely affective force.[8]

A LAST DISCIPLINARY REFLECTION: 'SLOW CINEMA'?

The question is therefore one of memory in the age of speed – or of perception by shock, as described by Benjamin (1968: 161–2). It is not for nothing that the novelty of Ceylan's cinema is often described in terms of the *slowness* of its narrative pace. The concept of 'slow cinema', apparently modelled on the ecological concept of slow city, draws on the careful identification of a number of formal features, which describe a certain style of filmmaking common to a number of filmmakers: the frequent use of long takes, descriptive pauses or dead time in the works of Béla Tarr, Tsai Ming-Liang and Nuri Bilge Ceylan (Antonioni and a few others are also counted as forerunners).[9] Since my analysis to follow might have certain similarities with the analyses developed from within this concept (especially in terms of the questions of image and time), I would like to elaborate on the elements in Ceylan's work that distinguish it from 'slow cinema.'

Although it is often described and praised as a critical trend in opposition to hegemonic commercial narrative cinema, I wonder if the concept of slow cinema is a disciplinary invention of a distinct genre by the discipline of film studies. We could at least consider the possibility of its being an invention born out of a disciplinary anxiety of making readable by classification what appears to come under the empty abstraction of 'arthouse film', or an oppositional anxiety of finding an alternative to mainstream cinema. One can certainly find the privileging of several formal features such as long takes and descriptive pause in the works of these filmmakers. Indeed a number of film scholars have offered valuable analyses of these formal features, involving close readings of

Distant.¹⁰ But the moment we give such features the name 'slow cinema', we do something quite different indeed: a varied artistic search is written back into a set of binarisms of slow vs fast, intellectual vs popular, high vs low, art vs commerce, aesthetic vs technological, natural vs artificial. Hence, although the proponents of this category approach what I would describe as challenging questions of time and image in a new way, the answer is already given in the concept of the 'slowness' of the *movement* of images.¹¹ A series of formal analyses are thus reinforced by a concept safely grounded in well-intended anti-technological politics. But the concept of 'slowness' falls short of what must be regarded as an artistic search. This is not simply to honour individual artistic creativity. Rather, one must join these diverse artistic searches in scholarly activity, whose job should not be limited to description. As I have tried to show in the above short analysis of *Cocoon*, Ceylan's cinema is a search tracing the power of the image, especially in its relationship with finitude. We should perhaps call such films, in more modest terms, simply 'cinema'.

FAR NEAR

Ceylan's turn to narrative is inevitable as far as the cut of the image also calls for another image, whether continuous or discontinuous with the previous one. There is here a struggle that needs to be appreciated rather than comprehended in a formally and scholarly sanctioned concept of slowness. While it was relatively safe to establish the relationship between time and image in the discontinuous time of memory, or to adopt the interruptive memory in the familiar experience of a quasi-photographic flow in *Cocoon*, there is nevertheless the slow emergence of narrative exigency. Once you are out of your cocoon (photographic tissue/film), there is now a life to be lived, *a story to be told*. The question then becomes how to negotiate this search for images with the exigency of narration.¹² The latter might turn out to be a predatory species: unless one finds a way of taming it, one's search is bound to slip through the film frames in the narrative necessity of 'the confusion of consecution and consequence' as Roland Barthes described it: 'what comes *after* being read in narrative as what is *caused by*' (1977: 94). Although this confusion is necessary to the narrative, it also implies that narrative happens *in time*. Far from giving up on the question of time, or simply resolving it for the ease of narrating a story, there is a struggle to reformulate it. First, the story must be close to one's own experience, something familiar, so that the force of narration (its unfolding in time, its inevitable turns) will come under control. Secondly, it must be kept at a minimal level, as ordinary as possible: the story refers to a new kind of event which happens *within* as well as between the images.¹³ This second aspect makes unfamiliar the familiarity of the story based on experience. A new, alien dimension is thus opened within the image itself, a dimension in which the image takes its own time. Hence a new experience of time, brought about by the formal devices which produce the effect of slowing down: long take, descriptive pause, dead time. But such devices cannot be taken in isolation from what needs to be told. There is a story, content to be told, even though it is a story that can only be told by these formal means. Something like a solution emerges in the focus on a different sense of time, which is also a different sense of living: *the everyday*.[14] What kind of time is the everyday? The first characteristics that come to mind are its repetitive, familiar and event-less character. But are all these features of the everyday not also responsible for the feeling of a strange void or distance, which traverses it? Drawing on Henri Lefebvre's work, Maurice Blanchot developed an uncanny approach to this most familiar passage of time: 'the everyday escapes' (1993: 240).[15] It is without a subject (I am anyone in the everyday), and without an objective (even when I use the washing machine, or I prepare a trap for the mouse in all seriousness as in the *Distant*, these are acts which substitute an indefinite presence). In its ever-closed indetermination, the everyday secretes discontinuity by its continuity.

Who are the characters that appear in the unfamiliar familiarity of the everyday? They appear out of a content or sense which calls for the style, i.e., the formal devices; but in turn, this is a style which has already made them appear as different figures, i.e., bundles of gestures, words, looks. It is as if the search into the powers of the image can only be conducted as far as one brings a *social difference* into it. Like in almost all of Ceylan's feature films, the narratives in the trilogy are traversed by two kinds of difference, which together foreclose any possibility of a pure or commanding origin in a kind of impossible exchange with each other: a spatial difference between the country and the city on the one hand, and a social difference between the middle class and the working class on the other. These two sets of difference, overdetermined as they are in various stories, constitute a unique differential force field of gestures, words and images, which has now become Ceylan's signature as auteur.[16] When Ceylan referred to his 'lonely and beautiful country' in an acceptance speech at Cannes, some interpreted this as a concession to nationalism or part of a publicity campaign, others as idealist nostalgia. It seems however that the 'country' meant in such a phrase is not a usual place, not a referent territorially unified under a flag, but the strange 'atopological' topography of a singular differential force field, a cinematographic rendering of what is conventionally called a national culture: working class mannerisms, petty bourgeois voices, failings to say, impossible conversations, empty streets, love at last sight, the corner of a building, leaves blowing in the wind. It is neither country nor city, neither the dominant class nor the other class, but their difference. If, as we learn from Benedict Anderson (1991), nationalism's imagined community requires the production of homogeneous, empty, linear time in newspapers and novels, the imagined national is the use or abuse of the fact that everyone is born into a language and into a locality, that is, the use or abuse of the familiar, of what is most intimate to me (the words I speak, the corner I turn every day). Ceylan's cinema teaches us that such intimacy involves an irreducible heterogeneity.

It is this register of differences, and especially class difference, which keeps coming back and haunts Ceylan's cinema. As many critics have rightly emphasised, in *Distant*, the photographer Mahmut is irritated by what he sees in his cousin Yusuf: his own lower class, rural background. It should be noted however that he himself also appears on the other side, as a major figure in Yusuf's affective investment. Speaking of his desire to find a job in international cargo ships, Yusuf says: 'you have seen all around the world. I want to see the world too!' The affective register of class is stronger than the kinship tie. In the incongruous topography made by difference, the near is far, the far near. And it is in this immeasurable distance, in this intimate void, that the film takes the measure of their humanity.

IN RUINS, OUT OF PLACE: IMMEASURABLE

Mahmut and Yusuf are figures of their separate communities: Mahmut's petty bourgeois community of artists and Yusuf's family and community in the small town he left behind. It is customary to approach such a story in a sociological problematic of 'transition' from a rural community to an urban society. I would like to argue instead that what is at stake, the so-called migration from rural to urban areas, is a transit, i.e., a structural feature of global capitalism, and *not a transition to it*. Raymond Williams' fascinating critical history of English literature, *The Country and the City*, is a significant work that comes to mind in this context. In this classic work, Williams read precisely the same class and spatial differences in the English novels in the nineteenth century (Williams 1973). There is a good deal of historical and cultural difference between Williams' (or his novelists') England and Ceylan's Turkey. While Williams evokes, to some extent, the sociological distinction between society and community (the former characterised by opacity and formality of relations, the latter by transparency and informality), his well-known and much-discussed concept of 'knowable community' puts the emphasis on *the perspective* from which the community is known.[17] His concept of community is therefore neither given nor nostalgic, but critical: Jane Austen's community is 'outstandingly face-to-face' but this reveals 'a moral grammar' rather than social reality – a grammar Williams read through 'a look, a gesture, a stare, a confrontation' (1973: 166). Ironically for Williams, the knowable community as a method of novel writing emerged at the historical moment when the community in question entered a process of transformation.

We might also speak of an interesting articulation of bourgeois moral grammar in *Distant*. In the film's perspective, however, such a bourgeois grammar is shown to be the displaced effect of an individual crisis rather than being originated in an epistemological assurance. Almost all the affairs, which allegorise the insufferable relationship between Mahmut and Yusuf, revolve around the issue of the order in the house. Although expected as a guest, and tolerated as close kin, Yusuf remains an outsider, an intruder who disrupts the order of the house in Mahmut's view. He keeps replacing his dirty pair of shoes; he berates him for leaving the apartment untidy, for failing to clean the toilet after using it, or for smoking inside; and finally, he insinuates that he has stolen an old watch he uses as a prop in his photographic work. All these instances position Yusuf on the side of disorder: he is a nuisance, an idler, and a parasite. Although Mahmut is typically middle class in his defence of the order, there is nevertheless some ambiguity that surrounds the social and cultural aspect of his character. As an artist, he belongs to a petty bourgeois intellectual world, which is, as legible especially for the Turkish audience, a typically left-wing environment, i.e., the small community we see at the party at his friend's house. In sharp contrast, in the scene in which he berates Yusuf for asking him a favour, his tirade is the hegemonic Turkish urban bourgeois discourse on the migrant from the rural areas. Yusuf is violently de-individuated and seen as belonging to a category which consists of those who come to the big city and expect to have a job and status without the slightest effort, asking for favours and looking for easy gains. Here, what Williams would have called 'perspective' is an instance of *free indirect discourse*, i.e. the narrative angle that implies the redundancy of Mahmut's speech: a dominant (class) enunciation, frequently articulated in the press and on TV, is internalised and mobilised by Mahmut as a displaced effect of his own crisis: with his unresolved relations with his ex-wife and his secret relationship with a married woman, his emotional-sexual life is in ruins, and with a commercial job that he hates as an artist and with his fading passion for artistic work, his professional life is no less so.[18] While his economic well-being is at the expense of a life misspent, he presents himself as an ideal by which he ascertains Yusuf's moral and subjective failure.

As for Yusuf, although he does his best (asking permission to use the phone or to put his wet shoes under the radiator, anxiously tidying up the living room), he always forgets something or does something wrong. It is as if he cannot locate himself in this place, which involves *a measure he cannot figure out*. All his life seems to be a series of distances he fails to estimate: on his first day in the big city, he leans on a parked car and makes the alarm go; he looks intimidated and puzzled, out of place, while listening to the conversations between Mahmut and his friends at the party; as soon as he makes a move to talk with the woman he likes, to finally cross over the enthralling boundary, he realises she is there to meet her boyfriend.

'TIME TO DIE'[19]

But perhaps there is also a place for Yusuf, or rather a kind of no-place at the margins of the urban (and, at the same time, filmic) frame into which he is trying to fit himself. What we may call the film's allegory of the mouse shows that this place involves a certain kind of time, or a certain sense of time that is radically uncertain.

The mouse Mahmut has been after for a long time finally gets stuck on the glue trap set at the kitchen door. Waking in the middle of the night because he is so disturbed by Mahmut's insinuations, Yusuf finds the poor animal struggling to free itself from the sticky pad. He watches the mouse, the abject animal par excellence, that little enemy of our urban civilised life, just like he watched the fish in their death throes on the fisherman's stand: *how long does it take to die? What happens in that strange duration between life and death?* (Is it the same question Mahmut is asking, when he wakes up from the nightmare in which he sees his apartment on fire because of a lampshade falling?). After a little discussion on what to do with the mouse, Mahmut asks Yusuf if he could wrap the poor animal in the sticky pad, put it in a plastic bag and throw it in the garbage bin outside the building – a task he would leave to the doorman to do tomorrow morning, were it not for the animal's crying the whole night. When Yusuf goes out, however, he sees the cats around the garbage bin, and instead of leaving the still living mouse there as a prey, he kills it himself by banging the plastic bag on the wall.

How to interpret this sequence – the consecution of trapping a mouse and the consequence of the dead one? (As the rule of narrative says: if there is a mousetrap in the story, it will catch a mouse at a later point.) With his uncontrolled, childish laughter, his idle wanderings in the city, his constant failure to keep the proper order, Yusuf is surely closer to, and is associated with, the animal in the unspoken (i.e., civilised) order of things. It is his supposed intimacy with the uncivil, natural world of animal violence and misery, which gives him his lot: the dirty business of getting rid of the animal, eventually killing it out of pity, as if he finally found a job as the doorman's stand-in. The sequence can be read as a successful metaphor of Yusuf's predicament at the cutting edge of living, allegorised by the mouse trapped.

The predicament is further complicated by the emphasis on the struggle of the mouse: it takes time to die. As there is no way of freeing itself from the sticky pad, the mouse is already dead. And, as death has not yet arrived, it cannot but struggle to free itself from the sticky surface. When Yusuf takes it to the garbage bin and sees the cats there, he decides to kill it himself, i.e., he enunciates its death in a silent speech act. Watching the fish in their death throes on the stall, or the poor mouse crying and struggling on the sticky pad, Yusuf would like to know, like all of us, how long it takes to die. How does one die? What is it that one goes through when one dies? While these questions arise out of his experience, they are foreclosed to him: he is given the task of bringing the death to an end, deciding the time of death of the mouse, as *his share* of humanity.

VANISHING IMAGE OF HISTORY

It is Ceylan's subtle, careful and close critique of sheer class difference registered on the affective level, which enables him to recognise Yusuf's ordeal, the non-place and the paradox of his humanity. The search for the relationship between time and image finds a reference in social difference. But, far from taking it as an answer, artistic exploration gives a new force to this difference. To make better sense of this, I must turn to Gilles Deleuze's shrewd observation of a thought-provoking difference between 'classical' and 'modern' cinema:

> ... classical cinema constantly maintained this boundary which marked the correlation of the political and the private, and which allowed, through the intermediary of an awareness, passage from one social force to another, from one political position to another: Pudovkin's *Mother* discovers the son's real object in fighting, and takes it over; in Ford's *The Grapes of Wrath*, it is the mother who sees clearly up to a certain point, and who is relieved by the son when conditions change. This is no longer the case in modern political cinema, where no boundary survives to provide a minimum distance or evolution: the private affair merges with the social – or political – immediate (Deleuze 1989: 218).

Deleuze then offers Yılmaz Güney's *Sürü/The Herd* (1978) and *Yol/The Way* (1982) as his examples.[20] We know that Güney is one of Ceylan's favourite filmmakers, but we should not look for continuity or influence here. It is a question of the erasure of the boundary that separates the private from the social, and its merging with it, which these two 'modern' (in Deleuze's sense) filmmakers share. The awareness or consciousness which marked classical cinema was epistemological, a matter of knowledge. Perhaps the loss of this epistemological passage is no reason for sadness, but a new condition that is now forcing the artist to reformulate his task in search of a new image – an image that interrupts representation rather than delivering the truth of it or the knowledge of its transformation. No knowable community, no moral grammar from Ceylan's camera angle. On the contrary, the meticulous tracing of a differential force field of gestures, words and images (unheard of speeds), which reveals no judgment but produces the affective force of an ethical interruption of representation. One can surely find numerous examples of such an interruptive image, a memory work in search of its involuntary force, in search of a figure without representation, in Ceylan's work. The final scene of *Distant* offers one of the best instances.

As their relationship reaches an impasse with the episode of the misplaced watch, Yusuf, realising that Mahmut searched his luggage, leaves Mahmut's apartment. We find out that he did so however, when Mahmut realises to his surprise that Yusuf left the keys hanging on the hook. He then checks the room and sees the already made bed on the floor and the absence of Yusuf's belongings, except for the pack of cigarettes. We notice the slightly affectionate expression on Mahmut's face. We then see him sitting on a bench by the seaside and lighting a cigarette he takes out of the same pack, 'a sailor's cigarette' he refused to smoke before. The ending is much praised by critics because it shows how Mahmut was able to sympathise with Yusuf only after Yusuf left: despite all the daily quarrels with someone close, we understand the significance of their place in our lives only after their disappearance – a universal human experience. But, to my knowledge, no one has asked where Yusuf has gone. Is there not also something of a failure in the film's (and the critics') exclusive focus on Mahmut's affection, which also implies an easy acceptance of Yusuf's absence? Is that the end, really? If this is an end however, it is also one we have not seen: we should speak of success so far as the film does not show where Yusuf has gone. Where did he go? We do not know, nor does the filmmaker. Out of work, out of place, unexpected guest, involuntary memory. Remaining a figure without representation, Yusuf is the vanishing image of our present.[21]

NOTES

1. Suner's aim is to further develop Naficy's concept of 'accented cinema' by demonstrating the amplitude of its field of application (2006: 365). Does Suner also assume that a single focus on geographical displacement is already a critique of the concept of national cinema without any critical treatment of this concept itself? There is no reason why Ceylan should not be read under such a concept, as his work is a meticulous undoing of the very concept of the 'national.'
2. Emre Çağlayan also confirms that the early trilogy is autobiographical and constitutes a single story (2018: 175–8). Why do these critics, who think Ceylan's cinema is non-narrative, struggle to give to his films a narrative continuity? Interestingly, there are moments in Suner's analysis, which seem to move in the opposite direction of the general thrust of her argument. Referring to the founding texts of Mary Ann Doane and Kaja Silverman, she argues that the sonic regime of dominant cinema anchors the sound to an immediately visible source and this kind of 'smooth alignment of sound and image fosters the reality effect that the mainstream cinema seeks to create' (2004: 318). This approach clearly goes against her concept of self-reflexivity since it is critical of the natural unity of the speaking subject in cinema. However, since Suner assumes that the critical agency anchored in self-reflexivity is *given* in the geographical-cultural displacement, she argues that the counter-hegemonic

strategy of 'dissonant voice' can be found in Ceylan's work. Her example, a scene in *Clouds of May*, in which the filmmaker is striving to shoot a scene with his father as actor shows indeed *the impossibility of self-reflexivity*, as she admits: 'what appears to be "natural" in the scene, the father's failure in performing himself, is already a successful performance' (Suner 2004: 320). There is no dissonance. Not surprisingly, Suner's following last resort is the prompt in the same scene: 'the words that actually belong to the father are prompted by an external voice. Such a dissociation of voice and person serves to destabilise assumptions about having a smooth and self-integrated identity' (Suner 2004: 320), *as if* the character who *acts as the prompt* is not *within* the fictive space of diegesis, not to mention the fact that the actor who plays this role is quite successful too, just like the father! If there is praise to be given to this scene, we must talk of its graceful and humorous showing of the *mundanity* of filmmaking – an activity that is not privileged by Ceylan, whose position *vis-à-vis* mainstream cinema does not seem to be a simplistic opposition at all.

3. http://www.bbc.co.uk/bbcfour/cinema/film_award/shortlist/uzak.shtml One also needs to underline that such a use of the concept of autobiography is uncritical. Auto-bio-graphy (self-life-writing) is a rationalisation of 'the ideological demand that we should consist as coherent and recognisable subjects in relation to a particular knowledge' (Smith 1988: 105–6). Assuming the imaginary identity of the subject of enunciation (writing or filming subject) and the subject of statement (written or filmed subject), autobiographical text is indeed an ideological form of self-reflexivity.
4. Freud's classic account can be found in the chapter 5 of his case of the 'Wolf Man' (2002). For a fascinating reworking of the concept through literature, psychoanalysis and philosophy, see Ned Lukacher 1986.
5. My reading of primal scene is influenced by Lukacher to some extent (Lukacher 1986: 23–4).
6. I borrow Michel Foucault's elegant formulation (memory without souvenirs) from a reading of Marguerite Duras' work, which he developed together with Helene Cixous in a fascinating interview. I do not claim that there is similarity between the works of Duras and Ceylan, but perhaps an intersection in respect of a certain characteristic.
7. 'Sensations, percepts and affects are beings whose validity lies in themselves and exceed any lived' (Deleuze and Guattari 1994: 164).
8. Jacques Derrida has argued that cinema (and modern image in general) is the return of ghosts (Derrida and Stiegler 2002). This technological condition also reveals the spectrality of memory.
9. One can find the most interesting and productive uses of the concept of 'slow cinema' in the following works, even though I find the category problematic: Çağlayan (2018), Jaffe (2014) and Lim (2014).
10. Ira Jaffe examines the specificity of the 'long shot' in Ceylan's *Distant* and *İklimler/ Climates* (2014: 67–86); Çağlayan develops rich formal analyses of selected scenes in *Distant* and *Bir Zamanlar Anadolu'da/Once Upon a Time in Anatolia*, (2018: 161–220) and Song Hwee Lim offers interesting observations on the use of long shots and time in *Distant* (2020: 19–20).
11. In their well-known work, *A Thousand Plateaus*, Gilles Deleuze and Felix Guattari have demonstrated that there are always differential and comparable speeds, some of which are indeed speeds in stillness (1987: 75–6). 'It is a question of speed,' they write, 'even if the movement is in place' (1987: 187). Trinh-Min-ha is of the same opinion: 'It is in stillness that one may be said to find true speed' (Trinh Min-ha quoted in Beckman and Ma 2008: 10). From this point of view, we may well speak of the unusual speed of Ceylan's images: the 'stillness' in Çağlayan's analysis of descriptive pauses in *Distant* might involve unusual speeds (the precipitation of words that cannot be said by Yusuf, the young woman's silent refusal to turn her body).

12. This exigency is 'Aristotelian' before being commercial. (See Rancière 2006: 1–2.) However, I interpret it differently than Rancière.
13. Such decisions further complicate the relationship between time and image by relieving finitude or discontinuity from its immediate identity with death. Death returns nevertheless: in the scenes of Yusuf watching the fish as well as the mouse in the throes of death.
14. I do not claim to talk about a real development here. This is a retroactive construction, an order of presentation, in which I had to skip both *The Small Town* and *Clouds of May*.
15. In placing the unfamiliar in the middle of the familiar, Blanchot's approach resonates with Freud's concept of the uncanny (Freud 1999): 'Whatever its other aspects, the everyday has this essential trait: it allows no hold. It escapes. It belongs to insignificance; the insignificant being what is without truth, without reality, and without secret, but also perhaps the site of all possible signification. The everyday escapes. In this consists its strangeness – the familiar showing itself (but already dispersing) in the guise of the astonishing. It is the unperceived, first in the sense that we have always looked past it; nor can we introduce it into a whole or 'review' it, that is to say, enclose it within a panoramic vision; for, by another trait, the everyday is what we never see for a first time but can only see again, having always already seen it by an illusion that is constitutive of the everyday' (1993: 239–40). When Suner employs Freud's concept of the uncanny to understand the works of Ceylan and Zeki Demirkubuz, she is close to this kind of approach. But since she reads the uncanny from within the concept of genre, which is clearly not appropriate for these works, she finds herself in the position of trying to control the concept by describing their works as 'horror of *a different kind*' (Suner 2004).
16. Surely, Ceylan's image is also made by gender difference. Seemingly insignificant, it is another immeasurable difference, and requires a different analysis by itself. I should note however that, while the story shows the destabilizing force of sexual difference on both Yusuf and Mahmut, the women remain marginal in it. This brings up the question of whether marginality is a condition of the story itself.
17. 'Most novels are in some sense knowable communities. It is part of a traditional method – an underlying stance and approach – that the novelist offers to show people and their relationships in essentially knowable and communicable ways. . . . In changes like these any assumption of a knowable community – a whole community, wholly knowable – becomes harder and harder to sustain . . . we must be careful not to idealise the old and new facts of the country. For what is knowable is not only a function of objects – of what is there to be known. It is also a function of subjects, of observers – of what is desired and what needs to be known' (Williams 1973: 165).
18. 'The social character of enunciation is intrinsically founded only if one succeeds in demonstrating how enunciation in itself implies collective assemblages. It then becomes clear that the statement is individuated, and enunciation subjectified, only to the extent that an impersonal collective assemblage requires it and determines it to be so' (Deleuze and Guattari 1987: 80).
19. 'All those moments will be lost in time, like tears in rain. Time to die.' (The last words of the replicant Roy Batty's soliloquy in the film *Blade Runner* by Ridley Scott.)
20. *Sürü/The Herd* (1978), a realistic portrayal of Turkey in transition to capitalism, was scripted by Yılmaz Güney while in prison and directed by Zeki Ökten and *Yol/The Way* (1982), also written by Yılmaz Güney while he was in prison, was shot by Şerif Gören according to Güney's instructions. Both films expose the disintegration of the system of patriarchy, from the state to the family. In 1982, *Yol* shared the Palme d'Or at the Cannes Film Festival with *Missing* by Costa-Gavras (editor's note).
21. I borrow the metaphor of 'vanishing present' from Gayatri Chakravorty Spivak: 'the vanishing moment of sequential human temporality' (Spivak 1999: 53).

CITED WORKS

Anderson, Benedict (1991), *Imagined Communities: Reflections on the Origin and Spread of Nationalism.* New York and London: Verso.

Barthes, Roland (1977), *Image Music Text,* ed. and trans. Stephen Heath, London: Fontana Press.

BBC Four: 'Interview with Nuri Bilge Ceylan' http://www.bbc.co.uk/bbcfour/cinema/film_award/shortlist/uzak.shtml (no longer available)

Beckman, Karen and Jean Ma (2008), *Still Moving: Between Cinema and Photography.* Durham: Duke University Press.

Benjamin, Walter (1968), *Illuminations: Essays and Reflections,* ed. and int. Hannah Arendt, New York: Schocken Books.

Blanchot, Maurice (1993), *Infinite Conversation,* trans. Susan Hanson, Minneapolis: University of Minnesota Press.

Çağlayan, Emre (2018), *Poetics of Slow Cinema: Nostalgia, Absurdism, Boredom.* Cham, Switzerland: Palgrave Macmillan.

Deleuze, Gilles (1989), *Cinema 2: The Time-Image,* trans. Hugh Tomlinson and Robert Galeta, Minneapolis: University of Minnesota Press.

Deleuze, Gilles and Felix Guattari (1987). *A Thousand Plateaus,* trans. Brian Massumi, Minneapolis: University of Minnesota Press.

Deleuze, Gilles and Felix Guattari (1994). *What is Philosophy?* trans. Graham Burchell and Hugh Tomlinson, New York: Columbia University Press.

Derrida, Jacques and Bernard Stiegler (2002). *Echographies of Television: Filmed Interviews,* Cambridge: Polity.

Freud, Sigmund (2002), *Wolf Man: from the History of an Infantile Disease,* trans. Louis Adey Huish, London: Penguin.

Freud, Sigmund (1999), 'The Uncanny'. In *The Standard Edition of the Complete Psychological Works of Sigmund Freud, Volume XVII (1917–1919): An Infantile Neurosis and Other Works,* London: Vintage, 217–56.

Foucault, Michel (2008), 'On Marguerite Duras, with Michel Foucault', in Helene Cixous, *White Ink: Interviews on Sex, Text and Politics,* trans. Susan Sellers, Stocksfield: Acumen.

Harvey-Davitt, James (2016), 'Conflicted selves: the humanist cinema of Nuri Bilge Ceylan', *New Review of Film and Television Studies,* 14: 2, 1–19.

Jaffe, Ira (2014), *Slow Movies: Countering the Cinema of Action.* London and New York: Wallflower Press.

Lim, Song Hwee (2014), *Tsai Ming-liang and a Cinema of Slowness.* Honolulu: Hawaii University Press.

Lukacher, Ned (1986), *Primal Scenes: Literature, Philosophy, Psychoanalysis.* Ithaca and London: Cornell University Press.

Naficy, Hamid (2001), *An Accented Cinema: Exilic and Diasporic Filmmaking.* New Jersey: Princeton University Press.

MUBI (2020) https://twitter.com/mubi/status/1326923710557728770

Rancière, Jacques (2006), *Film Fables.* trans. Emiliano Battista, Oxford and New York: Berg.

Smith, Paul (1988), *Discerning the Subject.* Minneapolis: University of Minnesota Press.

Spivak, Gayatri Chakravoty (1999), *A Critique of Postcolonial Reason: Toward a History of the Vanishing Present.* Cambridge, Massachusetts and London: Harvard University Press.

Suner, Asuman (2006), 'Outside in: "accented cinema" at large' *Inter-Asia Cultural Studies,* 7:3, 363–82.

Suner, Asuman (2004), 'Horror of a different kind: dissonant voices of Turkish cinema' *Screen,* 45: 4, 305–23.

Williams, Raymond (1973), *The Country and the City,* New York: Oxford University Press.

CHAPTER THREE

Portraits and Landscape: *İklimler/Climates* (2006)

Cecília Mello

This chapter offers a close analysis of Nuri Bilge Ceylan's *İklimler/Climates* (2006) from the point of view of its intermedial relationship with photography and painting. Ceylan's fifth film, *Climates* follows a couple, İsa and Bahar, played by Ceylan himself and his wife Ebru Ceylan, undergoing a relationship crisis. The intention of this chapter is to discuss the film's relationship with the art of painting and with the art of photography, noticeable in two opposing but complementary types of shot: close-ups of faces and establishing shots of the landscape. As I will suggest, *Climates* exaggerates the filmmaker's gesture – already evident in his first short *Koza/Cocoon* (1995) and recurring throughout his oeuvre, of employing close-up shots that linger on his characters'/actors' physiognomy as if in search of their singularity and interiority. This gesture harks back to pre-sound cinema's fascination with the close-up (Balázs 2010; Epstein 1998) and opens a discussion about Deleuze's 'affection-images' (1997), that is, those images that inhabit the interval between perception and action, foregrounding emotions, desires, needs. It also calls forth cinema's relationship with the art of portraiture – proper to painting's crystalized time and photography's fixed instant rather than to duration and the temporal frame. This leads to the expanded notion of 'moving portraits' (Schultz 2014; Oliveira Junior 2017), which co-exist in *Climates*' sophisticated editing structure alongside shots of natural and historical landscapes, another authorial gesture present in Ceylan's cinema that brings into the equation the issue of cinematic scale and proportion.

A FILM IN THREE MOVEMENTS

Climates can be regarded as a crucial film within Nuri Bilge Ceylan's career, signalling at least three 'firsts' for the director: it was his first film to be shot in digital, with a Sony F900 HDCAM by award-winning cinematographer Gökhan Tiryaki; it was the first time, after *Cocoon*, *Kasaba/The Small Town* (1997), *Mayıs Sıkıntısı/Clouds of May* (1999) and *Uzak/Distant* (2002) and before *Ahlat Ağacı/The Wild Pear Tree* (2018), that the predominant locale of his film was neither Yenice in the province of Çanakkale in northwest Turkey where he had spent his childhood, nor Istanbul, his birthplace and primary residence; and it was the first (and thus far the only) film in which Ceylan directed himself, taking on the role of the male protagonist and implicating his own body into his filmic universe. This personal gesture was exacerbated in the film by the casting of his wife, who had appeared briefly in *Distant* and who on this occasion took on her first and only protagonist role, playing the on-screen wife Bahar.[1] There have been, of course, frequent occasions in cinema history when a filmmaker has directed his wife (Rossellini, Cassavetes, Fellini, Vadim, Welles, to name but a few), but less so of directors directing both themselves and their partners (notable examples are Welles/Hayworth, Chabrol/Audran, Allen/Farrow, Branagh/Thompson, Jolie/Pitt). *Climates* is one of these notable examples, inevitably leading to questions about how much of a couple's real-life story is portrayed in the fictional universe of the film. Adding to this highly personal cinematic world is the film's dedication to Ceylan's son Ayaz and the brief appearance of the director's photogenic parents Fatma and Mehmet Emin Ceylan, familiar faces to faithful audiences of Ceylan's oeuvre, having appeared before in *Cocoon*, *The Small Town*, *Clouds of May* and *Distant*.

Dönmez-Colin observes how Ceylan's first films centred around issues relating to homecoming and escape from home, while '*Climates* is about an escape from a sense of establishing roots and belonging to someone' (2008: 200). This escape from establishing roots seems to be both an emotional and geographic impulse in the film, which takes the characters through separations and fleeting reconciliations, and through journeys across the country, to the southwestern province of Antalya via the ruins of Sardis in Manisa Province, Istanbul and finally Ağrı Province in Turkey's far east. These emotional and geographical journeys also signify the changing seasons of summer, autumn and winter, with the missing season coming courtesy of Bahar's name which translates as 'spring'. This builds on a continuing tradition in Ceylan's cinema of incorporating meteorological elements, with weather appearing as an atmospheric phenomenon and as a metaphor for his characters' moods.

The film, therefore, unfolds in three movements, comprising three different seasons and three different regions of Turkey. The first movement, lasting 28 minutes, starts in Sardis and ends in Kaş, a small tourist town in Antalya Province, southwestern Turkey, during a sweltering summer. It opens with what could be considered a prologue, an extraordinary sequence of the couple visiting the Temple of Artemis in Sardis, originally built by the Greeks in 300 BCE and later renovated by the Romans in the second century CE. There, İsa, a university lecturer, takes photographs for what seems to be a research project. The film then moves to Kaş, where the couple stay in a hotel overlooking the sea. İsa is seen stretched on the bed with his head inside a drawer – a possible relief for his neck pain – while Bahar sits in the balcony, framed by the door. Their increasing disconnection, suggested in the opening sequence and inside the hotel room, is further evidenced by their constant bickering as they dine alfresco with friends Arif and Semra, a sequence conveyed in a five-minute static long take. This boils over in the final part of the first movement, which opens with a shot of the sun, followed by a close-up of Bahar sleeping on the beach, covered in sweat. She dreams that İsa is burying her alive with sand, in a forthright reference to how she feels suffocated by him, and yet incapable of moving forward. Back to reality, she goes for a swim, and he rehearses a break-up speech. The editing plays a sort of trick by moving from a close-up of İsa to a semi-subjective shot of him sitting with his back to the camera, watching Bahar swimming in the distance, and finally to a medium close-up of his profile, which suddenly moves to reveal Bahar sitting next to him, making the otherwise rehearsed break-up all too real. On their way back to town, Bahar's misery impels her to cover İsa's eyes as he drives a scooter through a winding coastal road, causing an accident. But they both leave unscathed, and she finally returns to Istanbul by coach, with İsa staying behind for more pictures of ruined temples.

The second movement, which also lasts 28 minutes, takes place in Istanbul when autumn is punctuated by torrential rain. İsa teaches architecture in a college, shares an office with a colleague and is trying to finish a thesis. He has an encounter with another woman, Serap, who is going out with a friend of his, but whom he sleeps with on occasion. They meet by chance at a bookshop, and later that day he waits for her outside her house. They have violent sex, tearing each other's clothes and wrestling on the floor. Yet their second encounter is marred by the news of an earthquake and, more importantly, by talk of Bahar who, as İsa finds out, is now in the East working on a television drama. Later in his office, İsa chats with his colleague about going somewhere sunny for the winter holidays, but he instead flies to the snow-covered Ağrı Province to find his estranged partner.

The third and final movement unfolds in a small town covered in snow – the film was shot in various parts of Ağrı and Erzurum provinces, including Çat and Doğubayazıt. The fact that these are some of Turkey's poorest regions, affected by border tensions both historically and presently, is not the main concern of Ceylan in *Climates*. Rather, he purposefully softens the contrast between the country's regions by keeping the focus on the characters' inner feelings, mirrored by the weather, with internal and external moods, and not social issues, taking the front seat (see Jafaar 2007). This is the longest part of the film, running for forty minutes. After one hesitant, slightly awkward meeting in a café, İsa looks for Bahar and suggests that she leave her job and return with him to Istanbul the following day, claiming he is a changed man. She asks him if he had slept with Serap during their break-up. He lies, but only after a long pause that denounces his untruthfulness. This scene is conveyed in a long take (five minutes thirty seconds) and happens inside a minibus. The couple are constantly interrupted by crew members from the television drama, who open the door to deposit film equipment. They will meet one more time but, in the end, he leaves, and the break-up is once again final.

As Dönmez-Colin argues, even if the disintegration of the relationship makes up the core of the film's narrative, *Climates* ultimately sides with the male character, 'a macho Mediterranean male with difficulty relating to women, especially if they are gentle like Bahar' and who 'cheats on her with a woman who will give him violent sex and who can beat him at his own game' (Dönmez-Colin 2008: 166). In the moments of interaction between the main couple in the first and third movements, İsa, whose deceptiveness is somehow reminiscent of Antonioni's male protagonists in his incommunicability trilogy (*L'Avventura/The Adventure*, 1960; *La Notte/The Night*, 1961; *L'Eclisse/The Eclipse*, 1962), indeed shows himself to be authoritarian and slightly manipulative. It is his crisis – as well as his whims – that comprise the seasons and dislocations that move the film forward. But these are complicated by Bahar's sensibility, her 'female gaze', her refusal to always oblige and her subconscious that comes out in dreams.

The fact that İsa is a photographer in the film, as well as mirroring Ceylan's other metier, says something about the desire to capture and control the world, reducing it to its representation, to a parcel deprived of movement and the inexorability of time, a point to which I will return towards the end of this chapter. Overall, photography plays a key role in Ceylan's film career, notably in his first films *Cocoon, The Small Town, Clouds of May, Distant* and of course *Climates*. The transitions between the first and second and the second and third movements happen through the recourse to photography – the first from the ruins of an ancient city in Sardis, where İsa is taking pictures, to a projection of his pictures in the classroom. The cut goes from the enormousness of the real location, rendered in a long shot that conjures up the big cinema screen, to the precarity of the slide projection, which renders the imposing ruins as small and faded, accompanied by the sound of thunder that announce the change of season. Later in the film, the transition from the second to the third movement also happens through a photograph, this time the shot of a travel brochure suggestively entitled *A la carte*, filled with pictures of idyllic beaches and sunny locations. İsa holds it and stops at a page of a couple sitting on a beach with their backs to the camera, facing the turquoise sea. But the cut replaces this shot with the shot of an aeroplane, flying through heavy snowfall.

The connection between film and photography in Ceylan's cinema gains yet another dimension relating to the art of painting. Commenting on some of his photographs exhibited at the Thessaloniki International Film Festival in 2007, comprising images of country roads, farms and villages, as well as cityscapes and people, all shot with a digital panoramic camera, Geoff Andrew noted how they looked very much like paintings. This 'painterly effect' was achieved by printing with archival pigment ink on cotton rag paper, and later by coating the prints with archival varnish, giving the colours and texture an 'extraordinarily rich' effect (Andrew 2007). That Ceylan's photographs resemble paintings, and that his cinema opens to photography, both explain and validate the choice of approach and methodology in this chapter, which hopes to discuss *Climates*' relationship with photography and painting as instances of intermediality, working as crucial aesthetic and narrative devices. To this end, it is useful to evoke Ágnes Pethő's three modalities of intermedial 'border crossings',[2] the first in which media are fused, combined or integrated to form a complex multimedia or hybrid entity, the second in which media (forms, characteristics, products) are represented or referenced by other media, and the third in which media characteristics are transposed, transmediated, trans-semioticised, transformed or remediated (2020: 41). The present analysis considers the second and third modalities, by which photography is represented and referenced in *Climates* and by which characteristics of photography and painting are transposed to it. As I will suggest, both instances of intermedial border crossings are noticeable in how Ceylan interweaves close-up shots of faces and long shots of landscape in the film, enacting photographic and painterly gestures that interconnect atmospheric faces and landscape.

THE AMBIGUITY OF MOVING PORTRAITS

Cinema has been obsessed with the human face since its early days. As Mary Ann Doane observes, 'the close-up is often the site of a hysterical performance of faciality, of exaggerated expressions and hyperbolic affects' (2009: 65), and it is no wonder the non-narrative cinema of attractions served as a privileged tool for physiognomic studies, including an early genre of so-called 'facial expression films', made up entirely of close-up shots of faces (Gunning, 1997). The pre-narrative close-up soon gave way to D.W. Griffith's dramatic use of the device, employed narratively to evidence a character's emotion and becoming common currency in the Hollywood cinema from the end of the 1910s onwards. What ensued was to be one of the main obsessions of the first great cinema theorists in the 1920s, that is, the praise of the close-up as an instrument of unprecedented psychological-physiognomic knowledge, and of the filmic image as capable of revealing one's psychology or subconscious, a magical source from which emanated 'a kind of invisible, auratic, ethereal radiation [rayonnement]' (Aumont 1992: 24). Foremost among these approaches was that of Jean Epstein, who famously claimed that the close-up was the soul of the cinema, and who cultivated a faith in the cinematographic camera's revelatory powers. Yet for Epstein the close-up was necessarily tied to the conception of photogénie:[3] 'It may be brief, for photogénie is a value of the order of the second. If it is too long, I don't find continuous pleasure in it' (1988: 236). For him, it is the camera, rather than the human face, which contains the wonder of operating microdramaturgies.

More useful to this study of close-ups in Ceylan's work is Béla Balázs's notion of the close-up as a cinematic device able to reveal the occult forces of life. For Balázs, good close-ups are lyrical; they speak to the heart and not the eyes. They are dramatic revelations about what is really happening under the surface of appearances, or perhaps an expression of the unconscious:

> The play of expressions expresses feelings; in other words it is lyrical. It is a form of lyricism that is incomparably richer and full of nuance than literary works of whatever kind. Facial expressions are vastly more numerous than words! And looks can express every shade of feeling far more precisely than a description! And how much more personal is the expression of a face than words that others too may use! (Balázs 2010: 33).

Climates' close-ups are less Epsteinian and more Balázsian in that they linger on each characters'/actors' physiognomy as if in search of their singularity and interiority. Ceylan's command of style reaches a maturity in this film that translates in his preference for static long takes, allowing the actors space and time to work through an entire range of subtleties, enacting nuances that translate complex emotions and convey meaning. The film's prologue in Sardis is an eloquent example of this authorial trace, lasting six minutes and composed of ten shots. The sequence is articulated in the edit by the eyeline match and the 'Kuleshov effect' and traces a complex geometry of looks and movements that suggest proximity and distance. It opens with a close-up shot of Bahar, whose exquisite face is framed next to a stone pillar. The shot itself can be 'read' graphically as comprising three columns, the one on the left made of white, partially eroded marble, the second comprising her face leaning against the cold stone and the third on the right containing the out-of-focus suggestion of a background of ruins. İsa then appears in a subjective shot, observed by Bahar as he takes photographs and moves around the huge columns of the stunning ruins of the Temple of Artemis. The Kuleshov effect continues until they are seen together in a single shot. He asks her if she is bored; she denies it and climbs a hill towards a vantage point. A long take unveils a view of the temple's ruins, with a stunning mountain in the background. Geography, history and the diminutive human figure compose this landscape where the couple seem at once together and apart. Robin Wood has commented on how the ruins of the temple and its remaining pillars are equally the display of ruined phalli as a metaphor for the film's subject matter (2006). Bahar observes the broken pillars of the temple as İsa trips and falls to the ground. She smiles tenderly at the sight of her partner's clumsiness, but the shot lingers on, another close-up of her face with a blurred background held for nearly two and a half minutes. Duration works to reveal a range of reactions translated as subtle facial expressions, moving in time and emotionally, from a loving gaze at the vulnerable İsa, dwarfed by the weight of history amidst the ruins, which transmutes into melancholy and erupts in silent tears. The close-up ends with a fly that buzzes and lands on Bahar's long and thick auburn hair, its sound then replaced by Scarlatti's (1685–1757) 'Piano Sonata in F minor, K. 466', segueing into the credits sequence and continuing through to a shot of the couple driving in a country road at sunset. The music then goes from extra-diegetic to diegetic as Bahar, who is driving the car while İsa sleeps in the passenger seat, interrupts it by switching off the car stereo.[4]

The use of the static close-up in this initial sequence is repeated throughout the film, employed to reveal Bahar, İsa and Serap's faces. This authorial gesture opens a discussion about close-ups as *affection-images* in the Deleuzian sense, that is, those images that inhabit the interval between perception and action, foregrounding emotions, desires, needs. Deleuze famously wrote that 'the affection-image is the close-up, and the close-up is the face' (1997: 86), further reiterating that 'there is no close-up of the face, the face is in itself close-up, the closeup is by itself face and both are affect, affection-image' (1997: 88). For him, 'emotions arise from images of faces which communicate the unfilmable intensive affects of the characters', at once a reflective surface and a combination of micro-movements that translate as emotions: 'Sometimes the face thinks about something, is fixed on to an object, and this is the sense of admiration or astonishment that the English word wonder has preserved' (1997: 88). Deleuze deemed Dreyer's 1928 *La Passion de Jeanne d'Arc/The Passion of Joan of Arc* (1997: 106), the affective film *par excellence*, praising its emphasis on close-ups of Renée Jeanne Falconetti. In 1962, Godard directed his then-wife Anna Karina in *Vivre sa vie/My Life to Live*, a highly intermedial film in which he attempts to compose a portrait of Nana/Anna with recourse to various other media and texts. These include the cinema itself, with Godard paralleling Nana's/Anna's lachrymose face with that of Dreyer's Jeanne/Falconetti. These paradigmatic close-ups, moving between admiration and astonishment in a sense of wonder, are the ghosts of Bahar/Ebru's face in *Climates*, and the manifold connotations of the film's opening shots entail a discussion about the borders between life and art, intermedial relations and affect.

Deleuze's conception of the affection-image/close-up is indebted to Béla Balázs's, and both see this cinematographic device as having the power or the effect of suspending individuation. Balázs had claimed that 'if we see a face

Figure 3.1 Bahar's opening close-up. (Source: screenshot from *Climates*, 2006.)

Figure 3.2 The ruins of the Temple of Artemis in Sardis. (Source: screenshot from *Climates*, 2006.)

isolated and enlarged, we lose our awareness of space, or of the immediate surroundings' (2010: 157). Likewise, Deleuze disputes the idea of the close-up as a partial object, detached from a whole, a notion that would favour a psychoanalytic understanding of the image as castration and a linguistic reading of the image as synecdoche, with the close-up being the mark of a fragmentation or a cut to be reconciled to film's continuity, or as a mark of its essential discontinuity. Conversely, he claims that

> As Balázs has already accurately demonstrated, the close-up does not tear away its object from a set of which it would form part, of which

it would be a part, but on the contrary it abstracts it from all spatio-temporal co-ordinates, that is to say it raises it to the state of Entity. (1987: 95–6).

The close-up as Entity in Deleuze's conception bears a relationship with the portraiture genre in art history, engaged in a study of faces from different angles of approach. As is well-known, a portrait is an artistic representation of a person or a group of persons in their singularity, and in which the face and its expression become predominant. The intent is, on one hand, to display the person's likeness, and on the other hand to capture their mood, their personality and ultimately their inner world. Oliveira Junior (2017) explains how, for Jean-Marie Pontévia (1986), a portrait is a frame that is organised around a figure, a representation centred on a face and the look it contains: 'If the portrait is articulated around a figure, it is essential: the rest – if there is a remainder – is subordinate to it, which generally occupies the centre of the composition' (1997: 185). Likewise, in photography, a portrait is generally not a snapshot, but a composed image of a person in a still position, looking directly at the photographer, placed frontally to engage with the subject most successfully.

Portraiture is thus proper to painting's crystalised time and photography's fixed instant rather than to duration and the temporal frame. Here, I would agree with Oliveira Junior, who suggests that a singular, isolated and ideal conception of the portrait, in addition to raising questions derived from the philosophy of the subject (what is the subject abstracted from their relationship with the outside world, with other subjects?)

> entails an avalanche of incompatibilities transposed to the cinema without substantial changes. Art of duration, of being in time, of editing, of the transience, of the 'free' spatial and temporal mobility of the narrator, cinema does not allow us to talk about almost anything in absolute terms. (2017: 187)[5]

In the cinema, portraits are necessarily moving, as explained by Corey Schultz in his analysis of Jia Zhangke's *Ershisi cheng ji/24 City* (2008):

> Although similar to other portraits in photography and painting, these long-take filmed portraits use time in order to create what I term 'moving portraits' – portraits that are moving cinematically as well as emotionally. These moving portraits seem to 'project' the living presence of these subjects, a presence that slowly unfolds during the long takes and becomes increasingly mesmerizing as time passes. (Schultz 2014: 277)

In tandem with Schultz, I have noted elsewhere (Mello 2019) how the temporality of the cinema portrait exists at the crossroads of film and photography, for they combine the pose and the pause of photographic portraits – suggesting stillness, with the movement and fleeting time of the filmic experience.

The notion of 'moving portraits' complicates Deleuze's claim for the close-up's abstraction from all spatio-temporal co-ordinates that would raise it to the state of Entity. Despite any close-up's initial resistance towards the homogenisation of continuity editing, and the detachment suggested by the absent or blurry background, close-ups in *Climates* seem to last long enough to undergo both the Deleuzian suspension of individuation *and* its reactivation. As 'moving portraits', they emerge from a painterly and photographic gesture but refuse the state of Entity in their persistent ambiguity. Moreover, they are employed by Ceylan quite often in concert with landscape shots, and derive their meaning from this juxtaposition, precluding the idea of an abstraction from off-screen space and time. So, in *Climates*, close-ups as 'moving portraits' contain a latent tension between the fragment and the whole, between the past and the present, between love and its absence, and between that which can and cannot be said. They are located somewhere between the emotion and its verbal translation, suggesting not only a spatio-temporal but also a linguistic dislocation, often emerging in the form of tears in the case of Bahar, an exaggerated laughter for Serap, and a vacant, emotionally disconnected stare for İsa. As such, they function as reminders that certain things will always resist articulation into language, harking back to cinema's technical birthmark of verbal silence. This instance of intermediality between the cinema and photography and painting thus functions, paradoxically, to return to a pre-verbal stage of the moving image. Moreover, it could be argued that the 'moving portraits' allow access to a subject's interiority, harking back to Epstein's and Balázs's belief in the cinematographic camera's magic powers and in a movement between the subterranean and the surface, between interiority and physiognomy. This also ties in with Bazin's belief in the cinema as being able to reveal spiritual states, as elucidated by Peter Wollen:

> Realism, for Bazin, had little to do with mimesis . . . There was, for Bazin, a double movement of impression, moulding and imprinting; first the interior spiritual suffering was stamped upon the exterior physiognomy; then the exterior physiognomy was stamped and printed on the sensitive film. (Wollen 1998: 92)

If much can be seized from observing the exterior, the 'moving portrait' device allows for different possibilities of reading a human face as the expression of a person's interiority, acquiring, through duration, different values, and different roles.

LANDSCAPE, SCALE AND A SENSUAL INTERMEDIALITY

In *Climates*, the close-up's ambiguity is often complexified by its pairing with shots of the landscape, be it the natural world or a built environment, contemporary or historical. The film promotes dislocations through Turkey, at first latitudinally from the north in Istanbul to the southeast of the country in Kaş, then back to Istanbul, and finally longitudinally to Ağrı Province in the east, suggesting a travelling, cartographic impetus that will be reiterated in the director's following films, shot in various parts of Turkey. Giuliana Bruno (2007) has famously written on how motion and emotion are interrelated in the cinema, the travelling narrative *par excellence*, and how dislocations through landscape also necessarily entail changes in one's internal landscape. This interconnection between exterior and interior, between the mind and the physical world, is evidenced in the film's 'first movement', happening on the beach in Kaş, with the haptic quality of the seawater scintillating in the sun mirroring Bahar's sweaty face, whose profile, in turn, resembles a topographical relief. Later, a shot of a stone block with a busy-looking wasp sitting on it is followed by a close-up of İsa looking awry, and then by a long shot of the ruins taken from a vantage point, with scattered pillars and stones amidst standing ones, a background of mountains and the human figure, now seen to be as small as a bug. In the third movement, the yellow hues of the sun, the sand, the archaeological ruins and the suntanned bodies are replaced by the white and grey hues of snow and the paleness of winter faces. An extraordinary shot of İsa over a bridge overlooking a frozen river, with an imposing grey sky falling over him, is followed by a close-up of his face, the overcast weather anticipating his sombre demeanour. And finally, İsa takes a taxi to Ishak Pasha Palace in Doğubayazıt, seen in one of the film's most extraordinary shots in which he stands at a vantage point with his back to the camera. His body takes over the whole central part of the frame, allowing a glimpse of the extraordinary landscape of snowy mountains ahead. He then takes a photograph and steps forward to reveal in the valley the extraordinary seventeenth-century palace, located on the Silk Road near the Iranian border. Walking back down the hill to where the taxi is parked, he decides to take a photograph of the taxi driver – young, virile, working-class, İsa's opposite – with the palace in the background. The young man poses to the camera and looks quite striking in the still image, displayed as an insert with the cut introducing the stillness of photography into the movement of the film, bringing forth the cinema's complex temporality (Mulvey 2006).

Béla Balázs has observed how the cinema can convey the effect of the pathos of the large like no other art:

> A raging sea, a glacier above the clouds, a storm-lashed forest or the painful expanses of a desert – in all these images we find ourselves face to face with the cosmos. Painting cannot achieve this overwhelming monumentality because its static nature enables the observer to adopt a standpoint, a firm position in relation to it. But the uncanny motion of these cosmic forces reveals the rhythm, the beat of eternity, in which the stupefied heart of mankind must perish. The stage is even less capable of such

monumental effects. . . . These are magnitudes on a cosmic scale; they can be depicted only in film. (2010: 98)

Climates' ambiguity certainly contradicts Balázs's enthusiastic belief in cinema's ability to show 'the face of the earth' (2010: 98), but his comment sheds a light on the issue of cinematic scale and proportion, whose manipulation is the fundamental property of the cinema. As Mary Ann Doane explains by evoking Jean Mitry's *The Aesthetics and Psychology of the Cinema* (1990), the cinematic convention of decoupage that breaks up space into diverse types of shots was conceptualised in relation to the human body:

> For Mitry, then, scale becomes the primary measure of the cinema's ability to penetrate and organize space, through close-ups, medium shots and long shots (which are ultimately, entirely arbitrary as distinctions). From this point of view, scale becomes distinctive of the cinematic project not only in relation to the scale of the screen – the 'bigger than life' quality of the movies – but internally, as the regulator of the organization of space in relation to a body – both that of the character and the spectator. (Doane 2009: 72).

Doane's analysis focuses on the impact on the spectator of the distortions entailed by the manipulation of scale inherent to cinematic composition and parallels this experience historically with the impossibility faced by human subjects of ever completely making sense of, or mapping out the totality of, the social forces that determine their position (2009: 63). Cinematic scale thus embodies the limited possibility of partial knowledge proper to the subject's reduced sensory apprehension of a lived space, which according to Henri Lefebvre is limited to a repressive visualization and a consequence of the advent of modernity and advanced capitalism that annuls the human body as measure (Lefebvre 1991: 309). What is lost in the intensification of technological mediation is the haptic, intimate spatial relations that allow for immersion rather than distance.

Yet, as Doane rightly observes, 'because the cinema continually puts into play variations of scale that are given as relations of proximity and distance, it also allows for perturbation, dissonances within the structuration of space designed to the measure of rationalization' (2009: 77). The cinema, for Doane, simultaneously stabilises and destabilises. It is double-edged, producing an illusory orientation in relation to an incomprehensible space as well as dissonances and disembodiments, without ever truly abandoning the human body as the measure of its scale. This tension related to space and scale in the cinema, between orientation and disorientation, embodiment and disembodiment, is enacted in *Climates'* unique combination of painterly and photographic 'moving portraits' and 'landscape views'. The fact that İsa is a photographer, and that he travels his country taking snapshots of its landscapes, occasionally including a person in the shot, can be understood as a play with scale and control. At this point, it is useful to return to the film's opening sequence (the prologue in Sardis) and to its final part, a sort of mirror image of the initial break-up that replaces the sweltering summer with the desolate winter. In both, İsa takes photographs of different sites, whose immense scale, already transformed once by Ceylan's film camera, is deprived of its duration by his still camera. These photographs of the Temple of Artemis in Sardis and other ruins in the South of the country, as well as of the Ishak Pasha Palace in the east, document historical architectural sites and are then seen as projections in a classroom or small icons on İsa's computer, in a stormy evening in Istanbul where he seems stuck in front of the screen, unable to write.

Both film director and photographer work in a sort of mise-en-abyme on location and negotiate the relationship between the human figure and landscape, history and the present reality. The first sequence is overtly built around architecture, harking back to Antonioni as a paradigm for the presence of architecture in the cinema (Bruno 2007; Pethő 2020). The couple's movement is enacted as one between proximity and distance, between affection and disconnection, and Ceylan manipulates the scale of the temple, evidencing its grandiosity by inscribing the characters into them in long shots or exacerbating its textures and haptic elements by showing them up-close, and usually in connection to the character's faces. The choreography of shots seen here is later mirrored by an extraordinary sequence played indoors, in İsa's hotel room in the east, with a water bottle on the bedside table taking the place of the phallic symbol of the ruined pillars at the start. Outside the window, the snow falls heavily. Against what seems to be bells one would hear in a Buddhist or Daoist temple and an eerie musical score, the couple is seen in a series of extreme close-ups, denoting the night spent together where sex is replaced by tentative affects: İsa strokes Bahar's stunning hair, his face coming into shot and resting against it; her face is shown in half, one eye looking up, the background blurred; there are shots in which one face obstructs that of the other, in a recurring gesture around the film that enacts point of view, partial visions, obstructions and revelations. More extreme close-ups follow, notably of a cigarette that burns like incense, and in the end, both are seen sitting in bed, Bahar with her eyes closed and İsa with his eyes open, seeming discontent and slightly fed up. He looks at his watch: time is up, nothing more can be achieved. This is confirmed in the early morning, when both sit by the window, with snow relentlessly falling outside. Bahar seems happy and tells him she had a lovely dream of flying over rolling green meadows. Dreams of flying are one of the fundamental cross-cultural archetypal dreams and have been interpreted in many ways, from a memory of childhood play, a desire for freedom or sexual arousal. Here, whatever the connotations of Bahar's dream, her openness is annihilated by İsa's crude practicality: he tells her she should not be late for work, completely contradicting his pleading of the previous day. Once again in close-up, Bahar's face changes from a soft, peaceful smile to utter disappointment and profound sadness.

Throughout the film, İsa captures reality and later classifies it, with landscapes reduced to small computer icons that he fails to comprehend. His manhood is about control, he is authoritarian, annoying, always telling Bahar what to do (put your coat on, do not be late for work). He tries to understand the enormousness of nature, of the weather, of history, of Bahar herself, which in the cinema is also the imposingness of scale rendered in long shots of historical and natural sites and close-ups of her face. But they are impossible to contain. In Istanbul, his encounter with Serap is dominated by a performance of manhood gone a bit wrong, as stale as the hazelnut he eats before they wrestle on the floor, with violence replacing seduction. The second time they meet in Serap's flat he learns that Bahar has left Istanbul without telling him, the loss of control leading to impotence. He then tries to enact the knight in shining armour, braving the snow to find his princess and rescue her, but these roles do not fit them. In her turn, Bahar seems both in and out of love with İsa, her complex range of emotions finally counterposed and replaced by fiction in the film's coda: out in the snow, the television drama's female protagonist cries over a grave. Her husband comes up and says: 'Aze, you are not crying again. Come on, that's enough now'. But his impatience is followed by promises that he will avenge her father, that he will stop her tears from falling, and that they will be able to walk with pride again. He is the knight in shining armour that the television melodrama can present, but that the realist cinema of Ceylan never could. The shooting of the scene is interrupted by an aeroplane – İsa is leaving Bahar. The metaleptic leap from the television drama to the film – with the reality of the couple Nuri and Ebru Ceylan perpetually haunting the screen – opens yet another dimension to the melodrama that unfolds. The film ends how it began, with a close-up of Bahar. A single tear falls down her face, which slowly disappears through a dissolve to a similar shot, with a slight change in the frame evidenced by the shifting presence of a minaret towering the snowy landscape. She is finally effaced.

In *Climates*, water in all states – clouds, rain, snow, tears and sweat – speaks of the changing climates of life, just as the shifting sands suggest impermanence, and just as the ruined pillars of the temple convey both the weight of history and its fragility. By embracing intermediality, the film also embraces a more corporeal, haptic and non-discursive mode of perception. This chimes in with Ágnes Pethő's call for a sensual experience intermediality, one that is aware of how the totality of the 'in-between' remains necessarily ungraspable. Pethő evokes Rancière's conception of the cinema as an art in which the sensible and the intelligible remain undistinguished. Intermediality, she argues, is not some-

PORTRAITS AND LANDSCAPE: *İKLIMLER/CLIMATES* (2006) 65

Figure 3.3 Bahar's final, disappearing close-up. (Source: screenshot from *Climates*, 2006.)

thing one 'deciphers'; rather, it is something one perceives or senses (2020: 67). *Climates* references and remediates photography and painting in more sensual and fragmentary ways by relying on cinema's own ability to manipulate scale, moving between the minute and the enormous, and calling attention to the very ungraspability of the whole when it comes to human relations, and the weather. By doing so, it creates meaningful parallels between Turkey's faces and places, physiognomies and geographies, its reality and its representation.

NOTES

1. With *Climates*, Ebru Ceylan began to collaborate more decisively with her husband, sharing the writing credits in *Three Monkeys* (2008), *Once Upon a Time in Anatolia* (2011), *The Winter Sleep* (2014) and *The Wild Pear Tree* (2018).
2. Pethő explains how 'the crossing of media borders is one of the most persistent metaphors in the study of intermediality', and calls attention to how these borders are 'admittedly constructed (historically, cognitively and conventionally) and perceivable on diverse levels as differences that frame each medium coming into contact with another' (2020: 40–1).
3. *Photogénie* is a concept that derives from the desire to explore the optical and psychological power of the cinematographic camera, seen as able to turn common objects, landscapes and people luminous and enchanted. This power translates as *photogénie*, seen as the specifics of the cinema, a philosophical machine capable of making us better understand the great categories of the universe: time, motion, causality.
4. Scarlatti's Piano Sonata will only return in the second movement of the film at 48 minutes, playing in İsa's study as he seems stuck with his academic work, and being interrupted by a call from Serap. It is finally heard very faintly in the third movement. As Heidi Hart (2019: 107) observes in relation to the use of Schubert's A major piano sonata no. 20 in *Winter Sleep*, rather than intensifying an emotional-narrative arc, Scarlatti's

sonata adds a critical dimension to the film, being repeated three times and becoming less and less intense along the film's trajectory.
5. My translation. Original in Portuguese: '. . . acarreta uma avalanche de incompatibilidades se transposta para o cinema sem substanciais alterações. Arte da duração, do ser no tempo, da montagem, da transitoriedade, da "livre" mobilidade espacial e temporal da instância narradora, o cinema não nos permite falar de quase nada em termos absolutos'.

CITED WORKS

Andrew, Geoff (2007), 'Painterly Precision', *Sight and Sound*, February 2007, available at https://www.nuribilgeceylan.com/photography/press-london.php (last accessed 12 October 2021)

Aumont, Jacques (1992), *Du visage au cinéma*. Paris: Cahiers du Cinéma.

Balázs, Béla (2010), *Béla Balázs: Early film theory: Visible man and The spirit of film*, trans. Rodney Livingstone, ed. Erica Carter. New York and Oxford: Berghahn Books.

Bazin, André (2002), *Qu'est-ce que le cinéma?* Paris: Les Éditions du Cerf.

Bruno, Giuliana (2007), *Atlas of Emotion: Journeys in Art, Architecture and Film*. New York: Verso.

Courtine, Jean-Jacques; Haroche, Claudine (2007), *Histoire du visage: exprimer et taire ses émotions, XVIe-début XIXe siècle*. Paris: Payot & Rivages.

Deleuze, Gilles (1997), *Cinema 1: The Movement Image*. Minneapolis: University of Minnesota Press.

Doane, Mary Ann (2009), 'Scale and the Negotiation of "Real" and "Unreal" Space in the Cinema', in Nagib, Lúcia and Cecília Mello, (eds), *Realism and the Audiovisual Media*. Basingstoke: Palgrave Macmillan, 63–81.

____ (2002), *The Emergence of Cinematic Time: Modernity, Contingency, the Archive*. Cambridge, Massachusetts, and London: Harvard University Press.

Dönmez-Colin, Gönül (2008), *Turkish Cinema: Identity, Distance, and Belonging*. London: Reaktion Books.

Epstein, Jean (2012), *Critical Essays and New Translations*, ed. Sarah Keller and Jason N. Paul. Amsterdam: Amsterdam University Press.

____ (1921/1988), 'Grossissement', in *Bonjour Cinéma*. Paris: Éditions de la sirène, 1921, pp. 93–108; translated by Stuart Liebman as 'Magnification', in Abel, Richard, *French Film Theory and Criticism: A History/Anthology, 1907-1939*. Vol. 1: 1907–1929. Princeton: Princeton University Press, 1988), 235–41.

Gunning, Tom (1997), 'In your face: physiognomy, photography, and the gnostic mission of early film', *Modernism/Modernity*, Baltimore, 4:1, 1–29.

Hart, Heidi (2019), 'Music, Narrative and the Moving Image: Varieties of Plurimedial Interrelations', in Bernhart, Walter and David Francis Urrows, (eds), *Music, Narrative and the Moving Image: Varieties of Plurimedial Interrelations*. Leiden and Boston: Brill Rodopi.

Jafaar, Ali (2007), 'Snow better blues', *Sight & Sound*, 17:2.

Lefebvre, Henri (1991), *The Production of Space*, trans. by Donald Nicholson-Smith. Oxford: Blackwell.

Ma, Jean (2008), 'Photography's Absent Times' in Karen Beckman and Jean Ma, *Still Moving: Between Cinema and Photography*. Durham/London: Duke University Press.

Mitry, Jean (1990), *The Aesthetics and Psychology of the Cinema*, trans. Christopher King. Bloomington: Indiana University Press.

Mello, Cecília (2019), *The Cinema of Jia Zhangke: Realism and Memory in Chinese Film*. London: Bloomsbury.

Mulvey, Laura (2006), *Death 24x A Second: Stillness and the Moving Image*. London: Reaktion Books.
Oliveira Junior, Luiz Carlos (2017), *Retratos em movimento*, in *Ars* 15: 31, 183–208.
Pethő, Ágnes (2020), *Cinema and Intermediality: The Passion for the In-Between* (Second, Enlarged Edition). Newcastle upon Tyne: Cambridge Scholars Publishing.
Pontévia, Jean-Marie (1986), *Écrits sur l'art et pensées détachées*. 2nd ed. Bordeaux: William Blake, v. 3.
Schultz, Corey (2014), 'Moving portraits: portraits in performance in 24 City' in *Screen* 55:2, 276–87.
Suner, Asuman (2010), *New Turkish Cinema: Belonging, Identity and Memory*. London: I.B. Tauris.
Wollen, Peter ([1969] 1998), *Signs and Meaning in the Cinema*. London: BFI.
Wood, Robin (2006), '*Climates* and Other Disasters: The Films of Nuri Bilge Ceylan', in *Artforum* 45:3, November 2006. Available at https://www.artforum.com/print/200609/climates-and-other-disasters-the-films-of-nuri-bilge-ceylan-11921 (last accessed 12 October 2021)

CHAPTER FOUR

Aesthetic Silences and the Political Bind: *Üç Maymun/Three Monkeys* (2008)[1]

Vuslat D. Katsanis

Nuri Bilge Ceylan's fifth feature film, *Üç Maymun/Three Monkeys* (2008) thematises class injustice through the scapegoating of a three-member low-income family in Istanbul: the mother, Hacer (Hatice Aslan), the son, İsmail (Ahmet Rıfat Sungar), and the father, Eyüp (Yavuz Bingöl). The film begins and ends with an emphasis on the difficult circumstances that compel the characters to take responsibility for crimes they did not commit. Eyüp agrees to take the blame for his politician boss, Servet (Ercan Kesal) at the beginning of the film in exchange for a hefty sum of money.[2] Likewise, when his son is implicated in Servet's murder at the end, Eyüp turns to the neighbourhood's migrant worker, Bayram (Cafer Köse) to offer him a similar deal. Aesthetically, *Three Monkeys* makes extensive use of silence, long takes and shifting points of view to evoke the feeling of these characters' entrapment. Diegetically, we sense that the family are bound by an unjust system with no resolution in sight and, extra-diegetically, we see a reflection of our own experiences of bearing witness to a slowly unfolding corruption.

My reading is informed by Gilles Deleuze's theory of the cinematic time-image, its valences in the recent scholarship on slow cinema and by the theories of silence as a political act in 'eastern' and subaltern studies more generally. In Deleuze's theorising of post-war European cinema, when characters are bound to situations in which they can no longer speak or react, the stillness of an image cut off from sensory motor links opens to an experience of time that is unbearable (Deleuze 1989). Yet, as Jason Bahbak Mohaghegh demonstrates through his reading of 'eastern thought', the bleakness of this experience of time also opens to 'a rare post-identitarian moment based on the principles of the unforeseen and untold' (Mohaghegh 2013: xii). How this moment of silence and inertia works within and against political power to in fact imagine the possibility of a new politicity is what informs my reading of the political aesthetics in *Three Monkeys*.

On the one hand, the shift from movement-image to time-image discloses cinema's problematic association with ontological realism (Deleuze 1989; Bazin 1967). The belief in the referential truth of the photographic image is no longer held, especially considering the paradoxical relation between photography and cinema as a technology of the illusion of movement (Mulvey 2006; Beckman and Ma 2008; Jaffe 2014). On the other hand, the cinematic time-image gains greater critical complexity when the filmic subject is time itself (Çağlayan 2018; Koepnick 2014; de Luca and Barradas Jorge 2015). Time, as the subject, lays bare the situation of the characters' idle defeat, if not their indifference, to historical outcome. For Jacques Rancière, this post-Brechtian break established the foundation of a new 'politico-cinematic approach', which was concerned with aesthetics as a 'study of the aporiae of emancipation' (2014: 105). In other words, by slowing down the image in silent durations or even freezing it, cinematic time-images seek to speculate what Mohaghegh calls the 'radical unspoken' (2013: xi), thereby opening its political reach 'within an ostensibly apolitical aesthetic' (Chaudhuri and Finn 2003: 38).

My understanding of the relation between aesthetics and politics in *Three Monkeys* is also anchored in the real-time context of the film's story, which unfolds during the time leading to the summer of the 2007 general election – the year when the film was in production – when the Justice and Development Party (Adalet ve Kalkınma Partisi: AKP) declared a grand victory, securing a second term in office. The film, within its first ten minutes, plays in the background a barely discernible televised announcement of the controversial election results as İsmail sneaks home with a beaten face. It is late evening and Hacer is asleep on the couch with the television left on. Despite the subtlety of the reference to the night of the national election results, this is literally and metaphorically the bloodiest scene in the film as well as the turning point for the family's demise. A long close-up shot lingers on the teenager's bloody face with a shot-reverse-shot of Hacer staring back at him in silence. Hacer's desperation to save her son leads her to seek Servet's help and, as we later discover, start their sexual affair.

The subtlety of Ceylan's citation style by way of a television report first appears in *Mayıs Sıkıntısı/Clouds of May* (1999), where the father is shown asleep on the sofa during a news report on the difficulties of forming a governmental coalition and repeated in *Ahlat Ağacı/The Wild Pear Tree* (2018) as well where Sinan (Doğu Demirkol) enters his grandparents' house during a TV broadcast of the still-ruling AKP administration and prime minister, Binali Yıldırım, to whom no one appears to be listening. While *Three Monkeys* may be the first of Ceylan's films to centre the diegesis of a current political event in Turkey, the same image of sleeping characters amidst televised national controversy – evoked nearly ten years prior to and ten years after *Three Monkeys* – seems to suggest Ceylan's understanding of an impending rupture. In fact, the rupture we see between İsmail and his mother is also one that exemplifies the rupture between the Turkish public's own difficult relation to political participation and historical outcome. And yet, the experience of viewing this slowly progressing film where nothing seems to happen and everyone is disinterested, stands in direct affective contrast to the extremely cruel situation in which it unfolds. The slowness in fact contrasts with the experience of living in Turkey under a rapidly advancing regime whose self-declared agenda of fashioning a 'New Turkey' – announced in the party slogan 'there's no stopping; keep going' – would have been well-known to the film's local and global audiences.[3] Viewers would undoubtedly be familiar with the party slogan and the frenzy of controversial decrees hastily passed by AKP to restructure public education, healthcare, housing, employment and the military, and which have led to mass incarcerations of opposition journalists and intellectuals as well as rampant media censorship since the second-term elections. By referring to elections during the country's general elections then adopting the same citation style in two more films later, as if to suggest historical continuum in the national timeline, Ceylan seems to position the film's spectators within the interstice of a *mise en abyme* of politics, cinema and the everyday. In all three films – *Clouds of May*, *Three Monkeys* and *The Wild Pear Tree* – the characters are tuned out rather than tuned in to the television announcement. 'The news' is not, in fact, news. This gesture of disregard for what is evident recalls an additional aspect of the way in which cinema discloses the contemporary public's complex relation to the political as well as cinema's own problematic emplacement within that discourse. It is at this difficult bind of having to represent, overcome, and perhaps cope with impossible situations that I offer to read the political thrust of aesthetic silences.

NURI BILGE CEYLAN AND THE NEW CINEMA OF TURKEY

In many ways, Ceylan's cinema follows the intellectual trajectory of Turkey's new cinematic wave over the past fifteen years before the release of *Three Monkeys*. Thematically and aesthetically, the films that have come to constitute this new wave reflect upon the incongruencies between identity, collective experience, and home (Vidler 1992; Dönmez-Colin 2008; Suner 2010) and explore the recurrent sense of homelessness and liminality as socio-political critique (Akbulut 2005; Çakırlar and Güçlü 2012: 167). Yet many critics from Turkey insist that Ceylan's aesthetics lack politics (Suner 2011; Tulgar 2008; Atayman 2012). Ahmet Tulgar wrote of Ceylan as someone who has 'distanced himself from political discourse, moreover, who stands remote, who flees' (2008). Tulgar's criticism that Ceylan's cinematic style consists of 'perception-making innovationism, nihilism, and cynicism and films that do nothing but reinforce provincial decadence onto the city and the urbanites' goes as far as to call his work 'reactionary' and a 'threat to the left artery' (Ibid). Similarly, Veysel Atayman equates Ceylan's silence with irresponsibility and surrender echoing the perception that Ceylan's 'lonely and beautiful country' films turn a blind eye on the troubled political situation in Turkey (2012).

Ceylan's body of work consistently prefers the subtle over the sensational, the obscure over the obvious and the dull over the dynamic. From the little boy in *Clouds of May* (1999) who is tasked with carrying a raw egg in his pocket for forty days without breaking it in exchange for a musical watch, to the father in *The Wild Pear Tree* (2018) who embarks on a Sisyphean mission to dig a well in a ground where it is known there is no water, the ordinary characters in Ceylan's films are each bound within a cycle of individualised struggle. Over and over again, it is failure, disappointment, and unending struggle that shape the lifeworlds of all Ceylan's films. And yet none of his characters seem to react. Frozen in time, their vacant looks and impassive stance recall Deleuze's description of post-war cinema as a cinema 'of the seer' (1989: xi). For Deleuze, when the situation is so unbearable that 'no possible reactions' are conceivable, all that remains is bearing witness (1995: 123). In this regard, *The Wild Pear Tree* is the same story as *Clouds of May* and *Three Monkeys* in so far as everyone is singularly occupied with the primacy of their own needs, alienated from and deceiving even the ones closest to them like fathers and sons or wives and husbands, struggling in silence despite anticipating failure and shifting the blame so casually, as if fraud has become routine. For Deleuze, the cinema of the seer confronted the impossibility of action by reflecting inwardly on its own limited capacity when, like Ceylan's characters, 'people no longer really believed it was possible to react to situations' (1995: 123). This impossibility, however, appears in Ceylan's cinema 'not [as] an obscurantist turning away from the political, but [as] the open-ended politicization of the image' (Chaudhuri and Finn 2003: 38). Indeed, once removed from the action–reaction laws of continuity editing, the image of time gives 'rise to completely novel ways of understanding and resisting'; to ways of refusing things as they are (Deleuze 1995: 123). The question remains: 'Are those who act and *struggle* mute, as opposed to those who act and speak?' (Spivak 1994: 70).

Accusations (of political apathy) and labels ('reactionary') miss the politicity of the narrative silences appearing within the context of an all-pervasive governmental regime. Uninterested in cinema that provides answers, the narrative silences in Ceylan's films open the terrain of inquiry, and with it, expose the faint traces of another discourse. Indeed, as Mohaghegh shows by way of what he calls the radical unspoken in the Iranian new wave poetic tradition, where exhaustion, abandonment, vulnerability, secrecy and delirium are the writer's constraints, the recurrence of silences 'overturns oppressive legacies of meaning, truth, and reality in exchange for an enigmatic threshold of silent becomings' (2014: xi–xii).[4] These silent inflections as Mohaghegh illustrates constitute the very core of the 'insurgent possibility reaching out from within the dungeons of marginalization' (Mohaghegh 2013: 71). One might add to the poetic intellectual trajectory the aesthetics of stillness of Iranian filmmakers like Sohrab Shahid Saless (1944–98), Abbas Kiarostami (1940–2016) or Shirin Neshat (1967–) whose prosaic slowness similarly opens onto the inquisitive in a non-affirmative gesture against the governed realism of their time.

A handful of local scholars, including Zahit Atam, have noticed that *Three Monkeys*' silent aesthetics in fact speaks loudly against the systems of persecution (2009). Aslı Atasoy and Ebru Yetişkin have also separately noted that most of Ceylan's films reject ideological didacticism and refuse to affirm political, economic, social and cultural expectations (Atasoy 2008; Yetişkin 2010). At the same time, scholars have addressed the politics of home as both an entrapping and an exilic space (Diken, Gilloch, Hammond 2018) and the reign of history wherein 'identification with the past and present as a political, cultural and social entity' contextualizes structural power differentials (Dönmez-Colin 2008: 9). The early scene in *Kış Uykusu/Winter Sleep* (2014) when the little boy first glares in silence at his parents' landlord then throws a rock at his car in defiance, makes the theme of struggle against the inequities of power the most evident thread running across Ceylan's body of films (Toper 2014).

THREE MONKEYS

Three Monkeys opens on the evening when Servet, a middle-aged politician running for office, falls asleep at the wheel and kills someone. Fearing the consequences of the accident for his election campaign, he bribes Eyüp, his usual driver, to take the blame. Eyüp accepts his boss' offer in hesitation and spends the next nine months in prison leaving behind his wife, Hacer and his teenage son, İsmail who grow financially and emotionally dependent on Servet. The film progresses to reveal the affair between Hacer and Servet and İsmail's witness to the deceit. In the final sequence, after Servet is found dead, a new narrative problem is introduced. Eyüp visits Bayram, a lonely underpaid migrant, who works and sleeps in the neighbourhood teahouse. Bayram confides in Eyüp: '[w]e manage in this misery . . . No mother, no father, in foreign lands, we work only for a full stomach'. Eyüp responds: '[t]he prison provides three meals a day. Winter is approaching. They have heaters in prison. You're still young. When you get out, you'll have a large sum of money to open your own teahouse'. Hence, just as Servet enticed Eyüp with the promise that money will secure his future, now Eyüp tries to bribe Bayram to take the blame for a crime he did not commit.

By its very title, *Three Monkeys* is suggestive of the proverbial 'see no evil, hear no evil, speak no evil' triad against moral irresponsibility. To be sure, none of the characters in this film are likable for they are all deceptive; and yet, neither can they be individually held culpable for the very system into which they are born and trapped failing them. On the one hand, the film's photographic stillness poignantly portrays the characters' 'captivity'[5] amidst deeply rooted political and economic injustice, akin to what Mohaghegh contextualised for the silent poetic tradition in Iran as emerging within the 'epoch of deception, ruin, and fragmentation' (2013: 71). On the other hand, having to bear witness to this cycle of violence, as viewers, heightens our own emplacement within the situation. Given the deep systemic corruption and class injustice that encases the lifeworlds of the films' characters and viewers, it is the aesthetic contradictions unfolding between action and reaction, referent and resemblance, speech and silence that become the film's main discursive points. As such, Ceylan's aesthetic choices of stillness and silence in *Three Monkeys* configure an experience of film viewing that is a metaphor for contemporary life in Turkey – an arresting space where life is bound in irresolvable constraint.

Yet, the film also develops a language of negation through those instances when, in the absence of narrative action, we find stubborn resistance. As will become clearer in the scene analyses to follow, *Three Monkeys* foregoes character action, dialogue and plot turning points in favour of weaving in non-reciprocity (between sound and image), and ambiguity (of plot line and time) as the primary features of cinema's complicated relation to politics. This language of negation is what I call the 'non-affirmative time-images' of Ceylan's political aesthetics.[6] The ambiguous relationship between perception and object, and between action and reaction can thus be read as an attempt to find a more potent space in which the experience of the impossible can gain critical visibility.

After release from prison, Eyüp begins suspecting his wife, whose mobile phone goes off at all the wrong moments. Whereas the husband and the wife rarely speak, the loud ringing of the mobile phone breaks the silence in many scenes. The lyrics are of a highly melodramatic arabesque break-up song by popular Turkish singer Yıldız Tilbe: 'I hope you love and aren't loved back. I hope you suffer from the pain of love, just like I suffer. I hope you yearn but never unite, just like how I cannot unite'. One day, Eyüp secretly picks up the call and finds Servet's scolding voice on the other end: '[w]hat business do you have coming to my house? Have you lost your mind?'. A few moments later in the film when Servet is found murdered, police track the call log and arrive at the family home. Hacer's phone activity implicates the family, whose frozen faces show neither shock nor worry. Back at home, İsmail confesses to his parents.

The shift-the-blame structure of *Three Monkeys* disallows conventional plot points through which conflict resolution could have been possible. It also binds the characters in paradoxical silence wherein their individual pain is at once removed from the collective and justified for its sake. Film critic Rob White wrote how the film perpetually shifts 'narrative focus and viewpoint between characters' as if to make the personal a part of the political (2011). The film begins and ends with the same situation of despair, thus trapping its characters in an unending cycle in which justice is perpetually omitted. The characters bear this situation silently and on their own, and it is unclear why they neither react nor simply walk away. And yet, what ought to be located in Ceylan's cinema, even and especially during those moments when action is conspicuously absent, is what Deleuze understood to be the contested territory shared by both cinema and philosophy (1992: 3–7). The cinematic image acquires politicity when it refuses photographic indexicality to truth or clarity. The deployment of still images and motionless sequences acquires political merit because of their nuances; for wanting not to affirm but to reassess, if not resist, the various actions and reactions that brought on this situation in the first place. Viewed from this perspective, Ceylan's cinematically captivating and photographically silent images leave no room for moral indictment of the individuals that play the three monkeys, as all measures of realism, morality, and consequence are rendered structurally unavailable. In that voided space, all that remains is 'provocation to the point of producing a radical inability to choose between injustices' (Rancière 2014: 112–13). Where people face precarious abandonment as the condition of life, they are left to fend only for themselves. Ceylan interprets this bind not in terms of complicity but as futility: '[i]n vain, [the characters] try to buy into their lies' (Ceylan 2008b). Deceit as a remedy for pain and loneliness as the substance of life, are reiterated in one of the film's most vocal moments, when Eyüp asks his son during a prison visit: '[d]o we have anyone except each other?'. Met with silence, he repeats the question: '[d]o we have anyone?'. This question, like many others, never finds an answer in the film. Prison bars frame the father and son in extreme close-up shots as they search for meaning in each other's vacant eyes.

The aesthetics of slowness and the lengthy silences in *Three Monkeys*, seen against the backdrop of an impoverished family home, reveal the overwhelming amount of pain and injustice that govern the characters' lifeworlds. In fact, normalised conditions of violence, hyperinflation, police surveillance, censorship and the threat of incarceration under which filmmakers produce their work should at least alert critics as to why and how silence and inaction have garnered such intense aesthetic interest in Turkey. It is not surprising to see that silence, inaction and nonparticipation were invoked as powerful and necessary tactics of protest in the 'stand still' movement started by the choreographer Erdem Gündüz through his 'standing man' protest during

AESTHETIC SILENCES AND THE POLITICAL BIND 75

Figure 4.1 İsmail during a prison visit, looking back at his father. (Source: screenshot from *Three Monkeys* 2008.)

the 2013 Gezi Movement (Carvin 2013). Neither can we ignore the explicit interventions that Ceylan made at various points in his career, including his dedication speech at Cannes for the demonstrators killed by police violence during the Gezi protests, his Twitter updates during the same period and his solidarity signature on the petition letter issued by the Turkish Cinema Guild. Expressed in his silent cinematic images is perhaps the refusal to give into the semblance of action as a decoy for change. As with the Iranian poetic context, 'Poetic silence is the bleak delirium of the abyss in its most emancipatory form, in this instance not the purveyor of a nihilistic despair but the instantiation of the forbidding possibility' (Mohaghegh 2013: 21).

The film also refuses a single narrative point of view. *Three Monkeys* opens with Servet's accident; then switches to Hacer's affair; to İsmail's confrontation with his cheating mother; to Eyüp's struggle to find a solution and finally, to the dilemma that awaits Bayram. The shifting of narrative points of view, however, does not occur in any sequential order, where one action logically leads to the other; rather, these shifts emphasize the depth of the characters' collective entanglement. Eyüp and Bayram share the same future in that they are asked to take the blame, though at different points in time. Servet eventually shares the same past as the person he killed at the film's beginning. The multiplicity of temporal layers collapses the personal onto the political while long takes and fixed cameras sustain the attention of viewers. Indeed, while extensive long sequences, still cameras, and fragmented, claustrophobic compositions fence characters in compositional gridlocks, the collapse of the linear time *vis-à-vis* the time-image allows the characters to receive closer, perhaps more perceptive attention to redeem some level of their dignity. Within the spectral space of the nation, at least as it might be affectively registered in new wave movements more widely, political nonparticipation becomes a mode of endurance. Sure enough, Ceylan not only questions what it means to be 'alone in the world' with this film, but he also amplified the sentiment at the Cannes Film Festival, where he won the Best Director prize for *Three Monkeys:* 'I dedicate this award to my lonely and beautiful country, which I love passionately' – a statement that echoes the desire to find solidarities in others, while holding onto love as what might be the most resilient shield against the alienating violence that arrests the people of Turkey today. Hence, Hacer's mobile phone ringtone – the one speech-act that cannot go unheard in the film – resonates as an irrefutable declaration of mutuality. The statement, *I hope you love and aren't loved back*, thus subverts the privacy of the struggle by calling out the convoluted present. In other words, if Hacer's mediated cry is the subaltern speech act, then we could read the narrative silences and aesthetic slowness in *Three Monkeys* in terms of the interval between the political and the personal, such that the individual or the everyday is symptomatic of a greater record of shared systemic injustice. To that end, as Rancière asserts, cinema critical of politics can merely display 'the limits' (2014: 15).

Three Monkeys consistently draws out non-affirmative time-images, refusing the language of a cinema that provides answers. In fact, the discrepancy between what you see/hear and what is there is the primary filmic experience. For example, as an Istanbul film, *Three Monkeys* exhibits none of the famous landmarks of the well-documented city. Furthermore, it affords little screen time to nationally acclaimed celebrities like the popular folk singer Yavuz Bingöl. By refusing to provide the expected, the film enters another representative regime where the experience of viewing 'national cinema' results only in estrangement. Therefore, Ceylan's view of Istanbul is both unusual and uncomfortable. This other view of Istanbul, where architectural landmarks are absent and buildings are in ruin, makes for a filmic image that 'gains further significance as outside events hasten the disappearance of the past and strengthen the political appropriation of time' (Mulvey 2006: 21). Viewers are then to inhabit and are inhabited by a cinematic time-image that dissolves rather than preserves life, as if to demonstrate Mulvey's description of cinema as the constant reminder of the death drive.

As in most of Ceylan's films, home in *Three Monkeys* is an integral site of meaning. The family dwells in a shanty apartment in Istanbul's poverty ridden Yedikule District (Ceylan 2008c). The impoverished ugliness of the neighbourhood does not fit with the priceless view of the beautiful Marmara Sea that it faces. One critic likened the building to a 'sail-less ship adrift in a wasteland' in the same way as Ceylan's cinemascope photographs of Turkey remind him of 'the remnants of a civilisation which has lost its rudder' (Crittenden 2010: 17).

Home – both as the building that houses the family and metaphorically as the collective space of the nation – works in the film as a kind of Adornoian waste product (Dallmayr 1997: 35). It is an excess of that which cannot be incorporated, a site of ruin from its very conception. From its disarray emerges another experience of inhabitation – one that is not simply gritty and unappealing, but visibly disorienting. Aesthetically, the home displays the signs of instability and crisis. We can see exactly where 'rooms have been added on its roof over time', like patches of 'scars' that adorn many of Istanbul's shanty constructions, without planning or permission (Suner 2011: 20). But the architecture also engenders the contradiction that any ruin is at once a site under construction. The demolition site is simultaneously a construction site; a vision of the past and future displayed together. This stepping into construction is at the same time a stepping out of ruins rendered visible by Ceylan's cinematic time-image.

NON-AFFIRMATIVE TIME-IMAGE

The first instance of the non-affirmative time-image occurs on the day after the elections. Servet sits alone in his office, upset at having lost the campaign. Hacer is also in the office to ask for an advance so that her son can buy a car and begin work. This sequence of exchanges between Servet and Hacer is interesting, for it marks Ceylan's clever use of manipulated film speed to collapse the sense of linear progression. This is also the first time we hear Hacer's mobile phone ringtone, which marks the actual duration of time in this sequence until movement falls out of sync with sound, and time becomes altogether arbitrary. For example, while Hacer frantically searches her purse for the ringing phone, Servet sits annoyed on the other end of the desk. As we continue to hear the

Figure 4.2 Exterior of the family home. (Source: screenshot from *Three Monkeys* 2008.)

ringtone, the scene cuts with a sound-bridge to Servet cooling himself with the electric fan across the room. Hacer's search for her mobile lasts almost an entire minute, but the sound bridge on the 45th second indicates a time lapse of much greater duration. The slowed film speed renders it diegetically impossible for the two characters to share the same time and space. Servet's attempt to cool down in front of a fan lasts an additional half a minute, but the second sound-bridge of the fan's noise reveals that Hacer has long left the building. Looking out of the window from Servet's point of view, we take an aerial glance at Hacer at the bus stop. It is both unclear and irrelevant how much time has passed since she has left, or what has happened in the meantime. The characters remain silent the entire time.

A few minutes later, Hacer and Servet ride in the car together, though each continues to experience the passing moments differently. In the car scene, Hacer and Servet finally begin speaking, yet the picture consistently fails to reciprocate their dialogue. Image falls out of sync with both movement and sound such that speech no longer matches characters' lips. Despite the classical shot-reverse-shot between Hacer and Servet, their nonsynchronous dialogue never affirms their communication. The unsynchronised effect has been interpreted as an expression of the characters' inner thoughts (Er 2010: 64). Whether or not the dissociation of sound and image can reveal any insight into the characters' minds, the lack of correspondence between them defines their situation. The very inability of the characters to share the same time and space, and the failure of all attempts at affirming their presence characterizes the situations Ceylan conceives in *Three Monkeys*. The non-affirmative time-image, in this case, suggests unmappable time, memory and lived event, where the false form of cohesion and correspondence resonates as both the power and the limit of the filmic world. Ceylan dissociates image from sound to do away with film realism whereby reality is merely an interstice between frames that dissolves into excess, further complicating the film's representative capacity. Likewise, the incoherent and non-conclusive speech pattern in the car scene is emblematic of the non-reciprocal dialogue that runs throughout the film, where questions are met with more questions. Given the inadequacy of the question–answer paradigm alongside manipulated film speed and non-synchronous motion, the film's negation of time as an irrelevant measure of reality suggests, instead, the viability of the space between frames as the realm of the unseen and the unspoken.

As Rancière aptly defines it throughout his book, the interstitial space between frames is freed from the impulse for the objective documentation of reality (2014). For example, seconds before we see the ghost of the family's younger son, Ceylan displays another signature close-up, now of İsmail's sweaty face. In this three-minute sequence, Ceylan gradually and subtly slows the film speed before playing back the shot in reverse, such that we observe

Figure 4.3 Hacer during a car ride with Servet. (Source: screenshot from *Three Monkeys* 2008.)

the drops of sweat on İsmail's forehead draw back as he stares out towards the ghost of his younger brother. The slow sequence is at first free of any other sound except that of an empty building. We then hear the ticking clock, the breeze through the open kitchen window, and finally İsmail's heavy breath. There then appears an off-focus figure emerging from the distance, taking steps into what sound like puddles of water. The combined visual and sonic effect reinforces the uncanny appearance of the ghost, pushing cinema further toward the realm of the speculative.

The ghost appears twice throughout the entire film, each time during moments of heightened anxiety. First, he appears to İsmail who has just learnt of his mother's affair with Servet; then he appears to Eyüp who learns that İsmail is Servet's murderer. Rob White interprets this spectral presence as disclosing 'a traumatic primal scene', indicating the characters' 'remove from the world: their inaccessibility, their locked-away hurt' (2011: 67). But the ghost also refers to a relationship of pure contradiction; when nothing makes any sense, things are – and never are – as they appear. The incapacity of the image to represent or clarify things recalls again Rancière's warning against an expectation that images reveal 'clarity of a disclosure' (2014: 13–14). The film does little to clarify the story of the dead son, and in each turn, structurally denies the characters a space to grieve for their loss. In the absence of that space, the family are left in silent and silencing isolation, wherein justice remains outside the equation altogether.

Another instance of spectrality is with Hacer's attempted suicide, which recurs three times, each with subtle but significant differences. The time-lapse and the three different versions of the same act suggest the confines of Hacer's life. On the first occurrence, we follow Eyüp's hesitant gaze and see Hacer on the edge of the rooftop. Eyüp stands back without interference. Much later, the scene recurs a second time. This time, we watch Eyüp come out of the doorway and command her to step down. Changes in the setting between the two occurrences are so subtle that they could go unnoticed. However, minor differences in the *mise-en-scène*, including a change in Eyüp's clothing, reveal that these events develop in entirely different timelines. Likewise, in the third version of the same scene, we no longer have Eyüp's gaze on Hacer. This time, the camera watches Eyüp come out of the doorway – by now we are familiar with the idea of suicide – yet instead of finding Hacer at the edge of the rooftop, we discover her seated at the table with İsmail. Suicide, both in thought and action points out unfathomable despair. Like the ghost of her youngest son, Hacer's grief remains unspoken, recalling Spivak's ground-breaking critique that if 'the subaltern has no history and cannot speak, the subaltern as female is even more deeply in shadow' (1994: 83).

Ceylan explained his take on silence in an interview with Geoff Andrew in 2004: '[t]he truth lies in what's hidden, in what's not told. Reality lies in the unspoken part of our lives' (quoted in White 2011: 66). The film's non-affirmative temporality opens a space in which another discourse could be imagined. For Deleuze, once the image is cut off from sensory-motor links, it becomes a 'pure optical and aural image'; the site of total noncompliance, or the image of pure resistance (1986: 52). Yet, the suicide scene, no matter how many times it is presented, reveals little about the reality Hacer endures.

Just as Hacer's body is decisively noncompliant, so too is her mobile ringtone, which becomes an empowering speech act that disrupts narrative continuity: 'I hope you love and aren't loved back . . . Don't turn back, I don't want it. I am not my old self. Life is a game with neither roles nor scenes. I hope you aren't happy either. I hope you love and aren't loved back'. When we finally hear more of Tilbe's singing in the film's later scenes, we hear the protest in the song's lyrics, and Hacer suddenly becomes the only character to advocate her stance. Let us not forget that the first time we hear the song is when Hacer sings it at the film's start. Dönmez-Colin is persuasive in her assessment that Hacer gets read as the 'underdog' in the film (2008: 95). Abused by all the men in her life, she embodies layers of hurt and pain. To that end, the delivery of the lyrics through a ringtone is also pertinent since digital communication anticipates a subjectivity whose experience of reality is inherently inconsistent with the one presumed by analogue fidelity. Hacer has no one; only the concrete slabs of the city, the rubble of the landscape, the walls of her crumbling house. In this case, contrary to the equation that silence is oppression, the invasive volume of her mobile's familiar ringtone is so enduring that audiences can still hear it in their minds long after the film ends.

The accident, the murder, the fight during the night of the elections – all the various forms of violence in the film – are also the events that remain offscreen. The hit-and-run that opens the film is placed out of our sight even though it sets the entire filmic premise. In a cinema of the 'seer' we paradoxically see extraordinarily little. This structural omission of events leads audiences to speculate the in-between time of the frames, thereby provoking to question what intervention looks like and where it occurs. Even if the characters are playing the three monkeys and are therefore presumably complicit, the series of disappointments is perpetuated by the cycle of violence in which they are bound. Eyüp's deal with Servet does not provide the family with a happier life; Hacer's decision to reclaim her sexuality only reinforces her sexual alienation; İsmail's success to get cash and buy a car proves his financial dispossession. Just as the family house can be read as a metonym for the struggle to preserve, reconstruct, or maintain a sense of stability on an inherently unstable ground, so too the out-of-placeness of the time-images reveal the failed promises of our own expectations.

What we are concerned with here is what Fred Dallmayr noted in his article, 'The politics of nonidentity: Adorno, postmodernism – and Edward Said', as the 'excess of being over knowing' (1997: 35). Ceylan lets loose an overload of social and historical contradiction within a binding narrative. Coherence is informed by corruption, morality by captivity, and violence is an everyday occurrence. By the film's end, we realize that cinematic time is the film's way of working through the discrepancy between loneliness and solidarity, of negotiating private pain through the public act of cinema spectatorship. As such, *Three Monkeys* is a political film, though its politicity is still unfamiliar; one in which a combination of possibilities is numerous, piety is punitive, and participation is duplicitous.

The film ends with a sequence focusing on Eyüp, after meeting with Bayram to take the blame for his son. Standing alongside Eyüp on the rooftop of his building, we stare out towards the silent Istanbul sea. We see the passing of freight ships, rows of cars, a train, and heavy clouds arriving with the turning of the seasons. A close-up shot reveals Eyüp's exhausted face before another long take of the impoverished landscape of Yedikule closes the film. The family house – defiantly though with great difficulty – manages to remain firm, though it is certainly vulnerable, alone, and on the brink of demolition.

NOTES

1. This chapter originally appeared as 'Non-affirmative time-images in Nuri Bilge Ceylan's *Three Monkeys* (2008) and the political aesthetics of New Turkish Cinema' in *New Cinemas: Journal of Contemporary Film*, 13: 2, pp. 169–85 and was thoroughly revised, updated and expanded for this volume with kind permission of the editors.

2. The symbolism of the first names should be noted. Servet, in Turkish, means fortune. Likewise, the family members each have names rooted in Abrahamic religious traditions: Eyüp is Job, Hacer is Hager and İsmail is Ishmael.
3. For a report on party slogans and timeline, see the newspaper article, '[AK Party seeks another term, others pursue revenge] party slogans reveal post-election intentions' (Anon. 2007).
4. Mohaghegh specifically reads the unspoken within in the poetry of Ahmad Shamlu (1925–2000), Forugh Farrokhzad (1934–67) and Sadeq Hedayat (1903–51).
5. For a theorisation of the relation between captivity and photographic capture, see Rey Chow (2015).
6. I am using this term after Foucault's reading of the 'non-affirmative' order of signification in Magritte's *This is Not a Pipe* painting, which he argued, refuses to forge a relationship between resemblance and referent. See, Michel Foucault's 1968 essay, 'Nonaffirmative painting' (1982).

CITED WORKS

Adorno, T. (2008), 'Being. Nothing. Concept', in R. Tiedemann (ed.), *Lectures on Negative Dialectics: Fragments of a Lecture Course 1965/1966*, trans. R. Livingstone. Cambridge: Polity, 55–64.

Akbulut, H. (2005), *Nuri Bilge Ceylan Sinemasını Okumak: Anlatı, Zaman, Mekân*. Istanbul: Bağlam.

Anon. (2007), '(AK party seeks another term, others pursue revenge) party slogans reveal post-election intentions', *Today's Zaman*, 21 July. (URL no longer available)

Atam, Z. (2009), 'Critical thoughts on the New Turkish Cinema' in D. Bayrakdar, A. Kotaman and S. A. Uğursoy (eds), *Cinema and Politics: Turkish Cinema and the New Europe*. Newcastle: Cambridge Scholars, 202–20.

Atasoy, A. (2008), 'Nuri Bilge Ceylan: "Bilen İnsan Rolü İlgimi Çekmiyor"', *Radikal Gazetesi*, 21 May, http://www.radikal.com.tr/radikal.aspx?atype=haberyazdir&articleid=878791(last accessed 9 June 2022)

Atayman, V. (2012), 'Yeni Psikanalitik Topik: Kasaba – Kent', *Modern Zamanlar*, 26: 5.

Bazin, A. (1967), *What is Cinema?* Berkeley: University of California Press.

Beckman, K. R. and Ma, J. (2008), *Still Moving: Between Cinema and Photography*. Durham: Duke University Press.

Çağlayan, Emre (2018), *Poetics of Slow Cinema: Nostalgia, Absurdism, Boredom*. London: Palgrave Macmillan.

Çakırlar, C. and Özlem Güçlü (2012), 'Gender, family and home(land) in contemporary Turkish cinema: A comparative analysis of films by Nuri Bilge Ceylan, Reha Erdem and Ümit Ünal', in K. Laachir and S. Talajooy (eds), *Resistance in Contemporary Middle Eastern Cultures: Literature, Cinema and Music*. New York: Routledge, 167–83.

Carvin, A. (2013), 'The "Standing Man" of Turkey: Act of quiet protest goes viral', National Public Radio, 18 June.

Ceylan, Nuri Bilge (2018), *Ahlat Ağacı/The Wild Pear Tree*.

—— (2014), *Kış Uykusu (Winter Sleep)*.

—— (2008a), *Üç Maymun/Three Monkeys*.

—— (2008b), 'Interview with Nuri Bilge Ceylan', *Three Monkeys*, DVD extras, Turkey, France and Italy: New Wave Films.

—— (2008c), '*Üç Maymun*: Kurgu Günlüğü' ('Three Monkeys: Editing journal'), *Altyazı*, 78: November, 1–32.

___ (1999), *Mayıs Sıkıntısı/Clouds of May*, DVD extra.
Choudhuri, S. and H. Finn (2003), 'The open image: poetic realism and the New Iranian Cinema', *Screen*, 44:1 Spring, 38–57.
Chow, R. (2012), *Entanglements: Or Transmedial Thinking About Capture*. Durham: Duke University Press.
Crittenden, R. (2010), 'Another cinema', *Significação*, 24: 9, 9–29.
Dallmayr, F. (1997), 'The politics of nonidentity: Adorno, postmodernism and Edward Said', *Political Theory*, 25: 1, 33–56.
Deleuze, G. (1995), *Negotiations, 1972–1990*. New York: Columbia University Press.
—— (1992), 'Postscript on the societies of control', *October*, 59: Winter, 3–7.
—— (1989), *Cinema 2: The Time-Image* (trans. H. Tomlinson and B. Habberjam). Minneapolis: University of Minnesota Press.
de Luca, T. and Barradas Jorge N. (eds) (2015). *Slow Cinema*. Edinburgh: Edinburgh University Press.
Diken, B., G. P., Gilloch and C. Hammond (2018). *The Cinema of Nuri Bilge Ceylan: The Global Vision of a Turkish Filmmaker*. London: I.B. Tauris.
Dönmez-Colin, G. (2008), *Turkish Cinema: Identity, Distance and Belonging*. London: Reaktion Books.
Er, F. (2010), '*Üç Maymun*: Cehennemde Bir Fotoğraf', in A. Pay (ed.), *Yönetmen Sineması*, Istanbul: Küre Yayınları, 63–77.
Foucault, M. (1982), 'Nonaffirmative painting', in J. Harkness (ed.), *This Is Not a Pipe*, trans. J. Harkness. Berkeley: University of California Press, 53–4.
Jaffe, I. (2014), *Slow Movies: Countering the Cinema of Action*. New York: Wallflower Press.
Koepnick L. (2014), *On Slowness: Toward an Aesthetic of the Contemporary*. New York: Columbia University Press.
Mohaghegh, J. B. (2013). *Silence in Middle Eastern and Western Thought: The Radical Unspoken*. London: Routledge.
Mulvey, L. (2006), *Death 24 X a Second*. London: Reaktion Books.
Rancière, J. (2014), *The Intervals of Cinema*, trans. J. Howe. London: Verso.
Spivak, G. (1994), 'Can the subaltern speak?' in P. Williams and L. Chrisman (eds) *Colonial Discourse and Postcolonial Theory*. New York: Columbia University Press, 66–111.
Suner, A. (2010), *New Turkish Cinema: Belonging, Identity and Memory*. London: I.B. Tauris.
—— (2011), 'A lonely and beautiful country: Reflecting upon the state of oblivion in Turkey through Nuri Bilge Ceylan's *Three Monkeys*', *Inter-Asia Cultural Studies*, 12: 1, 13–27.
Toper, O. (2014). 'O çocuk taşı neden attı?" *Yarın Haber*, 20 June, http://yarinhaber.net/yaklasimlar/15115/o-cocuk-tasi-neden-atti. (last accessed 10 March 2022)
Tulgar, A. (2008), 'Film Başlarken', *Bir Gün*, 19: 12, http://www.birgun.net/ haber-detay/film-baslarken-2094.html. (last accessed 11 May 2017).
Vidler, A. (1992), *The Architectural Uncanny: Essays in the Modern Unhomely*. Cambridge: MIT Press.
White, R. (2011), 'Nuri Bilge Ceylan: An introduction and interview', *Film Quarterly*, 65: 2, 64–72.
Yetişkin, E. (2010), 'Güncel Politik Sinemayı Yeniden Düşünmek', *Akademik İncelemeler Dergisi*, 5: 2, 95–116.

CHAPTER FIVE

The Aesthetics of Space and Absence: *Üç Maymun/Three Monkeys* (2008) and *Bir Zamanlar Anadolu'da/Once Upon a Time in Anatolia* (2011)[1]

Adam Ochonicky

Nuri Bilge Ceylan's *Üç Maymun/Three Monkeys* (2008) and *Bir Zamanlar Anadolu'da/Once Upon a Time in Anatolia* (2011) are set into motion by death. *Three Monkeys* begins with Servet (Ercan Kesal), a wealthy politician and businessman, killing a pedestrian in a night-time hit-and-run incident and then paying his personal driver Eyüp (Yavuz Bingöl) to assume responsibility. In *Once Upon a Time in Anatolia*, a deceptively simple plot – the search for the corpse of a murder victim in the Anatolian steppes – serves as the foundation for an investigation into the malleability of archives, the representation of mnemonic processes and mortality itself. Early in the film, Doctor Cemal (Muhammet Uzuner) predicts that 'not even one hundred years from now . . . Well, as the poet said, "Still the years will pass and not a trace will remain of me"'.[2] Ceylan complicates this lamentation by exploring how the past materialises within the present. While deploying and subverting crime film conventions in both films, Ceylan shows characters attempting to alter understandings of past violence. Yet the full erasure or negation of the past is impossible. Through the ongoing entanglement of past and present, Ceylan infuses each film with absence – that is, with a peculiar sense of things unseen or unspoken contaminating the contemporary moment.

This chapter examines Ceylan's interconnected treatment of space and absence. The centrality of death and the unresolved past are reflected in the aesthetics of *Three Monkeys* and *Anatolia*. Notably, Ceylan spatialises his concern with absence. In both films, a haunting vacancy – an unsettling non-presence – is projected onto the very spaces in which the narratives unfold. These landscapes of absence are physical sites that have been reconfigured as subjective realms. Here, I use the term 'landscape' broadly, as spectral traces of the past infiltrate the present within natural spaces and human-built structures alike. On the levels of narrative and film style, Ceylan draws attention to that which is missing through an interplay between the visible and the invisible. This troubling of perception is heightened by a masterful command of cinematic form. Through inventive uses of framing and focus, Ceylan injects a large degree of spatiotemporal abstraction into urban and rural environments, including interior and exterior spaces. Such frames of absence – shots in which large sections of the frame are empty or vacant – make absence present within the cinematic image. Beyond assessing how these films conjure up the past within the present, I also consider how Ceylan imagines the present as a site of temporal convergence with the future. It is not just that the present is haunted by spectres of the past; rather, the present itself is spectral.

Theories of temporality by George Herbert Mead and Jacques Derrida help to clarify the meanings of absence in Ceylan's films. Mead is an important figure in American pragmatism and social psychology, and I see his writings on time as having under-examined applications for the study of temporality in cinema.[3] Of greatest pertinence is Mead's theory of the 'specious present', which denotes a temporal category that encompasses the ongoing past and impending future. In conjunction with Mead, I reference commentary by Derrida on spectrality, recording technologies and future absence. For Derrida, the awareness of one's future absence contaminates the present with a fear of the disappeared self. While there is minimal overlap between much of Mead's and Derrida's writings, juxtaposing their perspectives on temporality yields some intriguingly complementary results. Both theorists identify absence as a fundamental condition of the present – a temporal coordinate populated by past and future spectres. By considering *Three Monkeys* and *Anatolia* through the prism of Mead and Derrida, a hybrid concept emerges: what I describe as the 'spectral present'. Ceylan illuminates the spectral present through framings that emphasise overlapping temporal layers and transform realistic *mise-en-scènes* into landscapes of absence. Such locations appear to be largely vacant but hold traces of what has been and what will come; consequently, these two films challenge discrete notions of past, present and future.

CULTURAL AND CINEMATIC FRAMEWORKS

Ceylan's first several features are associated with the New Cinema of Turkey of the 1990s and early twenty-first century, but his career has progressed beyond the purview of that label. Gönül Dönmez-Colin explains that New Cinema of Turkey is distinguished by the 'search for an identity in a changing society, the threat to physical and/or mental space/territory and the general atmosphere of fear and not belonging when faced with the questions of identity: national, social, religious, political and sexual' (2008: 180). Asuman Suner observes that 'New Turkish films revolve around the figure of a "spectral home"', which is 'haunted by a nostalgic yearning for a long-lost childhood' (2010: 16). In line with these qualities, Zehra Cerrahoğlu describes Ceylan's first three films as preoccupied with identity and settings; these works have 'an almost autobiographical aspect' because 'the protagonists, locations and events are somehow related to Ceylan's personal life' (2019: 80). Beginning with *İklimler/Climates* (2006), Ceylan's films have broader emphases on 'social classes, superiority relations, oppression and bureaucracy-related issues with the setting of the suburbs or the province as background', as well as 'different production schemes' (Ibid: 81, 83). Whereas earlier films were low-budget productions with a 'small crew', 'family members' as cast, '[a]utobiographical locations', and '[p]ersonal stories', the later films are international co-productions with bigger budgets, '[p]rofessional actors', and more sophisticated narratives (Ibid: 83).

As the first two films released after *Climates* (which starred Ceylan and his wife Ebru Ceylan), *Three Monkeys* and *Anatolia* mark an important transitional period within Ceylan's filmography. Both Suner and Cerrahoğlu single out *Three Monkeys* as an especially notable break from Ceylan's early films in terms of narrative, themes and aesthetics (Suner 2011: 15–6; Cerrahoğlu 2019: 81). Increased recognition by international critics and film festivals – including the 'Best Director Award' for *Three Monkeys* at the 2008 Cannes Film Festival and the 'Grand Prix' for *Anatolia* in 2011 – accompanied Ceylan's evolution as a filmmaker. Zafer Parlak and Mehmet Işık identify a mixed or outright negative reception of Ceylan's work in Turkish mainstream media outlets partly due to his career trajectory that has involved changed production and financing methods, expanded subject matter and international acclaim (2018: 52–3).

For my purposes, I am interested in ways that *Three Monkeys* and *Anatolia* recall aspects of 1960s and 1970s European cinema, as well as art films from other eras and regions. In interviews, Ceylan is forthright about his influences and 'cites Ingmar Bergman, Andrei Tarkovsky, Robert Bresson, Yasujirō Ozu and Abbas Kiarostami among his major sources of inspiration' (Suner 2015: 133). Michelangelo Antonioni's iconic 'incommunicability trilogy' – *L'avventura/The Adventure* (1960), *La notte/The Night* (1961), and *L'eclisse/The Eclipse* (1962) – is another clear precursor to Ceylan's treatment of space and absence. Much like *The Adventure*, the narratives of *Three Monkeys* and *Anatolia* are propelled by absent figures. In *Three Monkeys*, Servet's unidentified victim is one of multiple absences. While incarcerated, Eyüp is physically absent from the apartment shared with his wife Hacer (Hatice Aslan) and son İsmail (Ahmet Rıfat Şungar). Ceylan gradually reveals that the family are grieving the loss of an unnamed son/brother (Gürkan Aydın), who appears to have drowned as a child. In several sequences, this deceased character manifests onscreen and is dripping water. In

Once Upon a Time in Anatolia, a caravan that includes two murder suspects – Kenan (Fırat Tanış) and Ramazan (Burhan Yıldız) – and a group of officials – Doctor Cemal, Commissar Naci (Yılmaz Erdoğan), Prosecutor Nusret (Taner Birsel) and others – attempts to locate the missing body of the murdered Yaşar (Erol Erarslan). Both Cemal and Nusret contend with the emotional ramifications of absent wives due to divorce and death, respectively.

Through various narrative events, Ceylan highlights the relationship between gendered power structures and historical memory. In their efforts to control contemporary and future knowledge of the past, male characters actively manipulate official records. *Three Monkeys* begins and ends with parallel bribes to shift the responsibility for death from one person to another. During Eyüp's imprisonment, İsmail pressures his mother to request additional money from Servet, who initiates an extramarital affair with Hacer. Shortly after İsmail discovers this affair and Eyüp returns home, Servet is killed; İsmail states that he 'did it', although the murder is not depicted onscreen. To avoid losing another son or returning to prison, Eyüp attempts to pay Bayram (Cafer Köse), a poor teahouse worker, to admit to the murder. In *Anatolia*, Nusret exhibits a remarkably flexible attitude towards veracity. Tasked with drafting an official account of the recovery of Yaşar's body, Nusret's narration belies what is depicted onscreen. He consistently fabricates witness statements in his report and produces a sanitised narrative that is less complex than actual events. This revisionist dynamic is further emphasised in the running conversation between Nusret and Cemal. Over several scenes, the prosecutor details a case in which a woman predicted when she would die and then mysteriously perished. Eventually, it is revealed that this story is about Nusret's own wife, who killed herself in the wake of his infidelity. The analytic Cemal continually questions Nusret's interpretation of these events until the prosecutor acknowledges his role in the death. As these examples suggest, absence – via the omission of actual occurrence – is inscribed into history, often by male authorities.

Whether it be nostalgic memories, a lost family member, censored records, or a hidden aspect of identity, absence is prominent in *Three Monkeys* and *Anatolia*. Repeatedly, these films brush up against the inaccessible. Personal histories remain invisible and exist beyond the parameters of the frame. When characters sombrely ponder circumstances in their lives, viewers are challenged to comprehend their interior psychological processes and motivations. This sense of perpetual haunted-ness establishes interiority as a form of cinematic absence. Ceylan explains that he 'like[s] to show the things that we hide' and that '[a]bove all, my films are about the inner world of people' (White 2015: 164–5). Along these lines, Haden Guest identifies 'the moral implied throughout [Ceylan's] films: that you can never fully know the person before you' (2012: 57). Although such concerns may seem removed from precise cultural or political matters, Suner asserts that Ceylan's films obliquely comment on Turkey's twenty-first-century status. Of *Three Monkeys*, Suner writes, 'The bizarre ordeal of the family . . . seems to mirror the present condition of Turkish society: that of living with the burden of oblivion and denial' (2011: 23). Precisely because the film 'does not refer to a particular historical event', Suner suggests that it has the ability to comment on forms of 'official censorship' and the cultural suppression of 'social memory' (2011: 23).[4] Such possibilities correspond with Argentinian filmmaker Lucrecia Martel's statement about her work: 'My films are political in this sense: to make a film is to share the doubt about our reality' (Matheou 2010: 32). Martel's provocative notion of the political is relevant for considering the uses of absence in cinema. To recognise that something is missing or obscured within the frame is, for Martel, to cast doubt on the stability of what is visible beyond the film, such as political and social formations. Like Martel's notion of doubt as political, Ceylan generates scepticism towards the blind acceptance of visible reality, including the veracity of the filmic image itself. Throughout their work, Martel and Ceylan – who are contemporaries – force audiences to scan the frame for traces of that which remains out of sight and just offscreen.

LANDSCAPES AND FRAMES OF ABSENCE

One of the ways in which Ceylan produces an awareness of missing or unseen presences is through the conspicuous recurrence of negative space in the frame. Because Ceylan's cinematic techniques frequently recall the films of Antonioni, the Italian director's aesthetics of space and concept of reality warrant further examination. Of these matters, Antonioni expresses the following sentiment:

> We know that under the revealed image there is another one which is more faithful to reality, and under this one there is yet another, and again another under this last one, down to the true image of that absolute, mysterious reality that nobody will ever see. Or perhaps, not until the decomposition of every image, every reality. (Brunette 1998: 120–1)

Antonioni suggests that images and reality are simultaneously proximate and distant from one another; any attempt to visually capture reality will serve only to expose the layered and inaccessible nature of an 'absolute, mysterious reality'. Many of Antonioni's films ruminate on the unknowability of others. Recurring elements such as interiorised performances and failing relationships highlight the limitations of visual perception. Even more applicable for understanding Ceylan's films are the ways in which Antonioni's evocative *mise-en-scènes* and manipulation of time reflect upon the accessibility of reality via cinema.

To better understand Ceylan's work, Seymour Chatman's foundational study of Antonioni is instructive. Chatman discusses how Antonioni renders physical spaces as entities with their own reality beyond the film's plot and characters. This treatment of space involves visualising absence within the frame:

> [Pier Paolo] Pasolini speaks of the prediegetic importance of the space that characters enter. But Antonioni features postdiegetic space even more prominently, by dwelling on what is left after characters depart . . . The prediegetic instance can often be conventionally attributed to the familiar conventions of the establishing shot, but the postdiegetic lingering is more immediately provocative because it seems on first viewing to be a mistake, a piece of sloppy editing. In either case, the whole meaning of *establishing* has been radically altered. What is established is not 'the same place' but the possibility that it is in reality 'another place', perhaps even an extradiegetic place. The scene is made portentous by a delay that challenges the whole tissue of fictionality . . . This kind of shot does not set the stage for some other shot, but . . . it is itself the scene . . . [T]he camera's lingering makes the place pregnant with significance. We contemplate intently, in a way parallel to but separate from the characters. We are engaged, even before they arrive or after they leave, in a scrutiny that we do not quite understand but that seems nonetheless urgent . . . It occurred to Antonioni to let the characters exit the frame and to keep on photographing what was left – to affirm that the background has its own esthetic and thematic autonomy. The effect is that the location is shown to possess an equal but separate reality. (Chatman 1985: 125–6)

Echoing Antonioni, *Three Monkeys* and *Anatolia* include scenes that begin too early or end too late. Such aesthetics evoke a similar sense of time to Antonioni's famed trilogy, as Ceylan invites viewers to reflect upon the 'autonomy' of onscreen spaces through prolonged shots of visual absence. Along with prominently featuring shots of pre-diegetic and post-diegetic spaces, Ceylan's characters are regularly fragmented or marginalised within the frame. These techniques accentuate the emptiness of the space occupied by characters. Ceylan troubles what it means to establish cinematic space, effectively undermining visible reality and surface-level appearances in his films.

As a brief aside, the unconventional framing techniques in *Three Monkeys* and Martel's *La mujer sin cabeza/The Headless Woman* (2008) are remarkably similar. Both films debuted at the 2008 Cannes Film Festival, just days apart; given their complementary narrative and aesthetic elements, they serve as fascinating companion works. Each opens with a hit-and-run collision that looms over the remainder of the proceedings. In *The Headless Woman*, there is sustained ambiguity as to whether protagonist Vero (María Onetto) killed someone while driving, but her guilt over the possibility (or even likelihood) informs every ensuing frame. Unlike Servet stopping to confirm his victim's death, Vero briefly pauses her vehicle, glances in the rear-view mirror, and continues driving. Martel includes numerous shots with absent space, which collectively underscore the film's thematic emphases on missing presences, historical and national amnesia and the incomplete erasure of the past.

In *Three Monkeys*, naturalistic exterior and interior environments are configured as subjective realms. Ceylan often shoots scenes with stationary cameras, and many shots are of lengthy duration. In conjunction with the *mise-en-scène*, these techniques produce frames of absence. For example, a heated encounter between Hacer and Servet is shot in an extreme long shot that lasts nearly three minutes. The static, distant camera presents characters as tiny specks within an expansive landscape. Natural elements of the *mise-en-scène* – craggy rock formations, a seaside cliff, mountains beyond the sea, slow-moving clouds above and gloomy, green-ish light – reinforce the scene's oscillating dynamic of menace and vulnerability. Intriguingly, the long take concludes with a cut to a second extreme long shot that insinuates a subjective point-of-view surveilling Hacer and Servet. An unseen character seems to be diegetically present but is visually absent in the frame. Soon after, İsmail claims that he murdered Servet. In hindsight, viewers might assume that this shot is İsmail's perspective, but the lack of definite attribution perpetuates the unsettling notion that something is always missing from the visual image. Finally, this scene is bookended by two shots of Hacer looking at herself in a mirror inside the apartment. As with several moments in the film, Hacer is associated with reflective surfaces that draw attention to the unknowable layers of her consciousness. Absence thus manifests onscreen in multifarious ways.

Inside the family's claustrophobic apartment, Ceylan creates odd perceptions of cavernous spatial depth and converging temporal layers. The apartment itself becomes a landscape of absence with, to borrow Chatman's phrase, a 'separate reality' that informs the fictional activities (1985: 126). Shooting on location, Suner notes that Ceylan 'rush[ed] the filming of the indoor scenes since the building was scheduled for demolition . . . The home at the center of *Three Monkeys*, therefore, is in fact on the brink of falling apart, both metaphorically and physically' (2011: 20). For scenes inside this evocative, crumbling space, Ceylan uses existing structural elements (such as windows and doors) to create subframes within the filmic image. Several bedroom and bathroom doors have frosted glass panes. Such elements produce a sense of characters simultaneously being on display and obscured. Major events happen behind panels and through frames, but specific details remain unheard or out of sight. For instance, Hacer often retreats into the depths of her bedroom for secretive phone conversations (presumably with Servet). At one point, İsmail unexpectedly returns home, hears muffled sounds from his mother's bedroom, and peers through the keyhole. Viewers never see what İsmail sees; Ceylan only shows the frosted glass panel and a close-up of İsmail's eye from the inside of the room. While it is apparent that İsmail is witnessing a sexual encounter between Hacer and Servet, the act occurs offscreen. As Suner observes, this is yet another form of absence in the film: 'the three events that advance the narrative – the accident, the affair and the murder – are not shown to the viewer . . . The key events, in other words, remain visually absent in the narrative' (2011: 19). Ceylan continually generates an awareness of missing content or unseen actions that are known primarily through their destabilising effects on the family.

Despite its cramped interior, Ceylan incorporates negative space into shots of the apartment. Such visual absences heighten the film's themes. When Hacer arrives at the apartment after first visiting Servet (and accepting a ride home), she walks to the far right of the frame and faces away from the camera. During an extended pause, Ceylan forces audiences to gaze at the primarily empty frame and ponder Hacer's internal thoughts. The frame's negative space thereby takes on subjective meanings, as the onscreen void reflects Hacer's inner turmoil and the unspoken implications of her encounter with Servet. Late in the film, Ceylan incorporates an especially notable frame of absence after Eyüp is interrogated by police for Servet's murder. Following a brief pan that shows Eyüp returning to the apartment and walking into the bedroom, the camera remains stationary for roughly eighty seconds. For several seconds after Eyüp exits the frame, the unmoving

Figure 5.1 The bedroom door frame, frosted glass door and mirror (which reflects Hacer sitting by a window) produce depth and portals within the crowded apartment. (Source: screenshot from *Three Monkeys* 2008.)

camera lingers on the vacant *mise-en-scène*, which features multiple frames within the film frame: the bedroom door frame, the frosted glass door, and a wall mirror that reflects an external window and empty chair. Like Chatman's pre- and post-diegetic spaces, Ceylan inserts a portentous pause during the scene. Hacer then enters the frame in the extreme foreground and moves back and forth. After physically exiting the frame, she sits in the off-screen chair that is reflected in the mirror. Once again, Hacer is linked to the loaded symbol of a reflective surface. As this scene demonstrates, Ceylan's framing renders the apartment's doors, mirrors and windows as portals that swallow up, conceal and/or reflect characters whose internal secrets and preoccupations remain unarticulated or invisible onscreen. This projection of spatial depth within the flat frames of the apartment reaffirms the domestic realm's status as a landscape of absence filled with hidden meanings.

The aesthetics of absence in *Three Monkeys* contrast interestingly with those in *Anatolia*. Whereas the earlier film utilizes the urban apartment's architectural elements to distort perceptions of space and create fragmented images of bodies, the latter features clear spatial relationships within a rural terrain. In *Anatolia*, Ceylan produces absence through scale, lighting and shot duration. Immediately after a preliminary scene in which Kenan, Ramazan and Yaşar converse in the latter's shop (and the opening credits), the film continues with a three-minute long take of the caravan driving on a road across the Anatolian countryside. The caravan stops to survey a site before progressing out of the frame. For the scene's duration, Ceylan's stationary camera shows the vehicles and performers in extreme long shot. Through such temporal dynamics, the naturalistic *mise-en-scène* is rendered as a space of absence. The shot begins with pre-diegetic space and ends with post-diegetic space; in other words, the countryside is an impassive backdrop that precedes and succeeds the narrative events. Like Antonioni's spaces, the Anatolian setting is presented as being 'independent of the characters and even of the narrative' (Chatman 1985: 125). Ceylan uses vacant space to establish the landscape as an entity in and of itself.

By shooting the Anatolian steppes in extreme long shots, Ceylan highlights the fragility and insignificance of the men travelling across its expanse. As the men scrutinise the land to no avail, the encroaching darkness further inhibits their ability to locate the missing body. Numerous shots of the countryside are distinguished by multiple planes of action in which characters drift in and out of light and shadows on the rolling surface. For instance, the two diggers responsible for unearthing Yaşar's body often seem to be on the verge of disappearing into the landscape. In extreme long shots, the tiny figures operate on the border between the flickering visibility produced by the cars' headlights and ominous darkness. During this protracted night-time section of the film, Ceylan's repeated use of long shots and extreme contrast lighting creates a landscape of absence that threatens to swallow up the caravan. There are also

THE AESTHETICS OF SPACE AND ABSENCE 93

Figure 5.2 The absent Anatolian countryside is both a pre-diegetic and post-diegetic space. (Source: screenshot from *Once Upon a Time in Anatolia* 2011.)

several quiet moments in which Ceylan luxuriates in the audio-visual textures of wind gently animating vegetation covering the vacant terrain.

The night-time lighting in *Anatolia* resembles the opening scene of *Three Monkeys* and creates some aesthetic continuity between the films. At the beginning of *Three Monkeys*, Servet's headlights are the only source of illumination as he drives along a shadowy, tree-lined road. The camera tracks behind the car and abruptly stops, which results in an extreme long shot of Servet's vehicle proceeding into the distance and becoming engulfed by darkness. Ceylan had intended to make *Anatolia* seem 'more naturalistic' by using natural light sources, but shooting in the steppes necessitated 'huge amounts of light' (Andrew 2015: 201). During the search, the men use their vehicles' headlights to brighten the landscape. Such efforts yield pockets of light encompassed by large swathes of impenetrable darkness. The resulting images show a space that feels more expressionistic and dream-like than naturalistic. Given the characters' objective, the darkness seems almost sinister – as if the physical setting itself is wilfully countering their search. What is sought remains just out of view, prompting suspicion that the missing body might be present but not perceivable.

Just as the aesthetics in *Three Monkeys* provide insights into the family's unspoken preoccupations, *Anatolia*'s landscapes of absence reflect the interior conditions of Cemal, Nusret and, to a lesser extent, Naci. Guest writes, 'The three principal male characters are each defined in terms of distant or departed wives who seem to float in a kind of netherworld, simultaneously absent and present' (2012: 58–9). Physically absent, these women are only known through men: Naci's phone conversations with his wife; Nusret's self-serving account of his wife's suicide; and Cemal's reserved discussion of his divorce. Eventually, Cemal emerges as the film's quiet protagonist. His role as introspective witness conceals past trauma that remains stubbornly present. Cemal openly states that he did not want children, which implies a potential reason for his failed marriage. The doctor's contemplative reaction to the central murder (which apparently occurred after Kenan told Yaşar that he was the father of the latter's son) draws attention to this character detail. It also establishes Cemal and his ex-wife's hypothetical child as yet another absence. While the precise circumstances of Cemal's divorce remain unclear, its lingering emotional effects correspond with Ceylan's focus on imperceptible depths beneath visible surfaces.

Cemal and Nusret's backstories create thematic continuity with *Three Monkeys*. Like Servet and Eyüp attempting to transfer responsibility for death to others, the personal details shared by the reticent doctor and talkative prosecutor are instances of men skewing facts while crafting more favourable 'public' stories. Along with a shared emphasis on the manipulation of personal and public records, both films are marked by pervasive absences in their imagery. Physical spaces are connected to the subjective states of characters consumed with past trauma and future uncertainty. Ceylan produces such landscapes of absence through the conspicuous recurrence of empty space within the frame, among other visual strategies. These vacant frames display pre-diegetic and post-diegetic spaces, which suggest multiple absences: the impending arrival or recent exit of characters, as well as more existential absences (missing bodies, lost spouses, or even the burden of historical memory on scales ranging from the national to the individual). Through the interplay of such narrative and aesthetic elements, these two films outline the spatiotemporal dimensions of absence in cinema.

THE SPECIOUS PRESENT AND SPECTRALITY

Three Monkeys and *Anatolia* are riddled with spectral presences. While these haunted films lack frightful depictions of the supernatural as in the horror genre, they still hinge upon disturbing intrusions of the past within the present. Indeed, ghosts manifest onscreen. In *Three Monkeys*, İsmail and Eyüp each encounter the drowned brother/son whose death continues to impact the family despite never being discussed aloud. In *Anatolia*, Kenan has a vision of the deceased Yaşar. Later, Cemal chats with townspeople who purport to have seen Yaşar after his death. The ontological status of these spectres remains unresolved: are they visualisations of characters' interior thoughts or actually supernatural entities? Either way, the deceased do not remain visibly or emotionally absent. For Ceylan, the past is ongoing and unresolved.

Components of Mead's and Derrida's temporal theories are useful for analysing the haunted spatiotemporal dynamics in Ceylan's films. Mead writes that the present 'marks out and in a sense selects what has made its peculiarity possible. It creates with its uniqueness a past and a future. As soon as we view it, it becomes a history and a prophecy' ([1932] 2002: 52). This quote encapsulates Mead's thinking about the flow of time. Throughout his writings, Mead emphasises the connectedness of the present to both past and future. However, he specifies, 'The present is not the past and the future' ([1964] 1981: 345). Instead, a specious present is expansive. It encompasses events that began in the past but continue in the present, as well as present events that will continue into the future.

Understanding the specious present entails recognising temporal continuity. In 'The Nature of the Past' (1929), Mead elaborates:

The actual passage of reality is in the passage of one present into another, where alone is reality, and a present which has merged in another is not a past. Its reality is always that of a present. The past as it appears is in terms of representations of various sorts, typically in memory images, which are themselves present. It is not true that what has passed is in the past, for the early stages of a motion lying within a specious present are not past. They belong to something that is going on. The distinction between the present and the past evidently includes more than passage. An essential condition is its inclusion in some present in this representational form. Passage as it takes place in experience is an overlapping of one specious present by another. There is a continuity of experience, which is a continuity of presents . . . What is taking place flows out of that which is taking place ([1964] 1981: 345–6).

Mead insists that the perceived passage of time obscures how past events persist in the present. What commenced in the past but continues in the present is part of the specious present – a temporal category that spreads across and includes numerous moments that, in their unfolding, are each contemporary or 'present'. Elsewhere, Mead further qualifies that certain aspects of the past are 'irrevocable' – that which 'must have been' – while other aspects of the past are actually present in that the past's 'presence is exhibited in memory, and in the historical apparatus which extends memory' ([1932] 2002: 47–8). In other words, the past consists of multiple elements: events that have objectively occurred and our ever-evolving perspective on those events. These latter processes also locate the past in the present.

Three Monkeys and *Anatolia* display several components of Mead's theories. Although the films' central deaths of an unidentified pedestrian, the unnamed son/brother and Yaşar are past, these absences remain present via their ongoing effects. The relationships that the living characters have to each death and to their personal histories keep evolving; past circumstances shape present experiences and perspectives on the future. Furthermore, the construction and revision of official records reflect Mead's emphasis on representations of the past. From Servet's cover-up (later replicated by Eyüp) to Cemal's omission of details from his autopsy report (to conceal that Yaşar was likely buried while still alive), the past is shown to be a production of the present.

Once Upon a Time in Anatolia visualises Mead's concept of time as a 'continuity of presents' ([1964] 1981: 346). During the search for Yaşar's body, extreme long shots depict the caravan's three vehicles traversing the dark Anatolian countryside. When considered through Mead's perspective, these shots exhibit a specious present by showing continuity from past to present and from present to future. Physical gaps separate where the cars have been, currently are and will be, yet all three spatiotemporal locations are visible. Due to the shots' duration, every fleeting instant is registered. The present spatial coordinate of each vehicle becomes its past location as the caravan steadily progresses into future locations; in turn, these future spaces become present locations when occupied by the vehicles. This continual movement within the frame demonstrates the logic of the specious present, as each changing spatial position is part of the same ongoing event.

After finally recovering Yaşar's body, Ceylan includes an intriguing shot of the caravan in the full light of morning. In the frame, segments of the road are visibly disconnected as the cars retreat toward town, and there are three distinct planes of action: the past is the foreground, the present occupies the middle ground, and the future is the background. While showing the ongoing nature of an event – the caravan's journey – the shot highlights the vacancy of the foreground space that was just occupied. The shot's immense scale and layering effectively results in a simultaneous vision of post-diegetic, current and

Figure 5.3 The Anatolian landscape is framed as a ripple of time in which past, present and future locations are simultaneously visible. (Source: screenshot from *Once Upon a Time in Anatolia* 2011.)

pre-diegetic spaces. Even if the physical continuity among each spatiotemporal coordinate is not fully visible from the camera's perspective, the connective segments of the road still exist. With this striking framing, Ceylan transforms the landscape itself into a ripple of time and creates a memorable image of the specious present.

Since both films are propelled by past violence and traumas, their future-oriented elements may be overlooked. Just as the specious present includes past events, so too does it encompass the future effects or continuation of contemporary circumstances. Mead observes, 'The irrevocable past and the occurring change are the two factors to which we tie up all our speculations in regard to the future. Probability is found in the character of the process which is going on in experience' ([1932] 2002: 45). Fittingly, both films end by suggesting an indefinite extension of absence and longing. In *Echographies of Television: Filmed Interviews* (2002), Derrida provides another framework for processing Ceylan's treatment of the future by theorising the temporal outcomes of audio-visual recording technologies. When discussing what it means 'to see spectacles or hear voices that were recorded at the beginning of the [twentieth] century', Derrida describes the experience as 'a form of presentification' that undermines '[w]hat we call real time' (2002: 129). Once a recording is made, the status of the present changes:

> [W]e are already in night, as soon as we are captured by optical instruments which don't even need the light of day. We are already spectres of a 'televised' ... Furthermore, because we know that, once it has been taken, captured, this image will be reproducible in our absence, because we know this *already*, we are already haunted by this future, which brings our death. Our disappearance is already here ... We are spectralized by the shot, captured or possessed by spectrality in advance. (Derrida and Stiegler 2002: 115-7)

According to Derrida, the creation of a televisual recording infects the present with an awareness of future absence. Because such recordings remind individuals of their eventual demise, the present becomes a spectral realm. Like Mead's specious present, absence stretches across multiple temporalities in Derrida's explication of spectrality.

Derrida contextualises his observations by referencing Roland Barthes's *Camera Lucida: Reflections on Photography* (1981). It is instructive to review Barthes's commentary on the temporality of photographic images: '[W]hat I see has been here, in this place which extends between infinity and the subject (*operator* or *spectator*); it has been here, and yet immediately separated; it has been absolutely, irrefutably present, and yet already deferred' (1981: 77). Just as Derrida later argues about television, Barthes associates the experience of looking at a photograph with present loss. Of this passage, Laura Mulvey asserts that Barthes's conception of 'the photographic image is a recording of absence and presence simultaneously' (2006: 57). These theorists reveal how the peculiar temporality of recorded images – whether moving or still – manifests absence within the present. Although Ceylan does not explicitly comment upon audio-visual recording technologies, the fear of future absence looms in his work.[5] The ongoing emphasis on manipulated records certainly speaks to this topic. In *Three Monkeys*, the expediency with which Servet transfers culpability to Eyüp carries an implicit threat that anyone could be made absent – written out of society – via legal or extra-legal means. In *Anatolia*, Ceylan similarly shows how a single individual – Nusret – chooses what is and what is not inscribed in official records. Multiple scenes expose Cemal's preoccupation with future absence. Through major narrative events and brief moments, Ceylan underscores the potential erasure of characters and the existence of many absences across both films.

THE SPECTRAL PRESENT

In their concluding moments, *Three Monkeys* and *Once Upon a Time in Anatolia* evince the spectral present. Following İsmail's confession, the three family members silently sit inside their apartment. Ceylan briefly cuts to a photograph of what appears to be Eyüp as a younger man with both of his, then-living, sons. For Eyüp, the photograph is a reminder of past trauma and provides an impetus to prevent new familial losses. Eyüp promptly leaves and solicits Bayram to assume responsibility for Servet's murder. There is a similar dynamic late in *Once Upon a Time in Anatolia*. In a fascinating example of the spectral present, Ceylan leads into the autopsy scene with a quiet moment of interiority. Upon returning to town, Cemal sits at his office desk. Ceylan then cuts to several close-ups of still photographs that sketch out a sparse chronology of Cemal's personal history. Each photograph shows a younger version of Cemal, from an image with his ex-wife to what appears to be himself as a child; both are now spectral presences. After the photographs appear onscreen, Ceylan cuts back to Cemal placing them into the desk drawer. The doctor glances out the window, turns, and stares directly into the camera. Ceylan lingers on Cemal's unblinking visage before cutting to a shot that reveals he is looking into a mirror. During this startling moment, the audience receiving Cemal's gaze is aligned with the mirror reflecting his image. Both the fleeting image of Eyüp with his two sons and the sequence of Cemal's photographs foreground absence. The former shows a child who has perished, and the latter reminds Cemal of the hypothetical child who may have caused a marriage-ending rift and of his own distant childhood.

Ceylan's use of photographs warrants deeper consideration. While analysing 'the fundamental, and irreconcilable, opposition between stillness and movement that reverberates across the aesthetics of cinema', Mulvey discusses the effects of incorporating still images into films (2006: 67). She argues, 'Although the projector reconciles the opposition and the still frames come to life, this underlying stillness provides cinema with a secret, with a hidden past that might or might not find its way to the surface' (Ibid). For Mulvey, the prolonged appearance of photographs within a film produces 'an illusion of stillness' that reflects upon the status of 'the moving image as filmstrip' and photography as a predecessor of cinema (Ibid). As such, the meanings of these still images range from narrative considerations to extra-diegetic contexts: a character's history, the film's actual production, or the medium's material attributes in general. Similarly, in a discussion of still images in Thai director Apichatpong Weerasethakul's films, Glyn Davis writes that such 'photographs serve as referents of the absent, distant or lost, resemblances of elements of the real and/or diegetic world located beyond the currently depicted scene' (2016: 103). Like Mulvey, Davis identifies how photographs may rupture the fictional pretence of a narrative film and engender a sensation of absence.

Comparable dynamics are discernible in *Once Upon a Time in Anatolia* via Ceylan's inclusion of still photographs and Cemal's ensuing gaze at the camera. On one level, this scene provides insights into the psychology of Cemal's character; personal history clearly influences his current behaviour. On another level, the sequence is overtly self-reflexive and challenges viewers to consider how cinema itself may be understood as spectral in nature. Ceylan draws attention to the fact that all figures onscreen are spectres of the past who, through the medium of cinema, manifest before audiences in the present. Accordingly, the concept of the spectral present encompasses aspects of film spectatorship. As Cemal looks at his mirrored reflection after seeing ghostly images of his younger self, the actor playing the doctor – Uzuner – stares at viewers from the 'real' past moment when the scene was shot. Cemal's review of photographs reflects the character's preoccupation with being forgotten, while Uzuner's direct gaze generates broader implications. During this contemplative sequence, Uzuner looks at the film's audience across time; like Cemal's wife, he is present in the recording but physically absent. Echoing Mead's notion of the specious present, a single film is something of an ongoing event. A film exists across numerous 'presents', including the times of its production and exhibition. Through these qualities, a film's performers and, indeed, its viewers are transformed into spectral presences whose future absence is confirmed. As viewers, we look at the film and when it looks back – as with Cemal's gaze at the camera – we are made aware of the many individuals who, at different temporal moments, will receive that gaze in our absence. In a much more understated manner, the photograph in *Three Monkeys* carries similar connotations of diegetic and extra-diegetic absences.

Once Upon a Time in Anatolia concludes with the autopsy scene, which has some symmetry with the film's opening sequence. The first scene features a nearly two-minute long take that begins with a close-up on the blurred glass pane of Yaşar's shop door. Inside, the figures are initially indistinct until the camera slowly moves forward and shifts focus. Yaşar gets up from sitting with Kenan and Ramazan and walks to the window, where he is framed in a close-up with his face distorted behind the glass. Even at this moment, Yaşar already seems to be not fully present. During the final scene, as Cemal directs the autopsy, his assistant Sakir (Kubilay Tunçer) notices dirt in Yaşar's lungs. Following an extended pause, Cemal dictates, 'No abnormalities were found in the trachea, oesophagus, or soft tissue of the neck'. Throughout the scene, Cemal compulsively retreats to a window and stares at a hillside and schoolyard. Shown in extreme close-up, Cemal seems to be holding back tears as he intently watches Yaşar's widow Gülnaz (Nihan Okutucu) and her son Adem (Fatih Ereli) cross this terrain. When the doctor exits the frame, the camera lingers on the vacated window. Ceylan's last shot mirrors the empty window of the film's opening scene, leaving viewers with another glimpse of post-diegetic space. This empty frame – a final image of absence – punctuates the film's emphasis on the impermanence of life and the unreliability of the visible.

Throughout *Three Monkeys* and *Once Upon a Time in Anatolia*, Ceylan engages with issues of memory, gendered power dynamics, the recording of history, and the spatiotemporal attributes of film. The connective temporal relations that Mead and Derrida theorise – particularly the ongoing nature of the past within the present and the unsettling recognition of future absence in contemporary moments – are made evident in both films. In *Three Monkeys*, Ceylan transforms a cramped apartment into a mysterious site of layered time by projecting hidden depths into physical frames (such as windows and doors) within the *mise-en-scène*. In *Anatolia*, Ceylan visualises the spectral present through extreme long shots that provide simultaneous views of the caravan's past, present, and future locations within the Anatolian steppes. Empty frames and negative space continually produce landscapes of absence onscreen. These shots of pre-diegetic and post-diegetic spaces visually affirm absence as a condition of the present, as do key sequences with still photographs. Overall, Ceylan's interconnected narrative and aesthetic elements reveal the spectral present as a realm haunted by overlapping temporalities and an unshakable sense of perpetual absence.

NOTES

1. An alternate version of this chapter was originally published in *Screening the Past* as 'The Spectral Present: Landscapes of Absence in *Once Upon a Time in Anatolia* and *The Headless Woman*'. It has been thoroughly revised, updated and expanded for this volume with kind permission from the editor, Anna Dzenis. See http://www.screeningthepast.com/issue-43/.

2. All quotations of dialogue from *Once Upon a Time in Anatolia* and *Three Monkeys* reference the English subtitles on the DVDs distributed by, respectively, Cinema Guild and Mongrel Media.
3. Mead briefly addresses cinema in 'The Nature of Aesthetic Experience' (1925–6).
4. Vuslat D. Katsanis also discusses how *Three Monkeys* engages with 'the contemporary Turkish public's difficult relation to the political' (2015: 172).
5. Craig A. Hammond suggests that Ceylan's filmography imagines 'that the future is an open and malleable space' (2018: 379). Within *Three Monkeys*, 'a latent and alternative possibility haunts [the characters] and lingers' (2018: 390).

CITED WORKS

Andrew, Geoff (2015), 'Journey to the End of Night: An Interview with Nuri Bilge Ceylan', in Robert Cardullo (ed.), *Nuri Bilge Ceylan: Essays and Interviews*. Berlin: Logos Verlag, 200–207.

Barthes, Roland (1981), *Camera Lucida: Reflections on Photography*, trans. Richard Howard. New York: Hill and Wang.

Brunette, Peter (1998), *The Films of Michelangelo Antonioni*. Cambridge: Cambridge University Press.

Cerrahoğlu, Zehra (2019), 'European co-productions and film style: Nuri Bilge Ceylan', *Studies in European Cinema*, 16:1, 73–89.

Chatman, Seymour (1985), *Antonioni: Or, The Surface of the World*. Berkeley: University of California Press.

Davis, Glyn (2016), 'Stills and Stillness in Apichatpong Weerasethakul's Cinema' in Tiago de Luca and Nuno Barradas Jorge (eds), *Slow Cinema*, Edinburgh: Edinburgh University Press, 99–111.

Derrida, Jacques and Bernard Stiegler (2002), *Echographies of Television: Filmed Interviews*, trans. Jennifer Bajorek. Cambridge: Polity Press.

Dönmez-Colin, Gönül (2008), *Turkish Cinema: Identity, Distance and Belonging*. London: Reaktion Books.

Guest, Haden (2012), 'Physical Evidence', *Film Comment*, 48.1, 56–9.

Hammond, Craig A. (2018), '*Three Monkeys* (2008): oblivion, anamnesis and the latent spectrality of hope', *Culture and Religion*, 19.4, 376–93.

Katsanis, Vuslat D. (2015), 'Non-affirmative time-images in Nuri Bilge Ceylan's *Three Monkeys* (2008) and the political aesthetics of New Turkish Cinema', *New Cinemas: Journal of Contemporary Film*, 13.2, 169–85.

Matheou, Demetrios (2010), 'Vanishing Point', *Sight & Sound*, 20.3, 28–2.

Mead, George Herbert [1932] (2002), *The Philosophy of the Present*. Amherst: Prometheus Books.

Mead, George Herbert [1964] (1981), *Selected Writings*, ed. Andrew J. Reck. Chicago: The University of Chicago Press.

Mulvey, Laura (2006), *Death 24x a Second: Stillness and the Moving Image*. London: Reaktion Books.

Ochonicky, Adam (2018), 'The Spectral Present: Landscapes of Absence in *Once Upon a Time in Anatolia* and *The Headless Woman*', *Screening the Past*, 43, http://www.screeningthepast.com/issue-43-dossier-materialising-absence-in-film-and-media/the-spectral-present-landscapes-of-absence-in-once-upon-a-time-in-anatolia-and-the-headless-woman/ (last accessed 31 August 2021).

Parlak, Zafer and Mehmet Işık (2018), 'Presentation of Nuri Bilge Ceylan and his Cinema in Turkish Media', *CINEJ Cinema Journal*, 7.1, 30–57.

Suner, Asuman (2015), 'Home, Belonging, and Other Aspects of Nuri Bilge Ceylan's Early Films', in Robert Cardullo (ed.), *Nuri Bilge Ceylan: Essays and Interviews*. Berlin: Logos Verlag, 123–52.

_____ (2011), 'A lonely and beautiful country: reflecting upon the state of oblivion in Turkey through Nuri Bilge Ceylan's *Three Monkeys*', *Inter-Asia Cultural Studies*, 12.1, 13–27.

_____ (2010), *New Turkish Cinema: Belonging, Identity and Memory*. London: I.B. Tauris.

White, Rob (2015), 'Nuri Bilge Ceylan: An Interview' in Robert Cardullo (ed.), *Nuri Bilge Ceylan: Essays and Interviews*. Berlin: Logos Verlag, 164–69.

CHAPTER SIX

Transnational Indistinctions: *Bir Zamanlar Anadolu'da/Once Upon a Time in Anatolia* (2011) and *Kış Uykusu/Winter Sleep* (2014)

Ebru Thwaites Diken

This chapter discusses Nuri Bilge Ceylan's cinema in terms of its transnational intimations, its contemplative dimension, its subtractive aesthetics and its approach to modernity through indistinctions rather than distinctions. I conceive of the 'transnational' in terms of a 'heterogeneous network' that cuts across cultures and geographies and binds together local contexts and global intellectual and political legacies (Latour 2005: 6). 'Transnational indistinctions' in this network refers to the dissolution of the demarcation line between the local and the global in spatial and temporal terms.

My discussion moves along three axes. The first axis situates Ceylan's filmmaking in a transnational network of artistic and intellectual production. His films produce decisive differences in their local repetition of Chekhovian, Dostoyevskian and Shakespearean themes. Ceylan de-territorialises the characters and stories and re-places and re-plays them in new contexts. His films are framed locally and networked globally. Secondly, through this repetition, Ceylan's cinema explores the universal within the singular. It explores the timeless, ahistorical and philosophical questions that relate to human existence. Universal affects such as envy, spite, resentment (which are, as Nietzsche and others have shown, constitutive of human sociality) are discussed through very personal, locally framed stories. Thirdly, through this movement where spatiality and temporality are displaced, Ceylan's cinema forces its audiences to contemplate the transition zones between reason and aesthetics, and between thought and taste. His films beautifully register the aesthetics of contemplative cinema, characterised by minimalist style, slow narrative pace, stillness and the density of Deleuzian time images. Ceylan's is an aesthetics of withdrawal, of 'preferring not to', rather than a cinema of action. Consequently, his films are crowded with unfinished projects, uncertain characters, incomplete enlightenments, criminalised judges, and other hybrid figures. In short, framed locally and networked globally, Ceylan's cinema is transnational in terms of a) its cross-geographical intellectual legacy, which produces a difference in repetition, b) the films' problematics, which pertain to the general human condition of late modernity such as loneliness, anxiety and evil, and c) their contemplative aesthetics, which often operates in a subtractive manner.

I focus on two of Ceylan's films that are European co-productions (as demonstrative of their transnational quality), *Bir Zamanlar Anadolu'da/Once Upon a Time in Anatolia* (2011) and *Kış Uykusu/Winter Sleep* (2014) to discuss how Ceylan moves from local distinctions to transnational indistinctions.

THE TRANSNATIONAL/TRANSAESTHETIC AS DIFFERENCE IN REPETITION

Auteurist readings of Ceylan's work often focus on the photographic film aesthetics and the national specificity of his films. I propose a different reading of Ceylan's cinema as a heterogeneous network that cuts across geographical and cultural territories in stylistic and thematic terms. In contrast to the imaginary of a solid national cultural identity envisioned by 'national cinema', the transnational cinema, conceived of as a network, consists of loose assemblages between local contexts and global intellectual, political and artistic legacies.

In this context, I draw on Latour's concept of the network, which suggests that all social relations are framed and networked at once; framed because one cannot have a social relation without separating it from the interference of other social relations and networked because there is a reminder of another spatiality and temporality in every social relation (2005). This perspective pertains to cinematic spaces and temporalities too. That is to say, the narratives in Ceylan's films necessarily have local and transnational dimensions at once. The stories in both films take place in remote, unconnected provincial towns in Anatolia. Although the characters are framed locally, they always refer to a transnational intellectual legacy. In both films, Ceylan borrows characters, dialogues and stories from Chekhov, Dostoyevsky and/or Shakespeare and reframes them in other historical and geographical contexts. To illustrate with an example, although the character İsmail (the tenant of the protagonist Aydın) in *Winter Sleep* is framed in the geographical space of Cappadocia, he partly resembles the 'drunken young fool' who burns the money in Dostoyevsky's novel *The Idiot*. In both the novel and the film, the act of burning money is an attempt to establish the 'moral norm of reciprocity' (Gouldner 1979: 161). This universal norm is repeated in the context of Cappadocia.

The interaction between the framed (locally/nationally) and the networked (globally) ascribes Deleuze's concept of repetition a central place in terms of how art and thought travel across time and space. As Deleuze suggests, every repetition creates a difference. Thus the 'new' is grounded repetition. Deleuze's example is clear cut: every time Shakespeare's play *Hamlet* is dramatised anew, it necessarily produces a difference in relation to previous dramatisations. Even when the same actor plays Hamlet several times, a difference emerges in each production (1994: 89–90).

All artistic endeavours are indeed repetitions of previous creations. The new emerges on the basis of repetition. This perspective stands in stark contrast to Malraux's claim that every work of art is creation *ex nihilo* (1978).[1] An *ex materia* account of artistic creation establishes all artistic events as repetitions of past events. No artwork can be entirely original. It is this repetition which makes Ceylan's cinema transnational. To give an example, *Once Upon a Time in Anatolia* bears resemblances to two short stories by Chekhov, 'Excellent People' and 'Perpetuum Mobile'. *Winter Sleep* is almost a direct adaptation from a short story by Chekhov: 'The Wife'. Ceylan suggests in an interview given to Romney that the main characters of *Anatolia* – the prosecutor, the doctor, and the mukhtar's daughter – are all Chekhovian characters (Romney 2012). The figure of the corrupt prosecutor in nineteenth century Russia comes to life in central Anatolia. Ceylan places this character in a murder story based on the twelve hours of a true event which has taken place in Keskin, Kırıkkale. In doing so, he de-territorialises Chekhov's stories and dramatises them in new settings. Neither Chekhov's nor Ceylan's characters are confined to the geographical spaces of Russia and Turkey.

Other transnational references in *Winter Sleep* include references of the protagonist Aydın (Haluk Bilginer) and the local schoolteacher Levent to Shakespeare in their conversations. It is no coincidence that, in real life, Bilginer is an actor with an international reputation, a graduate of The London Academy of Music and Dramatic Art, and he has taken the stage in the World Shakespeare Festival, performing in *Anthony and Cleopatra* at the London Globe Theatre in 2012. In the film, his retirement project, which is to write a book on the history of the Turkish theatre, locates him nationally. At the same time, however, Ceylan locates him globally by including Shakespearean exclamatory expressions and naming his hotel 'Othello', a reference to Shakespeare's famous tragedy, written most likely in 1603.

It is also significant that Aydın's sister, Necla, is a translator. She is framed locally, living in her family mansion; yet her job as a translator is symbolic of her transnational standing. This ironically recalls Yalçın Küçük's (2010) thesis on Turkish intellectuals: 'The Turkish intellectual is born in the translation room', a claim which reflects the influence of European intellectual life on the formation of the intellectual milieu in early Republic. While discussing her regrets about her divorce, Necla repeats in other contexts the timeless questions raised by theologians and philosophers hundreds of years ago. During a dinner table chat with her brother and sister-in-law, she invites them to think about the possibility of overcoming evil by not responding to it in the same way, wondering whether doing so would have made her ex-husband feel shame. Necla's query about non-resistance to evil has its origins in the Gospel of Matthew in the New Testament (the 39th verse of the fifth chapter). Chekhov refers to this idea in his short story 'Excellent People' and Ceylan re-contextualises it in a local setting in *Winter Sleep*.

These references to global intellectual legacies should not be thought of as simply Ceylan importing Russian realism and Shakespearean drama. Some parallels can be drawn in the configuration of cultural discourses in nineteenth century Russia and the late Ottoman Empire. Such discourses are historically contextualised in the peripheral positions of Turkey and Russia to Europe, their declining imperial pasts and engagements with Western modernization (Mathew 2019: 12). However, we cannot presuppose that Russian realism is *sui generis* and can be monolithically imported by a film director as such.

The intellectual exchange between Chekhov and Shakespeare adds another layer of complexity to the 'trans' quality of Ceylan's cinema. As argued by Sokolyansky, Chekhov was influenced by Shakespeare and used Shakespearean dialogues and themes in his plays (2001). Citing Roskin (1958: 131), Sokolyansky suggests that the exchange between Chekhov and Shakespeare is not limited to dialogues and themes, it also includes formal elements (Ibid: 110). Just like *Hamlet*, *The Cherry Orchard* includes 'extra-scenic characters' that help us grasp the 'pre-history of the fabula' (Ibid). They do not appear on stage, but the audience learns about them in the characters' dialogues. Such extra-scenic characters exist in *Winter Sleep* and *Anatolia* too. In *Winter Sleep*, we do not see Necla's ex-husband but learn about their past from her conversations with Aydın's wife, Nihal. Likewise, in *Anatolia*, we do not see the wife of the prosecutor Nusret, but learn about their relationship from his conversations with the doctor Cemal. The dialogues between the characters give us insight into their pasts and clues that explain their attitudes in their attempts to solve the crime. In a different way to these two films, in *Three Monkeys*, Ceylan's subtractive aesthetics and the characters' silences foreshadow the course of events. For example, when Eyüp asks his son, İsmail, if it was his wife who went to get the money from Servet, we feel his doubts from his silence. Eyüp's sceptical silence becomes a harbinger of the relationship that is yet to begin between Eyüp's wife, Hacer and his boss, Servet.

Another example of this transivity between Ceylan, Chekhov and Shakespeare concerns the scene in *Winter Sleep* when Aydın, looking up to Nihal's window, delivers his monologue: 'I have no one other than you. Actually, I missed you every minute, every second, but I could not say it, because my pride did not allow. We cannot go back to the old times when we lived as husband and wife. There is no need to anyway. Take me with you as your servant'.[2] For Mathew, this scene is reminiscent of the balcony scene in Shakespeare's play, *Romeo and Juliet*; while the quotations are directly borrowed from Josef Heifitz's film, *The Lady with a Little Dog*, which is an adaptation from Chekhov's story of the same name (Ibid: 22). Ceylan's use of similar camerawork to Heifitz, his direct adaptation of dialogues from Chekhov and their assemblage in a new setting endow his cinema not only with a transnational but also a trans-aesthetic character. In Mathew's words: 'While the Turkish context is never lost in these scenes, it is nonetheless striking how, at a purely formal level, a Russian realist antecedent inflects a scene that supposedly narrates the most specific and personal of exchanges' (Ibid).

This thematic and aesthetic transivity underlines the indeterminacy of the national and cultural specificities in Ceylan as well as in Chekhov and Shakespeare. Needless to say, there is no ownership of ideas. One cannot possess them as property or material items. Ideas are virtual in the sense that they are not reducible to actual identities. As the title of Gürbilek's book, *Benden Önce Bir Başkası/Someone Else Before Me* (literal translation) indicates, in the world of ideas, there is always someone else before one. In an interview, Gürbilek states, 'Kafka answers the question Dostoyevsky posed fifty years ago, "Am I a human or an insect?" But without Kafka's insect, we might not have noticed the insects that appear in almost every novel of Dostoyevsky' (2011).

The differences in repetitions may render Ceylan's stories and characters not only transnational, but also trans-identitarian, trans-sexual and trans-racial in the sense that, the characters re-appear in new contexts with different identity markers. For example, in terms of his alienation from his social surroundings and his contemptuous attitude towards the provincial people, the protagonist Aydın in *Winter Sleep* would be a typical intellectual figure in Chekhov, hence a repetition (Akın 2017: 85). However, Aydın is a Turkish intellectual with different problematics and a different social network that contextualise him. A Chekhovian intellectual would have been conditioned by the spirit of the intellectual climate against liberalism in the nineteenth century Russia, whereas Ceylan's figure of the intellectual takes issue with the problematics of late modernity, enlightenment and religion in the twenty-first century Turkey.

Another aspect of this transivity is the universal characters (the abject hero, the corrupt bureaucrat, the resentful slave, the cynical intellectual) that Ceylan, Chekhov, and/or Shakespeare share. For instance, in *Winter Sleep*, what makes İsmail a Dostoyevskian character is his spectacular abjection. If there is one thing that defines İsmail, it is his self-debasing attitude throughout the film. İsmail does so in order to debase everyone around him. His abjection ultimately becomes a weapon with which he turns the whole society into abjects. The resentful abject hero is a universal figure that can be found in numerous works of fiction and film, including in some of the other films of Ceylan. For example, in *Three Monkeys*, Eyüp symbolises Canetti's description of a resentful individual whose resentment is generated by his sense of inferiority (1984). Eyüp transfers his resentment to someone weaker than him (the poor migrant at the teahouse) through an act that can be understood with reference to the relationship that Nietzsche establishes between the sense of inferiority and the creation of morality as a justification for one's weakness. Herein lies the core of Nietzsche's master–slave morality as a foundational principle of human sociality. In *On the Genealogy of Morals*, Nietzsche contrasts master morality defined by pride and nobility and slave morality defined by mediocrity and ressentiment towards the master (2017). Pertaining to the nature of political power and the social psychology of the masses, Nietzsche's perspective on morality has universal significance.

The transivity between Shakespeare, Chekhov and Ceylan enables us to break away from the East/West binary that designates Chekhov and Ceylan as 'Eastern' and Shakespeare as 'Western'. When the international audience read the novel *Teneke/The Drumming-out* (1954) by Yaşar Kemal, the Turkish novelist whose books have been translated into more than forty languages, they do not read a story about Çukurova, but a story about the human condition, inequality and exploitation.[3] Likewise, when one watches a film by Ceylan, one not only watches a film on Anatolia, but sees a story on the atomisation of the individual, alienation, and the dissolution of the social bond in late modernity. As each repetition creates a difference, the 'new' in (New Turkish Cinema)[4] becomes a problematic term. The 'new' refers to the 'new' generated in the repetition, not 'new' in the sense of the authentic and the original.

A TRANSNATIONAL AESTHETICS OF CONTEMPLATION

The descriptive and critical capacity of the term 'transnational cinema' has been discussed in film studies in several ways by Higbee and Lim (2010: 8), Burgoyne (2016), Bergfelder (2005) and Ezra and Rowden (2006a). The term has been used to refer to the global production and distribution of films and funding structures as well as the new ways in which the films 'recode the world through transits, circuits and flows' (Galt 2016). As such, it has emerged in the historical and discursive context of globalisation, neo-liberalism and post-Fordism (Berry 2010: 112).

One can identify three distinct patterns as to how the concept is theorised in film studies (Berry 2010: 9). Given that cinema is an art and an industry at the same time, it has always been bound with economic and cultural formations that transcend the borders of the nation state (Ibid.). Thus, the first approach addresses the inadequacy of the term 'national cinema' for it cannot account for the movement of films and film makers across borders (Higbee 2000). In this prism cinema is already a transnational undertaking. The second approach emphasises the decisiveness of a common cultural heritage in the formation of film cultures. For instance, Nestingen and Elkington's analysis of transnational Nordic cinema accounts for the increasing mobility of people and talent and the governmental policies in Scandinavian countries fostering collaborative film production, a quality that is specific to welfare state policies and their cultural reflections on a regional scale (2005). Berry suggests that, since these two approaches could instead replace the term 'transnational' with regional or supra-national, the critical value of the term 'transnational cinema' lies in the third approach, which conceives of the term 'national cinema' as a Eurocentric term in its aesthetic and narrative conventions (2010: 9). Instead, transnational cinema encompasses exilic, diasporic and postcolonial cinemas. For example, Naficy argues that the films made by displaced directors from the 'Third World' share an interest in homelessness, identity, displacement, hybridity, non-places and transit spaces (2001). Being self-reflexive about their personal histories of migration, their films have an autobiographical touch and display an interconnectedness between the home and the host societies (Ibid.). Overall, Burgoyne's analysis beautifully registers the critical capacity of the term as an 'intellectual framework that explores the lines of connection' (2016).

This interconnectedness is partly due to the increasing number of global art house film festivals, which offer an alternative to commercial cinema in providing funding and networks. On the one hand, the international film festival circuit has enabled low budget independent art house film makers from the 'South/Third World' and women and LGBTQ+ filmmakers to reach global audiences. On the other hand, in this process of transnationalisation, the boundary between art house and commercial has been blurred.[5] Hollywood cinema has also opened to the world. Films such as *Babel* (*Iñárritu*, 2006) and *Slumdog Millionaire* (Boyle, 2008) allow for the representation of the non-English speaking world to global audiences and reflect an awareness of international conflicts (Sunde 2019: 19).

Against this background, Ezra and Rowden suggest that the process of transnationalisation encompasses two trends at the same time: 'The transnational comprises both globalization – in cinematic terms, Hollywood's domination of world film markets – and the counterhegemonic responses of filmmakers from former colonial and Third World countries' (2006: 1). I contend that Ceylan's filmmaking, which is heavily influenced by Yasujirō Ozu, could be situated among these counterhegemonic responses to commercial Hollywood, along with filmmakers such as Lav Diaz, Abbas Kiarostami, Apichatpong Weerasethakul and Tsai Ming Liang to name a few. These filmmakers share a visual style characterised by stillness, silence, long takes and durational looking (Jaffe 2014, Çağlayan 2018, Flanagan 2008). Jaffe and Flanagan call this contemporary aesthetic movement in independent filmmaking 'slow cinema'. The term was first used by Michel Ciment during a talk at the San Francisco International Film Festival and articulated in terms of Deleuze's concept of the time image. Çağlayan, in his book *The Poetics of Cinema*, points out that Flanagan describes the 'slow' in terms of the intensity of the narration, 'the employment of (often extremely long takes), de-centred and understated modes of storytelling, and the pronounced emphasis on the quietude and the everyday' (Flanagan 2008 as quoted in Çağlayan 2018: 5.) while Tuttle, criticising Flanagan on the grounds that not all slow cinema is thought provoking (Tuttle 2010b as quoted in Çağlayan 2018: 5), prefers to use the term 'contemplative cinema' instead of 'slow' (Çağlayan 2018: 6). Although Çağlayan partially agrees with Tuttle's views, he emphasises that, as the examples of *Blade Runner* (Ridley Scott, 1982) and *The Matrix* (Lana and Lilly Wachowski, 1999) show, not all thought-provoking films are slow (Çağlayan 2018: 6; Özyazıcı 2020: 198).

Koepnick (2014) contrasts a 'duration oriented aesthetics' *vis-à-vis* an agitated, action oriented aesthetics that is common to Hollywood commercial cinema underlines Çağlayan (2018: 15–16). Contemplative aesthetics captures the minute details of everyday life that escape the fast pace of modernity. Duration is a concept that relates to everyday life, in contrast to the world of systems which work according to chronological, linear time. In a world that elevates action and, even more so, fast action over slowness, slowness attains a particular value. The ability to slow down and the capacity to deactivate the mobile machine take on a different meaning (Ibid.). Perhaps this is why as early as the 1920s, Benjamin claimed – contra Marx or rather thinking with Marx – that revolutions are not the motor of history, but are rather the emergency brakes of history (2003: 42).

Broadly speaking, Ceylan's films are categorised among 'slow cinema' films. They often adhere to slow cinema aesthetics, are thought provoking, take issue with philosophical questions and display the human condition in intriguing ways. They focus on issues of displacement, migration, alienation and homelessness (see Dönmez-Colin 2008; Suner 2010). Daldal states that Ceylan's earlier films better suit the definition of 'slow cinema' (2017: 182). She compares *Clouds of May* with *Winter Sleep*, which includes many 'uncinematic dialogues' (Ibid.). Even though the dialogues constitute a significant part of the film (109 minutes), *Winter Sleep* has contemplative aesthetics that draw heavily on long static shots of wind and fire, and a focus on the characters' internal conflicts. In particular, the long, dream-like shots of wild horses evoke a sense of timelessness in the audience. *Anatolia* also fits within this category. As Daldal underlines, the film seems to focus on a murder story, yet the murder story is the context in which the director focuses on the characters' boredom and internal conflicts, and the everyday lives of the provincial people. The way in which the characters are presented turns the film into a story of the provincial people rather than an eventful murder story (Ibid.).

In terms of its contemplative aesthetics and transnational dimension, Ceylan's films could be compared to Lav Diaz's. Diaz does not only tell stories about the Philippines, but also takes issue with universal human conditions such as solitude, death and human greed, 'lending a sense of universality and timelessness to the locally rooted subject matter' (Jin Cho 2020). Like Ceylan, Diaz also writes philosophical dialogues (Çağlayan 2018: 23). Like Ceylan, he makes references to global intellectual legacies. For example, his film, *Norte, Hangganan ng Kasaysayan/Norte, The End of History* is visibly based on Dostoyevsky's novel, *Crime and Punishment*. Dostoyevsky was also the literary inspiration for Diaz's film, *Serafin Geronimo: Ang criminal ng Baryo Conception/The Criminal of Barrio Conception* (1998). The first sequences of *Norte* invite us to settle in to the slow pace of life in a coastal Philippine town and introduce us the Raskolnikov-like protagonist, Fabian, a law school drop-out whose discussions on good and evil with his professors echo those of Nietzsche. The film tells the story of a usurer's murder, yet uses it as a context to discuss inequality, nihilism, and the dissolution of society. Like Diaz's films, famous for their 'tableaux vivant compositions' (Jin Cho 2020), Ceylan's cinema has photographic aesthetics too. In other words, they share cinematic techniques that stand in stark contrast to an understanding of cinema based on action and mobility. They also share in common a transnational and a transaesthetic filmmaking that crosscuts over centuries and geographies.

ONCE UPON A TIME IN ANATOLIA

The film *Once Upon a Time in Anatolia* starts by drawing our gaze to the interiors of a workshop behind foggy glass at night-time. We hear distant voices, a barking dog, the sounds of a chain and stormy weather, which leave us with a sense of an anxious uncertainty. Soon after, the narrative sequence shifts to the visual of a car navigating slowly through narrow roads in vast, hilly landscapes. Rubin observes parallels between this scene and the opening scene of Abbas Kiarostami's film, *Bad Mara Khahad Bord/The Wind Will Carry Us* (1999). In both cases, the image of a small car being driven along curved roads in the dark is employed as a metaphor for the steep paths of life (Ibid).

The night travel underlines the non-specificity of the geographical context. Withdrawing information about the whereabouts forces us to focus on the characters and the story. The detainee accused of murder is accompanied by two officials, Doctor Cemal and the police officer İzzet. A senior police officer Naci and the driver called Arab Ali are seated in the front. The camera zooms in to the visual of the detainee's bowed face as we hear the others speaking about the mundane issues of everyday life, such as yoghurt, buffalo milk and prostate problems. The officials' haste and boredom underlie the whole investigation as a signifier of the existential crisis regarding provincial life. In between these casual conversations, every now and then, they question the suspect about where he has buried the body. Drunk at the time of the murder, all he remembers is a tree surrounded by ploughed land, and a fountain.

In the early sequences, Ceylan uses the colour contrast of light and dark. Rubin says that this contrast carries a theological significance. The light functions in the narrative as a symbol of the revelation of truth. As they stop at various locations to search for the body, they are always kept in the dark:

> at the third stop in the search for the body, the Doctor (who is the central character), stands away from the group, trying to relieve himself next to a rock. A lightning illuminates the rocks, and startles everyone. These rocks might be aligned with the Biblical sentiment that the murdered Abel's blood 'cries out' from the ground (Genesis 4:10), as well as Jesus Christ's suggestion that the rocks will "cry out" if humans fail to give proper praise to God (Luke 19:40). A little later Arab Ali pulls on the tree branch, and some apples fall. In what appears to be a metaphorical reference to the Edenic story (told in the Old Testament and alluded to in the Qur'an), "an apple rolls down a hill, enters a stream, and snarls in a swampy area of detritus and other rotting fruit'. (Robin 2016: 14)

In the film, there are also other theological signifiers. The name of the detainee, Kenan, alludes to the fallen apple in the Bible (Diken, Gilloch and Hammond 2017: 104). In Genesis, Kenan is the grandson of Seth, Cain's brother. The Biblical mythology (Genesis 4: 1–16) narrates the first murder in human history as the murder of Abel by Cain[6]. Abel is Cain's younger brother. God accepts Abel's sacrifice over Cain's, reversing the hierarchy between them. Out of jealousy, Cain kills his brother and buries him in the wilderness. He refuses to answer God's question: 'Where is your brother?'. 'I do not know, am I my brother's keeper?' answers Cain. Cain is punished by God, exiled from his farm and becomes a wanderer. Thus, the search for Kenan's victim is a 'Cainan-esque search for a body'. Kenan's murder and burial of Yaşar in the wilderness alludes to Abel's murder. Thus, Kenan is a 'possessor of a fallen family heritage'. During the search for the body, the camera follows an apple falling down the hill to join other fallen apples. Yet sweeping through them, it falls into the stream, cleansed by running water, an act in allegorical proximity to the ending of the Genesis story, that is, God's forgiveness of Cain (Ibid).

This act of being abandoned outside of civilisation in wilderness where there is no law constitutes the biblical genealogical roots of Agamben's concept of homo sacer, that is bare life as a biopolitical paradigm that can be sacrificed by the sovereign. In his book *Homo Sacer: Sovereign Power and Bare Life* (1998), Agamben calls for revisiting the theories of sovereignty in Western political history. He argues that, since the ancient Greeks, sovereignty has been based on the sovereign ban of bare life and exclusion from the political community. Hence, in Genesis 4:14,[7] wandering in the wilderness Cain says: 'Anyone who meets me may kill me'. Thus, the story in the film alludes not only to a Biblical story but also to a political theory of sovereignty that is foundational for Western politics.

Ceylan connects the local to the global by inserting universal mediators in the narrative. To illustrate with an example, as mentioned above, the geographical non-specificity in the early sequences bears the characteristics of what Grosrichard calls the 'Orient', the ground zero of all civilisations, a necessarily 'trans' space (1998). At the same time, the rock reliefs that startle Doctor Cemal render the place universally significant. They link a local murder story to a universal cultural heritage. In a place like Kırıkkale, an insignificant central Anatolian town, we see the traces of many civilizations that have experienced periods of rise and fall in history.

Another example concerns the use of humour in the film. As the prosecutor dictates the death report, he makes a humorous comment, likening himself to Clark Gable, an American actor who epitomised the golden age of Hollywood. As an aesthetic mode and a political allegory, humour is universal. Yet, the judge's humour comes unexpectedly in a serious situation like death. The 'out of context' nature of this pervasive humour invites a universal bodily reaction, laughter in people of all social backgrounds. It taps in to the universally human.

To open a parenthesis, I find Doru Pop's analysis of post-national film making practises in Romania and his use of Deleuze's (1987) concepts of 'de-territorialization' and 're-territorialization' inspirational for understanding some of the ways in which Ceylan incorporates Chekhov's stories in this film (2017). Based on an analysis of Bogdan Mirică's first feature film, *Câini/Dogs* (2016), Pop has observed that the directors of the Romanian new wave have deliberately abandoned using nationally specific images and picturesque representations of Romania. In fact, Pop suggests that new wave directors invent cinematic spaces in ways that are in no way related to actual Romania (Ibid: 258). The characters also become non-specific and transient. Pop calls Romanian new wave 'glocal' cinema, whereby the new wave directors de-territorialise the local narratives to 'make them part of a global culture' (Ibid: 265). Pop's reading of Romanian new wave may be seen as a heuristic tool to understand how Ceylan de-territorialises the story as a directorial strategy to render a local murder case a universal existential issue about justice and crime.

The film juxtaposes Kenan's murder with two other deaths. Nusret tells Cemal an extraordinary story about a woman who predicted her date of death. Cemal confronts him with his medical rationality. As the narrative unfolds, we learn that Nusret's wife committed suicide as an act of revenge for his infidelity. As Nusret did not order an autopsy on the body, the truth regarding her death, that she had taken an excessive dose of digoxin (a medication used to treat irregular heartbeat) ever came out. As someone representing the law, the prosecutor has concealed the truth. At the end of the film, we see Cemal performing an autopsy on the body of the deceased. His assistant detects some soil in his trachea, which indicates that he was still alive when he was buried. Cemal does not put this in his report, actively preventing further investigation of the murder. Law and unlawfulness emerge as two sides of the social bond. What bonds the prosecutor, the doctor and the murderer is not their commitment to law, but their participation in unlawfulness, which is universal.

WINTER SLEEP

The film begins with a long establishing shot of Aydın, the protagonist, standing in a narrow, curvy road in the midst of Cappadocia. Just as *Once Upon a Time in Anatolia* uses the contrast between light and dark as an allegory to the contrast between the revelation of truth and the hidden sin (a 'trans' event in the history of humanity), *Winter Sleep* uses the metaphor of fire under the snow to refer to the discontents of the human psyche disguised by the staged performances of everyday life. The film beautifully 'reveals the fire under snow' by unravelling the eruptions of a doomed marriage, inspired by Chekhov's story, 'The Wife' (Diken, Gilloch, Hammond 2017: 117).

The protagonist, Aydın, is an intellectual who runs an inherited cave house in Cappadocia. He writes a column for a local newspaper on issues such as the absence of aesthetics in Anatolia and the enlightenment of religious officials. His conversations with his right-hand-man, Hidayet, indicate that he has moved to Cappadocia after retirement. He lives with his much younger wife Nihal, who does charity work for the local school, and his divorced sister who translates literary works. Aydın frequently socialises with Suavi, who has a married daughter in London. Significantly, all characters in Aydın's immediate vicinity have some connection with the world outside of Cappadocia.

The setting of Cappadocia is also significant as a marker of a transnational narrative. Harbouring most of the early Christian legacy in Anatolia, Cappadocia is an important site for cultural tourism with a focus on conserving and appreciating the value of the authenticity of a place and universal cultural heritage. We hear Aydın declare in the film: 'I only wish those who appreciate the value of this place to come'. The place is also famous for its post volcanic landscape and wild horses. The name Cappadocia means 'the land of beautiful horses' in Persian.

One day, Aydın receives a letter from a teacher in the Garipçe village. Praising his story 'The Flowers Blooming in the Steppes' in a flirtatious tone, she asks for his help to complete the construction of a building to provide education for the illiterate. No matter how local this event may sound, the story of seduction through a letter is narrated in a Chekhovian fashion. Aydın reads the letter to Suavi and Nihal. Neither gives the reaction he expects. (Suavi: 'You are a creative man. You are an artist. Why do you waste your time on such matters? Mind your own business!'. Nihal: 'The local school's ceiling is leaking. You did not care at all. What made you so helpful?'). His sister Necla criticises him too, for considering the reader's praise a criterion for success.

In terms of his relationship with his wife, Aydın resembles Pavel Andreitch in Chekhov's 'The Wife' and, his relationship with his sister resembles that of Semyonitch in 'Excellent People' (Akın 2017). Aydın is an amalgamation of both characters. Despite their unhappiness, Aydın and Andreitch find it impossible to leave their wives. They both resort to charity work to regain their wives' respect, yet fail. Likewise, Aydın and Semyonitch are both in conflictual relationships with their sisters who debate about the possibility of overcoming evil by not responding.

The episode where the three men, Aydın, Levent and Suavi, gather in Suavi's house and discuss morality for almost eight minutes indicates that Aydın is a close reader of Shakespeare (Diken, Gilloch, Hammond 2018: 134). In this conversation, Levent quotes from Richard III: 'Conscience is but a word that cowards use, devised at first to keep the strong in awe. Our strong arms be our conscience, swords our law.' Aydın replies to Levent with another quote from Shakespeare: 'Our infallible fate is to be deceived in everything we attempt. I make brilliant plans each morning . . . and fool about all day' (Ibid). These Shakespearean exclamations are 'de-territorialised' to be put into use as an expression of Aydın's jealousy of Levent.

As mentioned above, the dialogues take almost 109 out of the 196 minutes in the film (Mathew 2019: 22). Therefore, we cannot declare the absence of dialogue a signifier of slow cinema. Ceylan also uses narrative techniques of conventional cinema such as shot-reverse-shot (Ibid). However, I contend that the film's visual style is still closer to slow cinema aesthetics than a cinema of action and mobility. Most of the conversations take place in dark interiors lit either by fire or dim light. The camera often focuses on the faces in close up, allowing the audience close engagement with the characters' emotions and thoughts. Although there is narrative action, the film uses this as a context in which to explore the characters' boredom and discontent. Aydın's actions also provide a context in which to explore the universally human. The film tells the story of Aydın's conflict with a tenant, İsmail, who cannot pay his rent. İsmail objects to his furniture being taken by the bailiffs and getting beaten by the police in front of his son. Nihal tries to compensate this by offering a hefty sum of money to İsmail. İsmail burns the money and Nihal fails in her attempt to ease her conscience.

The paintings that frame the conversations amount to the trans-aesthetic character of the film. As Aydın and Nihal argue (1:49 and 2:19 minutes), we see a faint image of Ilya Glazunov's painting, *At the Edge of the Ice-Hole*, an illustration that accompanies Dostoyevsky's unfinished work, *Netoschka*

Nezvanova/Nameless Nobody. The faces of the man and the woman in this painting are replaced by those of Nihal and Aydın and used as a film poster. Mathew states: 'As Nihal looks at the Glazunov painting, she activates a comparison between her Turkish present and its Russian precursor that simultaneously open both time-spaces' (2019: 22, 23).

Overall, this chapter has discussed how the selected two films by Ceylan have linked local stories to global intellectual legacies through the construction of plots and characters. Ceylan revisits Chekhov, Dostoyevsky and Shakespeare, dramatises their stories in new historical contexts and produces something 'anew' in these repetitions. It is in this context that I have discussed the transnational indistinctions in Ceylan's cinema, indistinctions that locate his films in a cross-cultural and cross-spatial heterogeneous network of artwork.

NOTES

1. *Creatio ex nihilo* is a theological doctrine which indicates God's creation out of nothingness. It suggests the idea that being originates from non-being. In modernity, art has replaced religion in terms of claiming the monopoly of creativity. Malraux suggests that art is *creatio ex nihilo* because artistic creation often requires the destruction of previous forms and styles (Allan 2009, 126–7).
2. Mathew interprets this scene in terms of how Ceylan imports Russian realism (2019: 21). I use his analysis to address the transivity between Ceylan, Chekhov and Shakespeare.
3. The novel, which tells the story of an idealist district governor who stands by the villagers in their fight against the landlords won the International Nancy Theatre Festival First Prize and was adapted into an Opera by Fabio Vecchi.
4. New Cinema of Turkey is a term coined by film scholars and critics to refer to a new wave of independent films made in Turkey after the 1990s that take issue with the country's conflictual past and issues such as memory, belonging, home, trauma and childhood.
5. See Moore's analysis on the use of gender as a transnational marketing strategy in Susanne Bier's cinema (2005).
6. The story of the first murder as narrated in the following two paragraphs is taken from the following source: https://www.bibleodyssey.org/en/passages/main-articles/first-murder (last accessed 16 March 2022).

CITED WORKS

Agamben, Giorgio (1998), *Homo Sacer: Sovereign Power and Bare Life*. Stanford: Stanford University Press.

Akın, Emrah (2017), 'Nuri Bilge Ceylan Sinemasında Anton Çehov Karakterlerinin İzi', Akdeniz Üniversitesi, Sosyal Bilimler Enstitüsü, Radyo Televizyon Sinema Ana Bilim Dalı, Yüksek Lisans tezi.

Allan, Derek (2009), *Art and the Human Adventure: André Malraux's Theory of Art*. Amsterdam, New York: Rodopi.

Benjamin, Walter (2003), *Selected Writings, vol. 4 1938–1940*, ed. H. Eiland and M. W. Jennings. Cambridge: Harvard University Press.

Bergfelder, Tim (2005), 'National, transnational or supranational cinema? Rethinking European film studies', *Media, Culture & Society*, 27:3, 315–31.
Berry, Chris (2010), 'What is Transnational Cinema? Thinking from the Chinese Situation', *Transnational Cinemas* 1:2, 111–27.
Brown, William (2015), 'Melancholia: The Long, Slow Cinema of Lav Diaz' in Tiago de Luca and Nuno Barradas Jorge (eds), *Slow Cinema*. Edinburgh: Edinburgh University Press, 112–22.
Bruno, Latour (2005) *Reassembling the Social: An Introduction to Actor Network Theory*. Oxford: Oxford University Press.
Burgoyne, Robert (2005), 'National, transnational or supranational cinema? Rethinking European film studies', *Media, Culture & Society*, 27:3, 315–31.
Canetti, Elias (1984), *Crowds and Power*. New York: Farrar, Straus, Giroux.
Chekhov, Anton (2016) *Excellent People and Other Stories*. London: Sovereign Classic.
Çağlayan, Emre (2018), *Poetics of Slow Cinema: Nostalgia, Absurdism, Boredom*. Basingstoke: Palgrave Macmillan.
Daldal, Aslı (2018), 'Ceylan's Winter Sleep: From Ambiguity to Nothingness', *Cinej Journal*, 6:2, 181–99
Deleuze, Gilles and Félix Guattari, (1987), *A Thousand Plateaus. Capitalism and Schizophrenia*, trans. Brian Massumi. Minneapolis: University of Minnesota Press.
Deleuze, Gilles (1994), *Difference and Repetition*, trans. Paul Patton. New York: Columbia University Press.
De Luca, Tiago and Nuno Barradas Jorge (eds.) (2016) *Slow Cinema*, Edinburgh: Edinburgh University Press.
Diken, Bülent and Graeme Gilloch, Craig Hammond (2018), *The Cinema of Nuri Bilge Ceylan: The Global Vision of a Turkish Filmmaker*. London: I.B. Tauris.
Dönmez-Colin, Gönül (2008), *Turkish Cinema: Identity, Distance and Belonging*. London: Reaktion Books.
Ezra, Elizabeth and Terry Rowden (2006a), 'General Introduction: What is Transnational Cinema?' in E. Ezra and T. Rowden (ed.), *Transnational Cinema: The Film Reader*. London and New York: Routledge, 1–12.
Ezra, Elizabeth and Terry Rowden (2006b) (eds.) *Transnational Cinema: The Film Reader*. London and New York: Routledge.
Flanagan, Matthew (2008), 'Towards an aesthetic of slow in contemporary cinema', 16:9, http://www.16-9.dk/2008-11/side11_inenglish.htm (last accessed 2 December 2021).
Galt, Rosalind (2016), 'Transnational Cinemas: A Critical Roundtable', Austin Fisher and Iain Robert Smith (ed.) *Frames Cinema Journal*, https://framescinemajournal.com/article/transnational-cinemas-a-critical-roundtable/ (last accessed 12 December 2021).
Gouldner, A. W. (1960), 'The norm of reciprocity: a preliminary statement', *American Sociological Review*, 25, 161–78, 1960. Washington University Press.
Grosrichard, Alain (1998), *The Sultan's Court*. London: Verso Books.
Gürbilek, Nurdan, (2011), Benden Önce Bir Başkası, Metis: Istanbul.
Higbee, W., and Song H. W. (2010), 'Concepts of Transnational Cinema: Towards a Critical Transnationalism in Film Studies', *Transnational Cinemas* 1:1, 7–21.
Jaffe, Ira (2014), *Slow Movies: Countering the Cinema of Action*. London: Wallflower Press.
Jin Cho, Hyun (2020), 'An Interview with Lav Diaz, the Filipino master of slow cinema', 4 October 2020, https://www.bfi.org.uk/london-film-festival/interviews/lav-diaz-genus-pan
(last accessed 4 December 2021).
Koepnick, Lutz (2014), *On Slowness: Toward an Aesthetic of the Contemporary*. New York: Columbia University Press.

Küçük, Yalçın (2010), *Aydın Üzerine Tezler*, Istanbul: Mızrak.
Malraux, Andre (1978), *Voices of Silence: Man and His Art*. Princeton: Princeton University Press.
Mathew, Shaj (2019), 'Travelling Realisms, Shared Modernities, Eternal Moods: The Uses of Anton Chekhov in Nuri Bilge Ceylan's Winter Sleep', *Adaptation*, 12:1, 12–26.
Naficy, Hamid (2001), *An Accented Cinema: Exilic and Diasporic Filmmaking*. Princeton: Princeton University Press.
Nestingen, Andrew and Trevor Elkington (2005) (eds.) *Transnational Cinema in a Global North: Nordic Cinema in Transition*. Detroit: Wayne State University Press.
Özyazıcı, Kurtuluş (2020), 'Nuri Bilge Ceylan and Slow Cinema', *Sinecine Journal of Film Studies*, 11:2, 193–225.
Pop, D. (2017), 'Deterritorialized Cinema, Dislocated Spaces and Disembodied Characters' Bogdan Mirică's Câini', *Caietele Echinox*. Issue 32, 252–66
Romney, Jonathan (2012), 'Nuri Bilge Ceylan: 'Death Was Always With Us – and That Is a Good Thing', *The Independent*, 17 March 2012, https://www.independent.co.uk/arts-entertainment/films/features/nuri-bilge-ceylan-death-was-always-with-us-and-that-is-a-good-thing-7576187.html, (last accessed 21 December 2021).
Roskin, A. (1958), *A.P.Chekhov.Stat'I Ocherki (Articles and Essays)*. Moscow: CIKhL
Rubin, Roysi (2021), 'Turkish Cinema From Nuri Bilge Ceylan's Point Of View', Lynn University, https://www.nuribilgeceylan.com/movies/ahlat/press-lynnuniversity.pdf, (last accessed 2 January 2022).
Sokolyansky, Mark (2001), 'Shakespeare and Iconicity: Shakespearean themes and motifs in Anton Chekhov's works' https://shine.unibas.ch/iconicity_sokolyansky.htm, (last accessed 22 December 2021).
Suner, Asuman (2010) *New Turkish Cinema: belonging, identity and memory*. London and New York: I.B. Tauris.
____ (2009), 'Silenced memories: notes on remembering in new Turkish cinema', *New Cinemas: Journal of Contemporary Film*, 7:1, 71–81.
____ (2002), 'Nostalgia for an Imaginary Home: Memory, Space and Identity in New Turkish Cinema', *New Perspectives on Turkey*, 27: 61–76.
Tuttle, H. (2010a), 'Slower or Contemplative? Unspoken Cinema', http://unspokencinema.blogspot.com/2010/03/slower-or-contemplative.html, 17 March, (last accessed 2 December 2021).
____ (2010b), 'Slower or Contemplative? *Unspoken Cinema*', March 17. http://unspokencinema.blogspot.co.uk/2010/03/slower-or-contemplative.html. (last accessed 16 March 2022).

CHAPTER SEVEN

The Politics of Dialogue and Ethics of Engagement: *Kış Uykusu/Winter Sleep* (2014)

Emre Çağlayan

During the Cannes Film Festival press conference of *Kış Uykusu/Winter Sleep* (2014), Nuri Bilge Ceylan was asked whether his film raised political and social issues in response to the then present situation in Turkey. In his response, Ceylan rejected not only the possibility but also the presumed necessity of cinema addressing contemporary political and social events. In contrast to looking at social or political issues directly, Ceylan defined his artistic motivation as the exploration of the fundamental qualities of human nature. The duty of the artist, Ceylan underlined, was not so much to facilitate a discussion or awareness in implementing social change, but to nurture and expand society's conscience and consciousness, injecting it with a broader range of empathic emotions. Cinema should nourish the soul and make its viewers confront their own weaknesses.

Ceylan's statement captures one of the most enduring fault lines in the debates of philosophical aesthetics: the extent to which artworks can teach us moralistic virtues through emotional engagement, and whether, under the illusion of fiction, art can permit, if not animate, social and political change. This chapter will explore the politics and ethics of Ceylan's cinema against a cultural background in which the very concept of a political film and the whole notion of what counts as moral behaviour are in crisis. While Ceylan's films are far from the kind of political cinema conventionally associated with formal experimentation or an explicit engagement with a political subject matter, they constitute political in their ambition, insofar as they aspire to affect and challenge their audience's system of beliefs, striving for the ancient tradition of eudaemonia, human flourishing. This chapter demonstrates this through a close analysis of how the films engage with our emotions and make ethical propositions, which contrast with the decline of mutual understanding and tolerance (and the rise of political conservatism) in contemporary Turkish society. It concentrates on *Winter Sleep*, which signals a shift in Ceylan's aesthetics from silence to debate and dialogue as primary modes of expression.

The analysis consists of three sections. The first section examines the theatrical release of *Winter Sleep* in conjunction with the shifts and debates of the political climate in Turkey in the 2010s, and outlines key tensions around the rise of authoritarianism and lack of accountability. Although the film does not directly engage with a specific political issue, it offers a measured narrative that reconfigures these tensions into a fictional story that is told in a way that instils a moral sensibility which has the potential for cultivating a more tolerant and civil society that is open to debate and dialogue. The second section focuses on dialogue as the film's most salient aesthetic device and demonstrates its functions in expressing alternating moral positions. The closing section looks at the ways in which the film stages an encounter with ethical questions on responsibility and complicates our emotional and moral allegiances through shifting structures of identification.

Despite Ceylan's consistent reluctance to identify his films as having any political undercurrent, several scholars have examined the political potential and virtues present in Ceylan's oeuvre. James Harvey-Davitt positions Ceylan in the lineage of humanist filmmakers and argues that his works 'focus on human subjectivity as a matter of conflict: between our notion of selfhood and the world around us', which provides 'a sincere reappraisal of our roles and responsibilities in society today' (2016: 250, 265). In contrast, Bülent Diken, Graeme Gilloch and Craig Hammond view Ceylan's cinema as 'fundamentally political', for it 'stages a conflict between different ways of seeing, between different regimes of sense' that produces in the critical viewer the possibility of 'affirmative transformations' (2018: 141, 142). I will build on these previous works with a sustained focus on *Winter Sleep* and the political context in which the film was released. My analysis will move through a synchronic conception of political cinema that takes into consideration the combined power of literary dialogue and emotional engagement and the ways in which such an aesthetic strategy can foster explorational possibilities in political and ethical thinking.

HISTORICAL AND POLITICAL CONTEXT OF *WINTER SLEEP*'S RELEASE

Winter Sleep premiered at the Cannes Film Festival on 16 May 2014, just three days after a mining explosion in Soma in Western Turkey that killed 301 miners. A day after the disaster then Prime Minister Recep Tayyip Erdoğan visited the town to a lukewarm reception from the Soma community, who protested at unsafe working conditions and the poorly organised rescue efforts and lamented their dead. Erdoğan rejected any liability, responsibility or accountability, and responded by citing nineteenth-century mining accidents to present what the miners and their families called a 'massacre' as a fatalistic, ordinary event that all developing nations have experienced during their economic development and accession to modernity (Hansen 2014). Amidst reports of Erdoğan slapping and insulting protestors, one of his aides was photographed kicking a protestor who was being held down by security officers. What made the Soma disaster a tragedy symptomatic of the moral bankruptcy of Turkish political culture in the 2010s was not only the sheer refusal to take responsibility, but also the lack of empathy or recognition of the unique experience of a marginal other. The tragedy of the loss of life and the ethical culpability of those responsible were further exacerbated by numerous reports from opposition figures that had warned of the safety concerns in the mining enterprise, which was privately run by a company with close ties to the ruling Adalet ve Kalkınma Partisi (Justice and Development Party – AKP). Scholars Adaman, Arsel and Akbulut explain the Soma disaster (and the social movements that failed to gain momentum in its aftermath) by considering a larger structural framework that consists of AKP's authoritarian populism, neoliberal developmentalism and extractivism, and conclude that the tragedy was not 'an exception' but an experience 'increasingly normalised in various ways across the country' (2019: 517).

During the 2010s, politics – and what it means to be political – in Turkey was in a rigid headlock that did not allow a dialogue between different sections of the political spectrum. One of the legacies of the Gezi protests the preceding summer was that they laid bare the fact that the AKP would crack down any form of peaceful dissent and critical disagreement with political violence and rhetorical demagogy. An extensive body of scholarly work identifies an authoritarian turn in Turkey's domestic politics in 2011–13, a period which saw momentous events and key policy decisions that were most vividly described as a devolution from 'a tutelary democracy into a competitive authoritarian regime' (Esen and Gumuscu 2016: 1582). Other scholars noted 'an accelerating pattern of authoritarian responses to increasing social and political instability as the AKP struggles to control and overcome the issues facing its continuity' (Yılmaz and Turner 2019: 693). Whatever the label, a growing consensus amongst political commentators indicates that the 'AKP is clad in the mantle of a decaying hegemonic force that relies increasingly on "coercion", rather than "consent", to enforce its policies and shape an ever-increasing portion of the everyday lives of Turkey's citizens' (Tansel 2018: 198). Recent developments, such as the prison sentences given to Osman Kavala, a leading philanthropist, and seven other activists who were accused of attempting to overthrow the government, by an unjust trial that has continued for years, are further evidence of the AKP's autocratic grip on the supposedly independent judiciary and intolerance towards civil liberty, the cornerstone principles of which are based on democratic dialogue and mutual understanding (see Michaelson and Narlı 2022). Viewed in this historical context, being political in Turkey is inseparable from taking an ethical stance that permits dialogue and understanding.

At Cannes, *Winter Sleep* attracted an additional level of journalistic attention because of the disaster in Soma. During solemn photoshoots, the cast and crew promoted the film by posing with placards displaying the hashtag '#soma' to commemorate the dead and send support to the families. The press conference was equally charged with political and emotional tension since memories of Gezi and those who perished during the protests were still fresh. The press engaged in a series of questions as a means of decoding Turkish politics but, as mentioned in the opening of this chapter, Ceylan refrained from defining his artistic motivation as a critical or political response to the contemporary events. Once the film was awarded the Palme d'Or Ceylan dedicated it to the young people who lost their lives, which was widely interpreted as a reference to the Gezi protests. Since Ceylan did not elaborate on his remarks, this was interpreted by some as further evidence of his reluctance to become an oppositional figure.

Several entry points in the film help decode the ways in which Ceylan's astute observations on typical patterns of behaviour (determined in this case by class and privilege) correspond to the authoritarian shift in Turkey that have pitted different social identities against each other. The characters are representative of conflicting ideologies that offer a panoramic view of contemporary Turkey. At the centre is a middle-aged former theatre actor Aydın (played by Haluk Bilginer, the name means 'enlightened'), who runs the Othello hotel in Cappadocia and lives comfortably off the rent from properties inherited from his father. Modelled after the liberal and bourgeois values associated with the Republican Party which was in opposition at the time, Aydın engages in intellectual discussions that reflect on what it means to accept responsibility to one's own community or what constitutes ethically productive action when faced with evil, but owing to his secular outlook he looks down upon the religious underclasses that characterise the AKP electorate. He boasts to one of his guests at the hotel that he is writing a comprehensive history of Turkish theatre, though the work does not materialise until the end. He also spends his free time writing an opinion column for the local newspaper, in which he deplores the lack of aesthetic beauty in the provinces and the absence of responsibility demonstrated by local community leaders. But the film gradually unveils the hypocrisy embodied by Aydın and the ways in which he publicly espouses a moral code that does not correspond to his actions in his private life.

Aydın shares the hotel with his divorced sister Necla (Demet Akbağ) and much younger wife Nihal (Melisa Sözen). Nihal has carved out a semi-independent life away from Aydın's manipulative supervision. She leads a charity project that aims to help refurbish a local school. Away from the hotel, brothers Hamdi, the local imam (Serhat Mustafa Kılıç) and İsmail, an unemployed alcoholic (Nejat İşler), invisible to their landlord Aydın, struggle to make ends meet. Throughout the film, we see how Aydın's ideals of ethical responsibility and conscience do not match the heartless indifference he shows to Hamdi and İsmail. Aydın delegates much of his responsibilities towards his tenants to his right-hand man Hidayet (Ayberk Pekcan) and to his lawyers. Early in the film, İsmail's son İlyas (Emirhan Doruktutan) throws a stone at Aydın's jeep to seek vengeance against the threats of eviction (blaming the landlord for humiliating his father), a narrative catalyst which ignites a chain of events that places varying combinations of the characters in mostly fire-lit chambers, talking to each other.

Indeed, the most obvious aesthetic feature of the film is its relentless and incisive dialogue, written in a novelistic style and staged in a way that is often described as uncinematically theatrical, unlike Ceylan's preceding works. Dialogue, spoken instruction and verbal storytelling have long been key features of popular cinema in Turkey, but the dialogue in *Winter Sleep* exceeds such traditional conventions both in terms of content (the varied discussions on responsibility, conscience, resisting evil) and delivery, intonation and performance. (Ceylan cast professional stage actors – another departure from his early films – who would accurately convey the literary complexity of the written text). In an interview with Geoff Andrew, he explained that it was not just the 'amount' but the 'kind of dialogue' and that the unnaturally 'literary' and 'philosophical' conversations in the film were part of his desire to capture a type of speech that existed in 'real life' though not necessarily is 'the language of the streets' (2014: 33). Indeed, the extensive dialogue present in the film stands in sharp contrast to the way Turkey's political culture has been marred with an absence of dialogue.

Ceylan's life-long obsession with Anton Chekhov was a strong motivation for adapting the latter's short story *The Wife* (1892) and replicating dialogues although *Winter Sleep* is an amalgamation of several Chekhov stories as a number critics have noted since, with additional references and allusions to Dostoyevsky, Shakespeare, Voltaire and Sartre. Detailing the film's literary connections to Chekhov and its connection to the nineteenth-century Russian context, Shaj Mathew writes that the dialogues 'are not designed to be short, amusing, or easy to follow. They are literary dialogues that compel a film-going audience to think in real-time about what concepts like "non-resistance to evil" might mean, or how altruism might only benefit the person doing the giving' (2019: 22). Mathew further elaborates: 'this film valorizes language – quite literally, since most viewers of *Winter Sleep* will have to rely on subtitles to understand the film – over the moving image that provides its form' (2019: 22). Some commentators even go as far as to characterise the function of dialogue as that of a weapon. Darragh O'Donoghue argues that 'words are not unproblematic carriers of narrative content – they are weapons, emblems of power, empty signifiers of moral impoverishment' (2015: 59). Another critic, Gabrielle O'Brien writes that Aydın 'wields language like a weapon, always desperate to have the final word' (2015: 58). But this aesthetic strategy has also invited detractors. Jonathan Romney identifies the film pejoratively as an 'ambitious, intellectually rigorous but rather laborious screen novel' (2014: 93). I claim that this uniquely overlapping experience of watching a film and reading literature, which could be characterised as watching a book unfold, and which is similarly explored in Ceylan's next film *Ahlat Ağacı/ The Wild Pear Tree* (2018), has political and ethical potential.

THE POLITICS AND ETHICS OF DIALOGUE

Dialogue and speech in cinema are notoriously treated negatively by film theorists, hence the common criticism levelled at *Winter Sleep* for having too much dialogue to bear in one sitting. Mary Devereaux critiques this theoretical position by charting the way sound cinema and the talkies were perceived by the early film theorists, in particular Rudolf Arnheim, who argued that the 'visual poetry' of silent cinema was obliterated by the invention of synchronised sound and that the complex language of bodily 'gesture and facial expression' was replaced, even interfered, by the directness of speech (1986: 39). Arnheim was writing at a time when silent cinema was gradually becoming outdated and he saw at first hand when the industry struggled to adapt to this modern technology: for him, the talkies were nothing more than a photographed play. But for Devereaux, Arnheim's commitment to the medium specificity argument – that an art form should capitalise on its unique materials – was no longer sustainable, since cinema now consisted of a newer technology that enabled the recording of speech synchronised with the moving image. Deveraux concludes: 'much will be gained in acknowledging that words, in their meaning, as well as in their intonation, accent, and rhythm, function stylistically and therefore deserve to be treated as a means of expression on equal footing with camera motion and other traditionally defined cinematic features of the medium' (1986: 45). Such a call for a reformulation of the 'cinematic' was unheeded for many years, up until Sarah Kozloff's book *Overhearing Film Dialogue* convincingly demonstrated the significance of dialogue in the art of filmmaking and mounted a defence against the 'field's long-standing antipathy to speech in film' (2001: 6).

Kozloff's book challenges the primacy of the image in film studies and constitutes a revisionist project in the sense that it recalibrates the role of film spectators from voyeurs and viewers to eavesdroppers and listeners. While film dialogue, and speech in broader terms, have often been relegated to secondary importance in cultural analysis (with respect to visual action), for Kozloff verbal communication is equally rich in the way it can trigger multiple avenues of interpretation. 'Speech is not some abstract, neutral communicative code', Kozloff writes, 'issues of power and dominance, of empathy and intimacy, of class, ethnicity, and gender are automatically engaged every time someone opens his or her mouth' (2001: 26). With an exclusive focus on American cinema, Kozloff sketches out extensive functions that dialogue can place in our experience of cinema, which encompasses a variety of narrative functions ('anchorage of the diegesis and characters, communication of narrative causality, enactment of narrative events, character revelation, adherence to the code of realism and control of viewer evaluation and emotions') and those that exceed narrative demands, such as 'exploitation of the resources of language', 'thematic messages/authorial commentary/allegory', and 'opportunities for "star turns"' (Kozloff 2001: 33–4).

What partly escapes Kozloff's schematic taxonomy is the type of literary and philosophical discussions, which she admits in her own words are 'atypical in American film', that feature extensively in *Winter Sleep* (2001: 62). In the film, the extensive dialogues are grounded in the fictional world and rendered plausible by the characters' individuality: Aydın as a former thespian and Necla as a translator. Take the example of Necla's proposition of not resisting evil, which is taken out of the Chekhov story *Excellent People* (1886) and is initiated during an evening in Aydın's study and then connected through an unnatural dialogue bridge to the following morning, when Nihal is also with them. Necla proposes a thought experiment, a world underpinned with a different moral order based on forgiveness that does not use force or punish the evil, and ponders whether such an act of non-resistance would naturally eliminate all evil or if evildoers would reach some sort of self-actualisation: a deeper, conscientious and remorseful understanding of what separates right and wrong. This blatantly idealistic world view is immediately dismissed and ridiculed by Aydın who refuses the logic of such a moral code arguing unreservedly that evil would prevail. He attempts to reduce Necla's imaginative question to a defeatist, hopeless point of view (with the claim that there is 'not much else to think about'). Next morning, Necla elaborates, but Aydın is distracted, first by the frozen honey on the breakfast table and later by Hamdi passing through in the distance, although he continues to parody Necla's proposition by provocation. Nihal, whose silent yet attentive listening the camera captures in close-up, later voices her disappointment and anger at Aydın's raucous, grizzly laughter. Despite Aydın's enthusiasm in putting Necla's moral theory in practice – by showing no resistance to Hamdi, who visits the hotel so that İlyas can deliver a formal apology – the discussion has little to do with what is at stake in the film's plot. But it is nonetheless an exercise in critical thinking and free imagination, of looking at the existing world from different perspectives. Indeed, within the context of Turkey's shift into an increasingly authoritarian regime, the very act of pondering how evil should be resisted could potentially constitute an act of resistance.

In their analysis of this debate, scholars Diken, Gilloch and Hammond argue the 'immoral core of Necla's morality' and the fact that her ethics is all but a perspective determined by the circumstances of her life and the kinds of judgements and assumptions arising from those conditions (2018: 127). Necla's desire to discuss non resisting evil and the debate's thematic function becomes clearer in a subsequent dialogue scene with Nihal, where we learn of the former's backstory. Having divorced her husband, who she hears is currently suffering from alcoholism, Necla now ponders what would have happened if she acted differently: if she had submitted with indifference and bowed down to her ex-husband's rotten behaviour and not filed for divorce, would she be have been able to help her husband confront his actions? Nihal responds first by saying not resisting evil would entail nothing but the evildoer feeling more entitled to their position and feeling righteous about their actions, but Necla speculates that her husband might be feeling remorse and then drops a bomb that pushes Nihal to respond in a different tone. Once Necla tells Nihal of her desire to ask her husband for forgiveness (in her mind, to make him feel ashamed), Nihal first reassures her that she is not the guilty one, but upon Necla's insistence mocks her by asking if she has been watching too many soap operas on television. Moments later, the conversation evolves into a tense stand-off. Nihal's remarks about the absurdity of Necla's proposition and emphasis on the obvious fact that she would solely be responsible for her actions drives Necla into a slightly more aggressive tirade that manifests her exhaustion at the derisive and subtly hurtful words that Nihal (and, by implication, Aydın, who has similarly mocked Necla's ideas) utters. It is hard to say where precisely the viewers' empathies reside in exchanges such as above, although clearly Necla's propositions are ridiculed not without reason as it becomes clear that Necla is hopelessly fooling herself to escape the hotel and return to her ex-husband.

The mocking responses by Aydın and Nihal function not only as a means of instilling a moral belief that is crucially significant (that evil must be resisted and confronted) but also unlock a richer dynamic of character relationships that adds weight and complexity to everyone's point of view. Ceylan captures these moments of revelation through a shot-reverse-shot structure that gives equal room to the speaker and the listener without privileging either perspective as the focus of emotional engagement or moral allegiance. These sequences are scaled in close-ups that magnify the characters' emotions and are paced with several pauses that, combined with repeated facial and aural expressions, produce empathic and ethical involvement. Several scholars have drawn attention to how reaction shots that portray characters responding to each other 'generate effective forms of empathy and sympathy' (Sinnerbrink 2016: 94).

Robert Sinnerbrink identifies this practice as cinempathy: 'an alternating of perspectives that opens up a deeper intersubjective understanding of the characters' situations from conflicting, yet intimately related, points of view' and one which prevents 'hasty moralizing judgment while inviting a deeper ethical responsiveness towards the context and dynamics of conflict' (2016: 100). While Necla's proposition of non-resistance to evil is clearly mocked, her sigh at the end, in response to the way Nihal's and Aydın's emotionally piercing remarks were thrown at her, counterbalances the privileging of any moral allegiance, even despite the viewer's disagreement with her ideals.

An unusually complex example of cinempathy occurs in a subsequent scene in Aydın's study, which begins with a discussion with Necla about a recent article Aydın published in the local newspaper. In this climactic tour de force that takes almost twenty minutes, Ceylan complicates the possibilities of empathic involvement and ethical evaluation through a few devices that include variations in shot scales, unusually blocking the bodies of characters when they are reacting to each other and an extensive repertoire of dialogue, whose nuances might be missed in its foreign translations. Whereas Sinnerbrink's emblematic example of cinempathy, a key scene from Asghar Farhadi's *Jodaeiye Nader az Simin/A Separation* (2011), features close-ups of facial expressions that vary from long takes to rapidly edited passages, which 'establish a kinetic rhythm that effectively conveys the increasingly antagonistic nature of [the characters'] argument', the scene in *Winter Sleep* is still and languorous, with select close-ups that are deployed only to intensify one character's response to the other (2016: 100). It begins with a frontal medium shot of Aydın working at his desk, and moments later we see Necla emerge from a nap on the sofa in the background. For most of the sequence, this shot is an anchor point because it frames both characters in the same image. Ceylan uses a few inserts with varying scales and angles that accentuate the dramatic evolution. The camera is most frequently placed between the characters, either facing Necla when she is vocally attacking Aydın's conceited, arrogant romanticism, or facing Aydın when he turns his back to respond to Necla's lethargic denigrations. But even among the two most frequent camera positions the scale ranges between medium shots and close-ups.

Even though Ceylan spent extra time working on the French and English subtitles for *Winter Sleep*, some of the nuances of class and culturally specific modes of articulations are inevitably lost for non-Turkish speakers. At the beginning of the scene, Necla criticises Aydın for expressing opinions outside his expertise and accuses him of 'ahkâm kesmek' translated in the film's English subtitles as 'pontificating'. However, the translation does not convey the substance of the word 'ahkâm', derived from the Arabic root 'hüküm' which means delivering a judgement or verdict. Whereas pontificating suggests an authoritative but pompous mode of speech, 'ahkâm kesmek' additionally conveys a lack of knowledge, consideration or empathy on the part of the speaker. This nuance is crucial, because it is both a critique of one's misplaced position of authority and inability to understand – even consider – the validity of other perspectives, and as such has been a common criticism levelled at positions of political power in Turkey. Indeed, once the phrase is uttered, Aydın responds to Necla by saying 'I see you found my articles worse than I thought', portrayed in a variation of the anchor shot mentioned above. But when Aydın asks Necla to clarify her statement, Ceylan inserts medium close-ups of the former where he, with a slightly embarrassed grin, makes several guesses ('Mediocre? Bloodless? Harmless?') though Necla responds ambiguously off-screen. As the scene evolves, Necla gears up her critique of Aydın's writings, with accusations of soppy romanticism, naivety and unconvincing self-belief, which unsurprisingly upsets Aydın and pushes him into a mode of self-defence that immediately receives another round of critique, where Necla, in a rare moment of close-up, calls out Aydın's shameless way of constantly justifying himself.

The scene then escalates into an intense argument between the siblings, who deconstruct and criticise each other's personalities and world view, often centring on similar themes of power, subjectivity and ways of relating to the external world. But the power of the scene and its politically productive function comes from its circular logic both in its visual structure and discursive development, which at one point Aydın characterises as an 'endless cycle'. For a few minutes, Necla continues her denigration of her brother, shot in close-up, throwing remarks. As Aydın listens with his back turned away from the camera, we are not given access to his reactions. Later, he turns around and replies to Necla, this time his upper body in close-up. Unlike in the scene discussed earlier, Ceylan refrains from showing reaction shots during these intense moments of vocal scrutiny. The viewers are made to align not with the listener (who is subject to criticism) but the speaker. But because the scene plays out in a circle, meaning each character takes turns in speaking to the other, there is something of a balance in alternating the different perspectives. It ends with Aydın saying 'We don't have to agree. Why do we keep arguing?' (though the first part could be more aptly translated as 'We don't have to think the same way on every topic').

In an interview with the Turkish film journal *Altyazı*, Ceylan speaks of the film as a series of interlocking tales that concludes its stories with characters confronting their weaknesses and that shows the audiences the injustices and inconsiderations each character makes to another (Aytaç, Göl and Yücel 2014). I argue that within the contemporary cultural context in Turkey, in which positions of political power continuously decline to accept social responsibility and accountability and do not take into consideration the circumstances of other perspectives by engaging in a dialogue, a film like

Winter Sleep offers the possibility of instilling in its audience moral attunement and political understanding. This is because the film engages its audiences by empathically involving them in a series of debates that side steps hasty moralising and instead opens its themes by giving equal weight to its characters' subjectivity. But instilling *Winter Sleep* with a political potential also requires a culturally specific understanding of how political cinema was defined within the discursive context of filmmaking in Turkey.

POLITICAL CINEMA AND EMOTIONAL ENGAGEMENT

The notion of political cinema has been a recurring debate among filmmakers and commentators in Turkey since the early 1960s. But a decisive understanding and influential form of political cinema only came about when actor-turned-director Yılmaz Güney made *Umut/Hope* in 1970. For Dennis Giles and Haluk Sahin, *Hope* is political cinema of a different, revolutionary order. In its re-appropriation of the aesthetics of social realism and rejection of didactic militant cinema, Güney not only 'diagnoses the disease of the socio-economic system' (Giles and Sahin 1982) but also places an emotive and revolutionary agency on individual liberty – with an emphasis on our choices, decisions and responsibilities in charting our fates and succeeding in our hopeful aspirations. In other words, Güney envisions a type of political cinema whose revolutionary aesthetics stems from the emotional resonances that it so delicately provides. According to Giles and Sahin, 'Güney has said that he considers revolutionary cinema not as a blueprint for action, but as a guide to thinking' (1982). This opens the possibility of a middle-ground political cinema that elicits emotional responses to contemporary problems to channel an awareness and a widening of perspectives. I argue that *Winter Sleep* holds a similar capacity by combining emotions and moral evaluation.

Despite huge critical success abroad, Nuri Bilge Ceylan has often been criticised for his 'apathetic stance on the ongoing political controversies in Turkey' and for revelling in personal stories that rarely deal with what matters in society. In response, Vuslat D. Katsanis claims that the 'affective dimension of his time-images' in *Üç Maymun/Three Monkeys* (2009), which could be considered as his most political film to date, 'offers a rich avenue for political reflection' (2015: 171). Asuman Suner reads the film's thematic concerns with collective amnesia, guilt and oblivion as 'mirror[ing] the present condition of Turkish society', which 'is haunted by the specter of horrendous acts of violence [. . .] perpetrated against its religious and ethnic minorities' (2011: 23). I would argue that while *Three Monkeys*' slow cinema aesthetics might allow such an allegorical interpretation, what is at stake in *Winter Sleep* is a more ethically exploratory mode of emotional engagement.

My approach to defining what a political film looks like and how it functions is inspired by two contrasting theories. According to Mike Wayne, political films 'address unequal access to and distribution of material and cultural resources, and the hierarchies of legitimacy and status accorded to those differentials' (2001: 1). As the saying goes, all films are political, but some are more explicitly so than others, which is why film studies has largely attended to political films that adopt the perspective of a Marxist, revolutionary or otherwise leftist point of view, primarily because the emergence of the discipline coincided with the burgeoning of a particular type of cultural analysis that was specifically inflected by these very traditions. Ewa Mazierska suggests broadening this historical contingency by theorising political films across two separate, though related, axes: (1) conformist or oppositional, determined by the extent to which the film in question accepts or rejects the status quo; and (2) marked or unmarked, the way in which the films reveal or hide those who hold power (2014). As in any rigid boundary, such divisions need to be considered as flexible spectrums, and Mazierska further notes that political films can be marked depending on the levels of their production, text, exhibition and distribution. Adopting a philosophical approach in the analytic tradition, Angelo Cioffi argues that 'a film is political when its intended aim is to i) persuade the audience about the validity of a political standpoint (the film has a rhetorical function) or ii) elicit reflection around a political issue (the film has an "explorational" function)' (2021: 32). For Cioffi, a film elicits reflection on a political issue when it actively engages its audiences and what is essential in this process is 'the activation and mobilization of our system of beliefs' (2021: 32). In my analysis, I combine Mazierska's distinctions with Cioffi's schema and frame *Winter Sleep* as a marked political film that is conformist while adopting an explorational function. While the film encourages reflection on questions of power (marking Aydın as representative of those who wield power), it does not actively oppose its unequal distribution and ends with a conformist tone that returns to the status quo. However, I argue that *Winter Sleep* succeeds in its exploratory function by showing us contrasting views, engaging in complex dialogues and refraining from moralising judgements.

To appraise the functions of political cinema, Cioffi suggests examining the way in which the film in question contributes to our system of beliefs. For this task, Cioffi proposes an analytical model with three dimensions: epistemic voice (the level of authority the film has toward its subject matter), epistemic merit (the way the film demonstrates evidence in support of a particular issue) and pedagogical method (the degree to which the film calls for the active participation of its audience in delivering a conclusion) (2021: 40–2). In terms of its epistemic voice, *Winter Sleep* correlates with what Cioffi calls a hesitant voice, because the film does not explore a single standpoint on a given issue and instead explores (hence the explorational function) several contrasting perspectives by letting other characters voice their opinions. This is perhaps the most obvious element of the film: although Aydın is marked as a protagonist, his authority is consistently and rhetorically undermined by other characters. Regarding epistemic merit, Cioffi writes: a 'work is epistemically meritorious if it brings a positive contribution to our system of belief, that is, it may yield true beliefs, or clarify some of our previously held beliefs, or it may foster our understanding of a complex issue' (2011: 40). The dialogues in *Winter Sleep* make us ask questions about social responsibility and how one should act in relation to their community. Throughout the film this broad question is progressively broken down into its smaller constituent parts: how should one act in the face of evil? In what ways can one show understanding and tolerance to one's siblings, loved ones and neighbours? To what extent should one follow a moral code by individual and sincere action? How does one make moral judgements of others? The film does not draw hasty conclusions to any of these questions but aligns its viewers with a leading character who we see espousing certain beliefs (through the writing of his column and conversations with others) though rarely acting upon them. In short, *Winter Sleep* does not conclude by putting emphasis on the right type of behaviour in taking social responsibility but instead uses dialogue to facilitate an emotional engagement that enables audiences to morally evaluate different points of view. As for pedagogical method, or what Cioffi identifies as the extent to which the work involves its audiences in weighing up the evidence in support of a particular issue, *Winter Sleep* uses character development and ambiguity as narrative devices that demand its audiences to connect the dots. When Aydın visits the home of his tenants, he makes remarks about its ugliness in a newspaper column as well as to his sister but he is mercilessly unmoved by Hamdi's pleas against eviction, the film has already prepared the grounds for portraying Aydın as a hypocritical landowner. Moreover, Necla's critique of Aydın taking on Hamdi as an easy target further strengthens the process of our moral evaluation. But no single character in the film is truly one-dimensional in terms of their moral compass, and as usual Ceylan masterfully develops complex characters with minute details that demand closer scrutiny.

Our combined processes of moral evaluation and emotional alignment are further complicated in a later scene when Nihal visits Hamdi, purportedly to inquire about İlyas. But Nihal's real purpose is to exercise moral authority and ultimate benevolence: having unexpectedly received from Aydın a hefty donation for her charity, Nihal presumably wants to help Hamdi by rebalancing the scales of inequality. She explicitly mentions that she does not want anything in return, nor does she expect Hamdi to pay it back. She says in her gentle voice 'think of it as help from a friend and please accept it', leaning under the warm lamp of Hamdi's cave-like room. This naive but benevolent action, as graceful as it may appear, is also her way of accomplishing divine justice and seeking revenge on Aydın. But Ceylan prepares for this moment with another shift in our emotional involvement. Before handing out the money, Nihal asks Hamdi about İsmail and we learn that İsmail was provoked into violence, spent time in jail and refused employment, all of which pushed Hamdi to provide for the whole family. At this moment, we finally understand why Hamdi had struggled to pay the rent and asked Aydın for extra time. Hamdi recounts these details through several long takes and with every pause Ceylan inserts close-ups of Nihal, whose affective and silent listening position us as another listener in the scene. We are encouraged to sympathise with Hamdi, something which is strengthened by virtue of his reluctance to accept Nihal's money.

The scene reaches its climax when İsmail enters the scene and is likewise surprised, trying to understand why Nihal is giving away such a large amount of money. He then takes the money in his hands and begins counting: 'for little İlyas who risked his life to mend his father's broken pride . . . for self-sacrificing brother Hamdi who had to go hand-kissing because he looks after five people . . . for the drunkard father İsmail who got beaten up in front of his son disgracing himself and his family' and finally 'for our heroine Mrs Nihal who tries to ease her conscience by doling out charity to those less fortunate than her'. While commending Nihal for doing the maths right, İsmail then calmly proclaims 'the person in front of you is a filthy drunkard incapable of appreciating all your kindness' and throws the money into the fire. With this transgressive act, Nihal is stunned. She breaks down in tears and the fire engulfing the cash becomes an apt metaphor for her misguided benevolence, which is not only rejected but destroyed completely. The scene ends with İsmail's calm gaze looking at Nihal and momentarily locates İlyas peering through the door. The shot reverse shot structure concludes with İsmail coming face to face with the camera, as if pleading directly to the viewers, having restored his pride in the eyes of his son. Once again, as audiences we are asked to reconsider our moral judgements. Which of these acts is the most devoted, self-sacrificing, ethically virtuous or the truest rendition of responsibility? Which deserves our utmost respect: Hamdi swallowing his pride to lackey Aydın for the sake of his family or İsmail's firm reassertion of his pride and refusal of the money? The film continuously shifts our emotional allegiances and makes us ponder the questions, rather than drawing authoritative conclusions.

A final few words should be said about the film's ending, which is crucial in getting to grips with how *Winter Sleep* fosters a political engagement with the theme of social responsibility. After a long debate with Nihal, in which he is accused of being selfish, spiteful and cynical, Aydın promises his wife to leave town for Istanbul. But along the way he changes his mind and spends an evening with his friend Suavi (Tamer Levent), who is accompanied by the local schoolteacher Levent (Nadir Sarıbacak). During a drunken debate, Levent insinuates that Aydın had been failing in his responsibility as a landowner, but Aydın defends his position and demands Levent consult his conscience before speaking. In response, Levent recites a passage from Shakespeare's *Richard III* (1593): 'Conscience is but a word that cowards use, devised at first to keep the strong in awe: Our strong arms be our conscience, swords our law'. The scene creates a strong parallel with the conclusion of Aydın's previous conversation with Nihal, where she says: 'Conscience, morals, ideals, principles . . . You're always saying these words. The words you always use to humiliate, hurt or denigrate someone. But if you ask me, if someone uses these words this much, he's the one to suspect'. Shot in Nihal's fire-lit chamber, the scene is composed of close-ups of both characters, though they primarily tend to favour affective mimicry and align viewers with Nihal because her teary face is illuminated, while Aydın is portrayed in medium shots concealed with shadows. After two hours of watching how Aydın behaves, the viewers cannot help but feel and think the same as Nihal, as her words vocalise our suspicions and strengthen the process of our moral evaluation. The film closes with Aydın returning to the hotel, where Nihal watches him from an upper window. Here, Ceylan resorts to a storytelling technique that he had avoided from the very beginning. While Chekhov's *The Wife* was written in the first-person, Ceylan did not adapt the story with a voice-over. But in the final scene, we hear Aydın speaking to Nihal, pleading that he is now a changed man ready to make compromises. There is, however, a level of ambiguity in Aydın's monologue. We cannot be sure whether he is speaking directly to Nihal or if these were words imagined and not yet articulated. But as many commentators argued, the film ends with a small victory for Aydın, with the prevailing of his smug indifference.

Even at its ambivalent ending, *Winter Sleep* demands its audience interrogate itself, it encourages manifold questions about whether Aydın will or can start accepting his true self and begin taking on responsibilities in a more sincere fashion. It would certainly be too far-fetched to characterise *Winter Sleep* as a revolutionary film, but through deploying dialogue in a strategically literary fashion, it demands an unusually intense level of attentiveness and participation from its eavesdroppers. Throughout the film, the dialogues shape the characters' moral compass, the words go beyond fleshing out their backstories and invite an examination of the relationship between responsibility, power and politics. Combined with an affective use of close-ups, the conversations align viewers with different perspectives; they challenge our assumptions and make us rethink our judgements. Within the political context of today's Turkey, where any dialogue between opposing viewpoints is less possible than ever before, a film that channels emotional engagement to sift through ethical discussions can be considered an example of political cinema. Just as in the case of Güney's *Hope*, such critical discussions need not point to a plan of action or a code of ethics but instead guide our thinking, which *Winter Sleep* succeeds in by portraying dialogue in unobtrusive yet densely complex fashion, giving equal weight to characters, their voices and their reactions. All that remains is for us to listen carefully.

CITED WORKS

Adaman, Fikret, Murat Arsel and Bengi Akbulut (2019), 'Neoliberal developmentalism, authoritarian populism, and extractivism in the countryside: the Soma mining disaster in Turkey', *The Journal of Peasant Studies*, 46:3, 514–36.

Andrew, Geoff (2014), 'Conversation Piece', *Sight and Sound*, 24:12, 30–34.

Aytaç, Senem, Berke Göl and Fırat Yücel (2014), 'Nuri Bilge Ceylanla Kış Uykusu Üzerine', *Altyazı* 141. https://altyazi.net/soylesiler/nuri-bilge-ceylanla-kis-uykusu-uzerine/ (last accessed 1 July 2022).

Cioffi, Angelo Emanuele (2021), *Philosophical Theories of Political Cinema*. London: Routledge.

Devereaux, Mary (1986), 'Of "Talk and Brown Furniture": The Aesthetics of Film Dialogue', *Post Script*, 6:1, 32–52.

Esen, Berk and Sebnem Gumuscu (2016), 'Rising competitive authoritarianism in Turkey', *Third World Quarterly*, 37:9, 1581–1606.

Diken, Bülent, Graeme Gilloch and Craig Hammond (2018), *Nuri Bilge Ceylan: The Global Vision of a Turkish Filmmaker*. London: I.B. Tauris.

Donoghue, Darragh (2016) '*Winter Sleep*', *Cineaste*, 40:4, 58–60.

Giles, Dennis and Haluk Sahin (1982), 'Yilmaz Güney: Revolutionary Cinema in Turkey', *Jump Cut: A Review of Contemporary Media*, 27, 35–37. https://www.ejumpcut.org/archive/onlinessays/JC27folder/YilmazGuney.html (last accessed 26 May 2022).

Hansen, Suzy (2014), 'The Mine Disaster That Shook Turkey', *The New York Times*, 26 November 2014.

Harvey-Davitt, James (2016), 'Conflicted selves: the humanist cinema of Nuri Bilge Ceylan', *New Review of Film and Television Studies*, 14:2, 249–67.

Katsanis, Vuslat D. (2015), 'Non-affirmative time images in Nuri Bilge Ceylan's *Three Monkeys* (2009) and the Political Aesthetics of New Turkish Cinema', *New Cinemas: Journal of Contemporary Film*, 13:2, 169–85.

Kozloff, Sarah (2000), *Overhearing Film Dialogue*. Berkeley: University of California Press.

Mathew, Shaj (2019), 'Traveling Realisms, Shared Modernities, Eternal Moods: The Uses of Anton Chekov in Nuri Bilge Ceylan's *Winter Sleep*', *Adaptation*, 12:1, 12–26.

Mazierska, Ewa (2014), 'Introduction: Marking Political Cinema', *Framework*, 55:1, 35–44.

Michaelson, Ruth and Deniz Barış Narlı. (2022), 'Philanthropist sentenced to life in Turkey in 'travesty' trial over Gezi Park protests', *The Guardian*, 25 April 2022. https://www.theguardian.com/world/2022/apr/25/philanthropist-sentenced-to-life-in-turkey-in-travesty-trial-over-gezi-park-protests (last accessed 30 May 2022).

O'Brien, Gabrielle (2015), 'Winter of Discontent: The Pensive Theatre of Nuri Bilge Ceylan's *Winter Sleep*', *Metro Magazine*, 184, 56–9.

Romney, Jonathan (2014), '*Winter Sleep*', *Sight and Sound*, 24:12, 93.

Sinnerbrink, Robert (2016), *Cinematic Ethics: Exploring Ethical Experience Through Film*. London and New York: Routledge.

Suner, Asuman (2011), 'A lonely and beautiful country: reflecting upon the state of oblivion in Turkey through Nuri Bilge Ceylan's *Three Monkeys*', *Inter-Asia Cultural Studies*, 12:1, 13–27.

Tansel, Cemal Burak (2018), 'Authoritarian Neoliberalism and Democratic Backsliding in Turkey: Beyond the Narratives of Progress', *South European Society and Politics*, 23:2, 197–217.

Wayne, Mike (2001), *Political Film: The Dialectics of Third Cinema*. London: Pluto Press.

Yılmaz, Zafer and Bryan S. Turner (2019), 'Turkey's deepening authoritarianism and the fall of electoral democracy', *British Journal of Middle Eastern Studies*, 46:5, 691–8.

CHAPTER EIGHT

Staying in the Primary Home, Relationships, Desires to Go and Roots: *Kış Uykusu/Winter Sleep* (2018) and *Ahlat Ağacı/The Wild Pear Tree* (2018)

Hasan Akbulut

Nuri Bilge Ceylan, much awarded by the various film festivals he attends, is a creative auteur, fed by the tradition of modernist cinema. He is a contemporary aesthete; the thematic structure of whose films articulate or explain each other. The formal and aesthetic aspects are interwoven into the long shots, wide landscapes, silences, the slow rhythm and the deep observations of the human spirit. Based on his earlier work, some scholars have considered him within the aesthetics of neorealist cinema (Daldal 2013) or a total filmmaker, as someone who writes, shoots, produces, directs and edits his own films (Knudsen 2016: 127). Deslandes and Maixent, on the other hand, state that Ceylan's films have a European identity in terms of 'his conception of cinematographic art, the introspective character of his scenarios and of the progress of his characters, and finally the metaphoric use of the different sceneries whether town or country' (2011: 89). In his work on slow cinema, Çağlayan states that 'Ceylan's main aesthetic strategy is his treatment of boredom in various levels across his films' (2014: 46). Along with the concepts such as 'Deleuzian time-image cinema, silence, a political aesthetic that expresses social problems' (Katsanis 2015: 169), Akbulut emphasises that concepts such as authorship, art cinema, modernism, self-reflexivity and contemplation are the guiding lights for analysing his cinema (2005: 11, 16). Dönmez-Colin finds *Kasaba/The Small Town* (1997) dialogic in a Bakhtin sense, while asserting that *Bir Zamanlar Anadolu'da/Once Upon a Time in Anatolia* (2011), 'from its very title to the clumsily buried corpse that a convoy searches all night to find, echoes (or 'refracts' according to Bakhtin) what Anatolia means with its rich (rocks resembling giant statues) but also dubious (the memories of the blood that was shed) past' (2014: 22–3). Using the changes of the weather or the seasons effectively in the construction of the Anatolian countryside and landscape as a political metaphor, Ceylan's work as a whole 'is inhabited by a kind of psychic meteorology' as Deslandes and Maxient underscore regarding *İklimler/Climates* (2006) (2011: 95).

The sense of loneliness, alienation, non-belonging and deficiency/incompleteness that appears in Ceylan's films constitute the main themes of *Kış Uykusu/Winter Sleep* (2014) and *Ahlat Ağacı/The Wild Pear Tree* (2018), the two films that I explore in this chapter using textual analysis supported by semantic, psychoanalytic and sociological criticisms.

PROVINCE AS PRIMARY HOME

One of the subjects that discussions about Ceylan's cinema focus on is the province both as the subject and the space of the narrative. The long and compelling sequences and the Chekhovian dialogues are mostly set in snowy Anatolia (Dupont 2014: 61) except *Uzak/Distant* (2002), *Climates* and *Üç Maymun/Three Monkeys* (2008) and even those have provincial connections.

The excluded and alienated state of the province requires being left alone by the centre and is defined as a settlement that is almost displaced as Giorgio Agamben states (2001: 228, 41–4). The province includes everything outside the centre, and the state of being outside inside requires grasping as 'experience and mood' (Gürbilek 2001: 138). For the province to distinguish itself as a province, it must be aware of another life denied to it, a centre from which it is pushed to the edge, to see itself through its eyes and feel incomplete and deprived in front of it (Gürbilek 1995: 52). Saffet in *The Small Town* and Sinan in *The Wild Pear Tree* each want to escape a small town that they regard as prison. Certain cinematographic techniques and themes such as expanding times, long shots, monotony and rural tranquillity accentuate such sentiment starting with Ceylan's earliest films. 'Rather than being an imaginary site of innocence and purity, the province in Ceylan's cinema is an ambivalent space where we can observe paradoxes of belonging in contemporary Turkish society' Suner underlines, (2010: 26). Whether in the rural milieu or in the city, the province creates an excess of meaning or produces a deep sense of incompleteness leading to an impossible quest. In *The Small Town*, cousin Saffet who wants to escape, Grandfather Nuri who returns home after fighting all the way to India, and the engineer Emin who comes back following his studies in the US, are similar; the impossible quest for roots between returning to the province and being stuck in the province makes them inactive. Thus, it can be said that Ceylan's characters, who experience a crisis of belonging in an impossible quest that prevents them from taking roots in the future are relatives of each other possessing the same contradictory spirits. The episode at the end of *Once Upon a Time in Anatolia*, which shows the doctor looking at himself in the mirror, reveals the loneliness and rootlessness of the contemporary man, which, according to Kicksola is 'the contemporary, post-secular icon of existential loss and despair' (2016: 28). In *The Small Town*, we see the first example of these images that pluck the characters from the moment and send them to a different time, when the young teacher breaks away from the lesson and watches the snow-covered outside from the classroom window.

Ceylan's early films, *Koza/Cocoon* (1995), *The Small Town*, *Mayıs Sıkıntısı/Clouds of May* (1999) and *Distant*, evoke the primary home and childhood not only through their themes but also through their titles They portray the primary home/the rural town of Western Anatolia where the main character was born and raised as a paradoxical space whose rhythm is connected to nature, where slow, calm, rural tranquillity dominates. In his later films, the characters are unhappy urban dwellers whose roots are in the province and who are tied to each other and their country by their deadlocks. In this aspect, I focus on two interrelated points, which could also be evaluated as a thematic summary of all Ceylan films: The first is the performance of relationships, which is prominent in *Winter Sleep*, and the second is the crisis of belonging in *The Wild Pear Tree*. I examine the difference between the characters as they really are and their staged performances, in other words, the presentation of selves through the dramaturgical theory of Erving Goffman. This approach is used to show that an effort to establish ideological, sexual and class domination underlies the 'masculinity performances' of the men in the film and this is related to the crisis of belonging. Both films present a wider and deeper panorama of Turkey through the individual stories of their characters, emphasising the determining power of Turkey's historical and social context on the characters/individuals. It has been stated that in Ceylan's films, personal history and collective past, personal memory and social memory coexist; having an identity also means a contradictory attachment to a place, geography, history and culture and an effort to confront the past.

Figure 8.1 Doctor looking at himself in the mirror. (Source: screenshot from *Once Upon a Time in Anatolia* 2011.)

WINTER SLEEP AS A PERFORMANCE OF RELATIONSHIPS

Winter Sleep is a film about the relationships between Aydın, a former actor, his young wife Nihal and his divorced sister Necla, and their relationships with others around them. Aydın, who runs Hotel Othello in Cappadocia and owns several rental properties, also writes a column for a local newspaper called *Bozkırın Sesi/The Voice of the Steppe* although he can neither be included in the Anatolian steppe nor move away from it.

Winter Sleep takes an objective approach to the characters without privileging any of them, although its focus is Aydın and his point of view as established during the opening sequences that show Aydın looking at his hotel from distance.

Aydın, who left Istanbul and returned to his father's home after a thespian career of twenty-five years, is unhappy in his marriage. From a distance he stares at his lonely young wife Nihal, who lives in a separate room and devotes herself to charity work. He tries to control her. He is jealous of the teacher Levent who assists Nihal in her charity work. He tries to make his work and his existence important by chatting with the hotel guests and reading the letters of praise from his followers to those around him. His sister Necla regrets returning to Cappadocia from Istanbul and considers reconciling with her ex-husband, who did evil things to her, as a better option than her life in Hotel Othello. Aydın's best friend Suavi is a wealthy but lonely man who lives a modest life after having lost his wife.

Aydın wants to be approved of, admired, respected and loved. He lives his daily life like an actor, performing the role of the good proprietor, the 'tolerant/ soft landlord' and the pensive intellectual. However, these are the performances that he fulfils as required by his role. At the beginning of the film, when Timur, his free-spirited guest, asks if the hotel has a horse, he says that the horse was advertised 'just for scenery'. This answer is important to understanding the difference between Aydın's outward personality and what he really is. He advertises his hotel with features it does not possess (horses) and presents himself with attributes he does not have. According to Harvey-Davitt, *Winter Sleep* focuses on the question of 'What if I am not who I think I am?' (2016: 264).

This question evokes Erving Goffman's dramaturgical approach to the presentation of the self in sociology by pointing to the artificiality and performativity of the construction of the self. Goffman states that the self, presented to others in everyday life, is 'the product of the dramatic interaction between actor and audience' and arises within the interaction where each team plays its routine for the other (Goffman 1956: 57 as cited in Ritzer 2011: 376). 'In other words, the self is a sense of who one is, that is a dramatic effect emerging from the immediate scene being presented and . . . it is vulnerable to disruption during the performance' (Ritzer and Stepnisky 2013: 120). The dramaturgy theory developed by Goffman argues that everyday life is like a drama show and every action is performed on a stage. 'In order to maintain a stable self-image, people perform for their social audiences' (Ritzer 2011: 375–6). In this dramaturgic perspective, 'we must continue to act out the tragedy or comedy of our lives; and the show must go on as long as we live' (Coser 2012: 495–6). It is not coincidental that Aydın is an actor, and he names his hotel Othello, one of the plays of Shakespeare, the author of the lines 'All the world's a stage, and all the men and women merely players' (Shakespeare 2004a: 83).

Aydın plays many roles in his life: a former actor, a hotel owner, a writer, a husband and an elder brother. But what marks these roles is his didactic, pedantic, patronising attitude and arrogance. According to Goffman, when an individual plays a part or puts on a performance he requests his observers/ audience to take seriously the impression that is fostered before them (1956: 10). 'The key point here is the actor's own belief in the impression of reality that he stages: the performer can be fully taken in by his own act or he may not be taken in at all by his own routine' (Goffman 1956: 10). By performing his acting profession, Aydın constructs his self as if he were performing on stage. As McAdams states 'the psychological self may be construed as a reflexive arrangement of the subjective "I" and the constructed "Me", evolving and expanding over the course of human life' (2013: 272). Thus, the psychological self 'begins life as a social actor, construed in terms of performance traits and social roles' (Ibid.). Aydın is often absent-minded; not hearing or ignoring what is said. Sometimes he reinforces the image of an intellectual immersed in contemplation, withdrawn from daily activities. Although he wants to know and control everything, he always delegates the ordinary tasks he finds beneath him, such as collecting rent and resolving disputes, to Hidayet; he watches events from a safe distance. Aydın's behaviour towards hotel employees also establishes him as a boss. When he sees an employee who is late to work, Aydın dramatically highlights his own activities (being early for work, taking care of the customers) and his role. 'For if the individual's activity is to become significant to others, he must mobilize his activity so that it will express during the interaction what he wishes to convey' (Goffman 1956: 19–20).

In the film's narrative, we first see Aydın chatting with his guests and then with Hidayet on the way to meet Ekrem, who has promised to find a healthy wild horse. After this meeting, Hidayet visits one of Aydın's properties to collect the rent, but returns empty-handed. The two men discuss the issue of overdue rents and Hidayet attributes it to Aydın's softness. Although Aydın uses the powers granted to him by the law, this is not enough for Hidayet who tries to shape Aydın's performance. Just then, little İlyas throws a stone at Aydın's vehicle and breaks its window. This shot without any cuts is so masterfully rendered that we see every detail. As Hidayet chases İlyas, the boy falls in a stream and gets wet. Through Hidayet, Aydın asks the boy why he has broken the glass. The fact that he does not even communicate directly with a child is a strong indicator of his arrogant personality, which protects him from risk. This arrogant attitude will soon reappear. When they take İlyas back home, Aydın's eyes, waiting for Hidayet outside, scan the pile of old and rusty items in the garden. These images, which we watch from the subjective point of view of Aydın, convey his thoughts on Anatolia, its squalidity and poverty. While recounting to Necla what he just saw, he blames the poor for their backwardness, which he describes as 'filthy' and 'messy'. In return, Necla, who is his only audience, comments half-cynically that she liked his article on the aesthetic deprivation and ugliness in Anatolian towns. Aydın, with his name meaning someone who guides the public with his thoughts and actions, blames the woman and the men of God. The 'crooked, shabby' state of Hamdi Hodja, the boy's uncle angers him; 'the men of God are supposed to be a model for the public'.

Aydın believes in the Kemalist modernisation project, which states that Western modernity, rationality, development and enlightenment should be brought to Anatolia by state employees such as teachers and men of God, but he is not seen taking such an action. Moreover, Aydın returns to the province not for the enlightened purpose of educating the people, but because of his failure in the city. He performs the roles of husband, writer and intellectual although he is now a withdrawn actor, having refused to appear in television series. He is the master of his own property, where he sets the rules and tries to teach roles and relationships by preaching 'to the people', both by dictating to those in his surroundings and by writing for a local daily newspaper. Aydın, who gets others to do the dirty or difficult work of daily life, is on the stage even if he looks like he is behind the stage.

Ritzer claims, '. . . even as they present that self, actors are aware that members of the audience can disturb their performance. For that reason, actors are attuned to the need to control the audience, especially those elements of it that might be disruptive' (2011: 377). While Aydın can maintain this control in his relationship with his employees, he cannot maintain it in his relationships with Nihal and Necla. In the face of Necla's destructive criticism, after she finds the newspaper article, which Aydın wrote with the desire to be liked, but which his sister terms 'cheap, riskless, romantic, insincere', his sympathetic tone changes to aggression. Aydın's articles contain acceptable average conservative values while he does not even have a practice related to religion and spirituality.

IMITATION PERFORMANCES

The expectation of being accepted and approved makes the imitation performance one of the main themes not only for Aydın but also for the other characters of the film. The role is played for others, through others. According to Goffman, who examines the relationships between people in daily life as unfocused and focused interactions, 'in [the] realm of unfocused interaction, no one participant can be officially "given the floor"; there is no official centre of attention' (1966b: 34). Focused interaction beyond everyday encounters 'occurs when persons gather close together and openly cooperate to sustain a single focus of attention, typically by taking turns at talking' (Goffman 1966a: 24). The characters of *Winter Sleep*, which is a performance of relationships, perform focused interactions which occur through words and behaviours such as sarcastic remarks, false compliments, or simple ignoring. The scene where Hidayet argues with İsmail about the stone thrown by İlyas is remarkable in this respect. 'What is all this, what is happening?' asks İsmail, with his harsh and angry eyes, while looking at Aydın, who watches them from a distance. Hidayet gives a roundabout answer: 'There is nothing wrong. Your child fell in the water, we brought him back, so he wouldn't get sick'. While relaying what happened, Hidayet tries to take an accountable stance with his hands in his pockets, one foot slightly inclined to the other. Although he tries to reinforce his performance of 'asking for an explanation' by sniffing from time to time, his stance, gesture and way of speaking cannot hide that it is an imitation, played purely to be watched. As Park points out 'in human society every act of every individual tends to become a gesture, since what one does is always an indication of what one intends to do' (as cited in Goffman 1966b: 16). On the contrary, İsmail's stance, his style, his sniffling, and his self-confidence emphasise that he is the one who asks for an explanation. Hidayet is aware of the role he plays; he plays for Aydın, not for İsmail and his family. His performance, mimicking the hands in pockets pose of Aydın and sniffling of İsmail, reveals an obvious fear.

It is İsmail's turn to play. İsmail performs an unjust bourgeois who pays the price for the stone by slapping İlyas in front of everyone. This performance is a lesson to Aydın and Hidayet, who should feel guilty about what happened. Shortly after, İsmail tries to take his anger out on Hidayet by attacking him. While watching all this from the seat of his car, Aydın scolds Hidayet for 'letting a drunk provoke him'. 'He's cursing, Mr. Aydın' replies Hidayet, in an attempt to justify what he did. We can say that in such a scene, Hidayet is happy to encounter a rival actor like İsmail. He has neither the courage nor the strength to deal with İsmail, but at least he can enjoy standing up to him as an equal opponent, sharing the same stage with him and giving a performance of confrontation and reckoning even though it is just a bluff. Finally, when Hamdi Hodja intervenes to separate them, he performs his soothing performance. He cannot accept their execution because they cannot pay the rent; by looking at Aydın, 'You could have talked to us first' he utters. Aydın does not deal with Hamdi either. He makes Hidayet the mediator to receive Hamdi Hodja's apologies and explanations. The relationship between these three men is mediated. According to Goffman, although people look at each other and talk when they meet in a setting, 'It is also possible for one person to treat others as if they were not there at all, as objects not worthy of a glance, let alone close scrutiny' (Ibid: 83–4). Aydın's attitude coincides with not having an interlocutor beyond the ritual of what Goffman calls 'civil inattention' (Ibid: 84). While Hamdi tells Hidayet about what happened, he wants to make his voice heard by Aydın and to be recognised by him. As explained by Goffman (Ibid: 113), Hamdi both demands a cognitive recognition by referring to his personal biography such as his name and his father's status, and expects social recognition from Aydın by way of a greeting ritual. Aydın, who does not want to make eye contact with Hamdi, who reminds him of the province, of being provincial, of being backward, shakes his head slightly. Although Hamdi comes to the hotel twice by walking the snowy roads to apologise to Aydın for what happened and to demand the cancellation of the execution, Aydın avoids getting involved in his problems, saying that he left these matters to Hidayet. What disturbs Aydın most from all that he has witnessed is Hamdi's 'crooked and shabby' appearance and the smell of his feet. Because foot odour confronts him with backwardness, poverty and the province within him.

Events in the film are related to Necla's notion of responding to evil with goodness to prevent someone from doing evil. Aydın takes on the charity works that Nihal organises without his knowledge, on the pretext that he is looking after her wellbeing, then he donates a large amount of money to the campaign. Nihal tries to take revenge on Aydın by giving this money, which was bestowed by Aydın with the intention of crushing her down, to İsmail; İsmail throws the money into the fire and teaches Nihal a lesson. While the power to buy things burns to ashes in the fire, Aydın comes back to Nihal; Necla, on the other hand, returns to her ex-husband Necdet to respond to his evil doings with kindness.

Benevolence, one of the main themes of the film, becomes the conversation topic of Aydın and the teacher, Levent, who get drunk at Suavi's farm, and it shapes their performances. Disturbed by Levent's sarcastic remarks on the benevolence of the wealthy, Aydın tries to ease his conscience by saying that he has helped a lot without giving his name. What lies behind his benevolence is not a humanist compassion, nor his discomfort with social inequalities, but the desire to be liked and approved by his power: totally a player's attitude. However, Aydın's attitude turns into an unsuccessful show after Levent performs like an actor while quoting the impressive lines on conscience from Shakespeare's *Richard III*, Act V, Scene 3 (Shakespeare 2004b: 148_9)[1]. Levent's tirade invites Aydın to respond: 'Our infallible fate is to be deceived in everything we attempt. I make brilliant plans each morning and fool about all day'.[2] This sentence reveals that Aydın admits defeat in the performance of relationships. His mouthful of vomit after the tirade is also metaphorical in the sense that he realises the personal reasons that have made him unhappy in his life. At the end of the film, when he considers with his inner voice apologising to Nihal, we can say that this tirade is at once a confession, an acceptance and a submission, as well as a moment of renewal, or perhaps another performance for Aydın:

> I didn't go away. I couldn't. [. . .] Please, don't ask me to go either. [. . .] Take me with you like a servant, like a slave. And let us continue our life, even if we do it your way. Forgive me.

Diken interprets this scene after Aydın 'hits the bottom' as 'a promise and a sign of liberation' because 'when, in the final shot, we see Aydın for the last time, he is noticeably calm. He finally starts to write his book *History of Turkish Theatre*' (2017: 103). Aydın, with the rabbit he hunts in his hand, looks helplessly at Nihal, who watches him at the window. His sorrowful stance is the physical expression of submission, regret and a demand for reapproval. His inner voice suggests that he adopts the role of the 'slave' who has chosen to obey, as opposed to the domineering, all-knowing 'master' role he performs. When we regard the Hegelian dialectic of slave and master as a process experienced not only in the people's relations with others, but also with themselves, we can consider Aydın's recognition of the 'slave' in himself as a test of maturity. It is a blessing of nihilism that finds life in submission, a submission to time and space. However, when the foils of acting flake away, we can see the helpless, lonely, and unhappy Aydın under his shell. Similarly, Nihal is confronted by İsmail with the petty-bourgeois compassion that underlies her benevolence. İsmail describes Nihal as 'a heroine who tries to ease her conscience by doling out charity to those less fortunate than her' in his impressive and bookish speech. This is a sharp class criticism of the benevolence of the wealthy and well-intentioned people.

Figure 8.2 Aydın, with his sorrowful stance at the end of the film. (Source: screenshot from *Winter Sleep* 2014.)

Aydın's benevolence is aimed at influencing Nihal, oppressing her and establishing control over her because Nihal is a spoilsport that he cannot control. She is like the wild horses that live freely in nature in Cappadocia. Those horses are only trained when needed and then released back to nature. It is therefore difficult to tame them. The wild horse is also a metaphor for İsmail as well as Nihal, as a motif connected to the themes of rebellion, wildness and irregularity. Neither the wild horse nor İsmail accepts to be tamed. İsmail is a disruptor who refuses to play his roles within the limits set by the social one law/power/rational mind. Nihal is imprisoned within the house and marriage; her disagreements with Aydın make us think that she is also a disruptor. The horse, which was caught for the customer to ride, is released by Aydın at the end of the film. For Aydın, this means metaphorically accepting the eccentricity of Nihal that he cannot control. In these aspects, they fall into the anomalous, contradictory category. According to Levi Strauss, who states that meaning is constructed through binary structures, anomalous categories share the qualities of structures that are in opposition to each other (1963: 161). Edmund Leach, who developed the concept, calls a category 'anomalous' 'when it overlaps another', blurring the 'clear cut and unambiguous' (1989: 155). According to Fiske, 'An anomalous category is one that does not fit the categories of the binary opposition, but straddles them, dirtying the clarity of their boundaries. Anomalous categories draw their characteristics from both binarily opposed ones, and consequently they have too much meaning, they are conceptually too powerful (1990: 118).

Aydın and Nihal can be seen as a contradictory category since they will continue their way as two separate people despite being under a marriage contract and staying in the same house. This contradiction is also about being both inside and outside the social and belonging.

CONFRONTING THE PROVINCE WITHIN US: *THE WILD PEAR TREE*

The Wild Pear Tree centres on Sinan, who dreams of becoming a writer, but cannot escape the fate of his father. After his graduation, Sinan returns to his poor family living in the Çan district of Çanakkale. He wants to build a life for himself different from his father's, in a country where educated unemployment is at its peak. Father İdris leads a life that does not befit a teacher and perceives the reality he lives in differently. Mother Asuman is angry with her husband İdris for losing his money to gambling and damaging his reputation. İdris, who had once seduced Asuman by drafting poems, has now turned into a man far from his ideals, whose word is unreliable and whose debit card has been taken away from him so that he will not waste his salary on gambling. For Sinan, this poor house, home to an unhappy mother and a high-school student sister enmeshed in the world of televisual images and a disgraced father they want to get rid of, is a place to escape from. He hates the province where he was born and raised to the extent that he says, 'If I were a dictator, I would drop an atomic bomb here'. He has no intention of wasting his life in places where there are 'a lot of small-minded, bigoted people who look like "peas in a pod"'. For him, the way to salvation is to be appointed as a teacher, or to enter a state job with a stable income and to write a book. After failing the general exam required to be appointed, he tries to enter the world of literature by publishing his book, *The Wild Pear Tree* about his observations of rural life. He sees himself as an 'intellectual person who will escape this world and transform his troubled experiences into the stuff of art, into a 'quirky, autofiction meta-novel' (Ebiri 2018). Criticising life and those around him ruthlessly, Sinan slams a local writer, whom he pretends to like but is jealous of, by asking provocative questions.

When locked out in his rural hometown as a young candidate writer, he can only pay for the printing costs of his book by selling Arab, the dog his father İdris loves very much. Even if his book is published, he can neither be recognised in the literary world nor would his book be sold. Having exhausted his possibilities, Sinan eventually goes to the army to do his compulsory military service. When he returns, he sees that the only person who has read his book, which his mother has left to rot in a sack, is his father. İdris, who is now retired, has settled in the village to engage in animal husbandry, again pursuing an impossible task: finding water in the well which is next to the wild pear tree. Although his father Recep believes that this effort of İdris will be fruitless, he does not hesitate to help him in removing the stone from the well as he is tired of İdris chasing empty dreams and the neighbours making fun of him. The diligence and rationality of his father creates a contrast with İdris's pursuit of inappropriate things.

Figure 8.3 The well that brings father and son together. (Source: screenshot from *The Wild Pear Tree* 2018.)

Film critic Geoff Andrew sees *The Wild Pear Tree* 'as an expansive, highly imaginative reworking of *Clouds of May*' (2018: 46), emphasising its relevance to Ceylan's other films on rural towns. Indeed, the film is reminiscent of Ceylan's earlier films with its slow, unhurried rhythm and the themes of returning to roots and belonging as well as the subject of the rural educated characters' returning to their small provincial hometowns. Even the characters look like as if they come from the earlier films. The roles of Muzaffer and Saffet in the *Clouds of May* and Mahmut and Yusuf in *Distant* could be divided between Sinan and İdris in *The Wild Pear Tree*. Sinan resembles Saffet in his desire to change and to live another life.

Ceylan reintroduces the theme of children resembling their parents in *The Wild Pear Tree*, which we have seen in his earlier films. Here, the film suggests not only genetic transmission, but also cultural transmission from generation to generation.[3] 'Intergenerational cultural transmission refers to the transmission of cultural ideas (e.g., values, beliefs, knowledge, practices) from one generation to the next generation' according to Tam (2015: 1260) and can be studied from different perspectives. Familial transmission, which is one of the many types of transmission, occurs through socio-cultural processes that expand the will of the individual, and on its basis is the family, the means of reproduction of the society. According to Lahaye, *et al*, 'the phenomenon of transmission realized by family provides the opportunity to give social, cultural and symbolic ties of belonging to younger generations; it also stimulates professional, political and value preferences' (2011: 40). Sinan's desire 'not to be like his father' is a challenge to this cultural transmission, but the socio-cultural and class roots of the transmission that go beyond individual boundaries make his desire impossible and cause him to act in accordance with his habitus. Such a habitus is influential in Sinan's choice of teaching profession, which is seen as a guaranteed job. However, both İdris's desire to do a different job from his own father and Sinan's dream and effort to become a writer emphasise the role of the actor/individual in cultural transmission. Although Sinan was born and raised in the province, he has no intention of being someone who has lost himself in the flow of life. For this reason, he can neither have a good relationship with his childhood friends nor respond to Hatice's erotic interest, which frightens him. As Hatice reminds him, as an educated person, he does not like them and those places. Sinan is also eccentric in his questioning of religious belief. Father and son, whose differences from their social environment are visible, are far from rational regarding accepted values, which results in their exclusion. İdris was excluded in the past when he wrote poetic love letters to his wife, and he is excluded at the present for his irrational habits such losing money to gambling. He is so alone that he cries after the disappearance of his only friend, his beloved dog Arab. He is out of the norm as a dreamer of useless work. Anomaly or non-normality gains meaning with the metaphor of the wild pear tree. Sinan describes the impossibility of escaping from the town and his resemblance to his father through this tree: 'Sometimes, things I see in you, me and even grandad remind me of a wild pear tree. We are all misfits, solitary, misshapen'.

The wild pear tree has an incompatible nature as it grows neither in the forest nor in the garden; it is contradictory, just like İdris and Sinan. With its shapeless, crooked and weak form, the wild pear tree is both a metaphor for the eccentricity, difference and exclusion of the father-son and a mnemonic figure that reminds us of what is forgotten or willed to be forgotten in the intergenerational transmission in Turkey. What it reminds us of is the failure of the modernisation adventure and the wounds of the past. This past is both individual in the sense that Sinan understands that he cannot be different from his father socially or psychically. Turkey confronts its province, the part that it left behind in the modernisation process. With this film, Ceylan draws a panorama of Turkey with its social and cultural characteristics and norms of class through family relations.

The modernisation that envisages the construction of daily life in Turkey in line with western standards, has been perceived as a process which is both desired and feared. This contradictory desire has been expressed in artistic products in the form of father–son conflict, on the axis of being different from the previous generation, more clearly from the father. The father–son conflict makes it possible to read this film both as an oedipal drama and as a broader socio-cultural drama. Despite Sinan's action/performance as an actor, it is seen in the film that cultural transmission shapes the lives of the characters as a means of social reproduction. Besides, Sinan's tendency towards the teaching profession, which he considers guaranteed, and like his father, his interest in literature, recall the idea of socio-clinical transmission, which states that habitus is internalised. In clinical sociology, the purpose of which 'is to analyse the socio-psychic processes characterising the complex and intimate relationships between individuals and society' (de Gaulejac 2014), transmission is thought to operate through the dialectical interaction of historical conditions and individual efforts. Accordingly, Sinan is aware of the historical (and class) conditions he was born into, but by interpreting it, he makes some psychic arrangements. 'These arrangements express the tensions experienced during integration with a changing society and the personal history inherited from the past' (Lahaye et al. 2011: 85). This tension, expressed by Sinan's identity crisis, cannot be separated from Turkey's painful and ambivalent modernisation process faced with the binaries of east/west and village/city. Similarly, this historical and social context is influential in the transformation of İdris. The father and son are individuals with different values, interests and ideals from the narrow social environment in which they live. The restrictive historical, social and economic conditions surrounding them do not allow their potential to be realised. The father, who seems to have failed in everything he touched but has chosen to live in peace with that, is at first a source of embarrassment for Sinan. When he realises his resemblance to his father, this embarrassment is replaced by an understanding, a strange kind of love. This feeling includes both accepting one's destiny and an effort to seek another meaning in life within this inevitable fate and to be happy with it. In the same way, Aydın's acceptance at the end of *Winter Sleep* is a renewal.

The Wild Pear Tree tells how the historical and social context of today's Turkey, where there is struggle for survival, poverty and unemployment in the background, steals the dreams of the characters, leaves their desires unsatisfied, and pushes them into intrapsychic conflicts. The intergenerationally transmitted economic, cultural and social capital of the family has a determining effect on the social position and status of the individual. Thus, demanding to be read as performances of units such as the family and the couple, as well as individuals, particularly in historical and social conditions, Ceylan's films require a reflection on the psychic conflicts, identity crises of the characters, and the social conditions that drive them to act in these ways. The interaction between social structures and psychic structures is narrated through the belonging and identity crisis of the individual. Precisely for this reason, his films can be read as clinical sociological narratives that 'draw attention to the individual, personal, psychic, emotional and existential dimensions of social relations' (de Gaulejac and Roche 2007: 10).

CONTRADICTORY ATTACHMENT TO ROOTS, BELONGING AND THE PAST

Much of the writing on Ceylan's cinema focuses on his ability to create wide landscapes that effectively emphasise the physical and social isolation of the characters. *Winter Sleep* and *The Wild Pear Tree* prove Ceylan's power in constructing realism in cinema by adding the ability to make the characters talk within their own class and social strata. According to Deleuze, 'Interactions make themselves seen in speech-acts' and talking cinema is an interactionist sociology in action, or interactionism is a talking cinema. Deleuze also states that sound brings a new dimension to the visual image in cinema, thus the sound film shows something new as the image heard: 'It is as if the visual image is de-naturalized. In effect, it takes on an era that might even be called human interactions, which are distinct from both previous structures and consequent actions or reactions' (2000: 227). This whole, according to Deleuze, better reveals pure forms of sociability through conversation (2000: 280). Although Ceylan's two films that are the subject of this study seem theatrical with their abundant and impressive dialogues, they are extremely cinematic in the Deleuzian sense because 'What cinema invented was sound conversation which, until then, had escaped the theatre and novel alike, and the visual or readable interactions which corresponded to conversation' (Deleuze 2000: 231). Ceylan's films, most of which take place in the province, demand to be read both visually and audibly with their desolate natural landscapes and the conversations of contradictory characters caught between the province and the city. These visual and audial images turn into a sociological and aesthetic text/experience, prompting a reflection not only on the characters who feel rural boredom as an experience and their moods, but also on the social, cultural and political climate of the country that produces this mood. Although the province is depicted as a place of non-modernity, poverty, backwardness and ignorance in *Winter Sleep* and *The Wild Pear Tree*, while making this description Ceylan criticises the view he mediates. In such a critical understanding, Ceylan makes Aydın see the disorder when he looks at his rental properties and feel uncomfortable with the smell emanating from Hamdi's socks. This untidy, disorganised landscape and Hamdi's ragged appearance and the smell of his feet, emerging from the forgotten sides of memory and settling in the present, remind Aydın and the audience where they are and when. As a divided intellectual whose body is in the East and the soul is in the West, Aydın suffers from 'belated modernity'. According to Gregory Jusdanis, 'belatedly modernized, is a system of thought that has come to accept its insufficiency before a modern one presuming to be superior, and a culture that has adopted an infantile role when confronted by foreign modern ideals' (1991, 150). In these two films, Ceylan, as an intellectual who is aware of Turkey's experience of belated modernity (Gürbilek 2003: 599), describes the sense of lack, cynicism, and endless and impossible desires for change created by this delay.

The belonging and identity crisis that Turkey has experienced in the process of historical and social change, the modernisation, the past and the province are carried to the present in Ceylan's films, making themselves visible with allegories and metaphors in the individual stories of the characters. In *Winter Sleep*, the province and the past appear in Cappadocia, where Aydın has made his refuge and a one-man stage, through a broken car window, the smell of the imam's feet, and a huge bundle of money thrown into the fire. On the other hand, *The Wild Pear Tree*, in which we feel the strong shadow of the past on the present and the future, can be considered as a summary of Ceylan films. 'Our father, whom we are ashamed to resemble, our provinciality that can never be concealed, our Orientalism that we recognize when we face the West, our anxiety about not being able to create something original and our state of being Turkish, which is woven with all these desires and conflicts, are all presented in this film' (Akbulut 2018: 27).

The past does not seem to stop following Ceylan. Because when the distant or recent past is not remembered, when the pain of past traumatic experiences is not dealt with, when these experiences do not turn into narrative and visual representation, the past which is tried to be suppressed will continue to appear sometimes under the snowy steppe, sometimes in the smell of feet, sometimes in a well which is hopelessly dug and sometimes in a formless wild pear tree.

NOTES

1. The tirade is as follows: 'Conscience is but a word that cowards use, devised at first to keep the strong in awe. Our strong arms be our conscience, swords our law' (Shakespeare 2004b: 148–9).
2. Although this aphorism is attributed to Voltaire in some resources and to Shakespeare in others, the identity of its author is uncertain. In my correspondence with Ebru Ceylan, one of the screenwriters of the film, she has stated that Nuri Bilge took notes from a book he had read during his university years, but he did not remember the source. It could be Voltaire, André Maurois or Andre Gide. Seçil Büker and some English Language and Literature experts identify a Shakespearean style even though it is unlikely that he wrote it. (I would like to thank Ebru Ceylan and Nuri Bilge Ceylan for their help.)
3. Mother Fatma's foot itch in *Clouds of May* is a typical genetic transmission. In *The Small Town*, the complex sense of belonging that brings the men of the family back to the town, even if they go to other parts of the world, suggests that this cultural transfer has a psychic dimension.

CITED WORKS

Agamben, Giorgio (2001), Kutsal İnsan, trans. İsmail Türkmen. Istanbul: Ayrıntı.
Akbulut, Hasan (2018), 'Bugünün Yeni Türkiye Sineması'nda Geçmişi Anımsamak', Panorama Kadir Has Üniversitesi, 29, Güz: 25–7.
____ (2005), Nuri Bilge Ceylan Sinemasını Okumak: Anlatı, Zaman, Mekân. Istanbul: Bağlam.
Andrew, Geoff (2018), 'Return of the Native'. *Sight & Sound* 28, 12: 46–9.
Çağlayan, Emre (2014), 'Screening Boredom: The History and Aesthetics of Slow Cinema', PhD thesis, University of Kent.
Coser, Lewis (2012), Sosyolojik Düşüncenin Ustaları: Tarihsel ve Toplumsal Bağlamlarında Fikirler, (trans.) H. Hülür; S. Toker; İ. Mazman. Ankara: de ki.
Daldal, Aslı (2013), 'The Impact of Neo-Realism in Turkish Intellectual Cinema: The Cases of Yılmaz Güney and Nuri Bilge Ceylan', *Academic Journal of Interdisciplinary Studies*, 2, 9: 181–6.
de Gaulejac, Vincent (2014), 'Pour une sociologie clinique du travail', *La Nouvelle Revue du Travail*, 4. https://doi.org/10.4000/nrt.1576, (last accessed 9 September 2021).
de Gaulejac, Vincent and P. Roche (2007), 'Introduction', in Vincent de Gaulejac and Fabienne Hanique (eds.), La sociologie clinique, enjeux théoriques et méthodologiques. Toulouse: Erès Poche.
Deleuze, Gilles (2000), *Cinema 2: The Time-Image*, trans. Hugh Tomlinson and Robert Galeta. London: The Athlone Press.
Deslandes, Ghislain and Jocelyn Maixent (2011), 'Turkish auteur cinema and European identity: Economic influences on aesthetic issues', *Journal of European Popular Culture*, 2, 1: 81–98.
Diken, Bülent (2017), 'Money, Religion, and Symbolic Exchange in Winter Sleep', *Religion and Society: Advances in Research*, 8,1: 94–108.
Dönmez-Colin, Gönül (2014), *The Routledge Dictionary of Turkish Cinema*. London and New York: Routledge.

Dupont, Joan (2014), 'History, Fantasy, and a Dog's Life: Cannes 2014', *Film Quarterly*, 67, 4: 61–6.
Ebiri, Bilge (2018), 'The Wild Pear Tree: Nuri Bilge Ceylan Gets Personal', *The Village Voice*, May 21. https://www.villagevoice.com/2018/05/21/the-wild-pear-tree-nuri-bilge-ceylan-getspersonal/ (last accessed 9 August 2021).
Fiske, John (1990), *Introduction to Communication Studies*. 2nd ed. London and New York: Routledge.
Goffman, Erving (1966a), *Encounters: Two Studies in the Sociology of Interaction*. 3rd ed. Indianapolis: Bobbs Merril.
____ (1966b), *Behavior in Public Places: Notes on The Social Organization of Gatherings*. New York: The Free Press.
____ (1956), *The Presentation of Self in Everyday Life*. Edinburgh: University of Edinburgh Social Sciences Research Centre.
Gürbilek, Nurdan (2003), 'Dandies and Originals: Authenticity, Belatedness, and the Turkish Novel' *The South Atlantic Quarterly* 102/2, 599–628.
____ (2001), Kötü Çocuk Türk. Istanbul: Metis.
____ (1995), Yer Değiştiren Gölge. Istanbul: Metis.
Harvey-Davitt, James (2016), 'Conflicted selves: the humanist cinema of Nuri Bilge Ceylan', *New Review of Film and Television Studies*, 14, 2: 249–67.
Jusdanis, Gregory (1991), *Belated Modernity and Aesthetic Culture: Inventing National Literature*. Minneapolis: University of Minnesota Press.
Katsanis, Vuslat D. (2015), 'On-affirmative time-images in Nuri Bilge Ceylan's Three Monkeys (2008) and the political aesthetics of New Turkish Cinema', *New Cinemas: Journal of Contemporary Film*, 13, 2: 169–85.
Kickasola, Joseph (2016), 'Tracking the Fallen Apple: Ineffability, Religious Tropes, and Existential Despair in Nuri Bilge Ceylan's Once Upon a Time in Anatolia', *Journal of Religion & Film*, 20, 1: 1–36. https://digitalcommons.unomaha.edu/jrf/vol20/iss1/13.
Knudsen, Erik (2016), 'The Total Filmmaker: thinking of screenwriting, directing and editing as one role', *New Writing: The International Journal for the Practice and Theory of Creative Writing*, 13, 1: 109–29. https://doi.org/10.1080/14790726.2016.114257.
Lahaye, Willy, Jean-Pierre Pourtois and Huguette Desmet (2011), Kuşaktan Kuşağa Aktarım. Çocuklarımız Çocuklarını Nasıl Eğitiyor? trans. Z. Canan Özatalay. Istanbul: İletişim.
Leach, Edmund (1989, [1964]), 'Anthropological Aspects of Language', *Anthrozoös: A multidisciplinary journal of the interactions between people and other animals*, 2, 3: 151–65.
Levi Strauss, Claude (1963), *Structural Anthropology*, (trans.) Claire Jacobson and Brooke Grundfest Schoepf. New York: Basic Books.
McAdams, Dan P. (2013), 'The Psychological Self as Actor, Agent, and Author', *Perspectives on Psychological Science*, 8(3): 272–95.
Ritzer, George (2011), *Sociological Theory*. 8th ed. New York: McGraw-Hill.
Shakespeare, William (2004a), *As You Like It*, eds Barbara A. Mowat and Paul Werstine. New York: Washington Square Press.
Shakespeare, William (2004b), *A Tragedy of Richard III*, eds Barbara A. Mowat and Paul Werstine. New York: Washington Square Press.
Suner, Asuman (2010), *New Turkish Cinema: Belonging, Identity and Memory*. London: I.B. Tauris.
Tam, Kim-Pong (2015), 'Understanding Intergenerational Cultural Transmission Through the Role of Perceived Norms', *Journal of Cross-Cultural Psychology*, 46, 10: 1260–6.

CHAPTER NINE

Of Fathers, Sons And 'Solitary, Misshapen' Trees: *Ahlat Ağacı/ The Wild Pear Tree* (2018)[1]

Coşkun Liktor

Nuri Bilge Ceylan has garnered worldwide acclaim with his slow-paced, meditative and visually evocative films, which have received numerous international awards and glowing reviews. Beginning with his feature debut, *Kasaba/The Small Town* (1997), Ceylan's films have been strikingly populated with alienated, emotionally impoverished and discontented male characters, including children and adolescents in conflict with antagonising paternal and maternal figures. A key theme running through Ceylan's oeuvre is the father–son relationship, which acquires an autobiographical dimension in his second feature, *Mayıs Sıkıntısı/Clouds of May* (1999), a self-reflexive film about an aspiring filmmaker, Muzaffer (Muzaffer Özdemir) returning to his hometown to shoot a film casting his reluctant parents. 'The starting point of *Clouds of May* was the desire to tell a story about my father' Ceylan stated in an interview, 'and only later it occurred to me to add the son Muzaffer as a stand-in for myself' (cited in Akbulut 2005: 20).[2] The father–son relationship plays a significant role in *Üç Maymun/Three Monkeys* (2008), which focuses on a dysfunctional family of three, where the father's failure to confront his wife openly about her betrayal leads to frustration on the part of the son, who feels burdened with the weight of his father's shame. Fatherhood is also a key motif in *Bir Zamanlar Anadolu'da/Once Upon A Time in Anatolia* (2011), a murder story concerned with the search for the corpse rather than the identity of the killer, who claims he is the biological father of the murdered man's son, a boy who would later throw a stone at him, his eyes shimmering with hate. A similar episode marks the narrative in *Kış Uykusu/Winter Sleep* (2014), a boy throwing a stone at the car of Aydın (Haluk Bilginer), not his father, but a father figure nonetheless, a wealthy landowner, much like the village *ağa* (a recurring derogatory motif in commercial Yeşilçam cinema from the 1950s to the early 1980s) and the landlord of the boy's family. The figure of the stone-throwing child representing hostility towards and rebellion against father figures in these films takes on an allegorical dimension considering that 'stone-throwing children' – as they were dubbed by the press – were a topical issue in the late 2000s, when the arrest and jailing of Kurdish children throwing stones at the police during anti-government demonstrations in Southeast Turkey caused much controversy both within and outside the country.

Ceylan's continual preoccupation with the fathers and sons finds its culmination in *Ahlat Ağacı/ The Wild Pear Tree* (2018), which centres on Sinan (Doğu Demirkol), a young graduate returning to his family home in Çan, a small town in northwest Turkey near the ancient city of Troy and the Gallipoli Battlefields of World War I. The location is not far from Ceylan's own hometown, Yenice, the setting for his first two features, *The Small Town* and *Clouds of May*. That Sinan is depicted as a restless young man deeply frustrated with provincial life reinforces the intertextual links between *The Wild Pear Tree* and Ceylan's first three features, *The Small Town* and *Clouds of May*, as mentioned above, and *Uzak/ Distant* (2002), considered by a number of critics as 'the provincial trilogy', which 'revolve around the same trope: real and imagined journeys of homecoming and escaping from home' (Suner 2010: 79). *The Wild Pear Tree* in particular bears a thematic resemblance to *Clouds of May*, Ceylan's earlier rural homecoming story, 'as an expansive and highly imaginative reworking' of that film (Andrew 2018: 46).

The Wild Pear Tree focuses on the fraught relationship between Sinan and his gambling-addicted father, İdris (Murat Cemcir), an irredeemable loser depicted in the film as a humiliated figure stripped of social and economic power. 'Whether we like it or not, we can't help but inherit certain defining features from our fathers, like a certain number of their weaknesses, their habits, their mannerisms and much, much more', Ceylan has said about the film, 'the story of a son's unavoidable slide towards a fate resembling that of his father is told here through a series of painful experiences' (cited in Raup 2016). Taking my cue from these remarks, in this chapter I explore the relationship between Sinan and his father using a psychoanalytic framework, with the aim of investigating the conflictual dynamics that eventually culminate in Sinan's becoming heir to a legacy of disillusionment and thwarted hopes. Focusing especially on the episodes that shed light on Sinan's ambivalent feelings towards his father, as well as the patricidal and filicidal impulses inherent in the father–son conflict, I attempt to analyse the predicament of Sinan, who must grapple with an ineffectual, humiliated father who fails to embody paternal authority. I draw upon Freudian and Lacanian theory to explain how İdris transforms from an object of contempt into an identificatory ideal for his son. In addition to the psychoanalytical dimension, I also examine the socio-political implication of the father–son relationship, which brings with it the possibility of interpretation of the film as an allegorical take on Turkish national identity and the present political situation in Turkey.

THE FRUSTRATED SON AND THE HUMILIATED FATHER

Based on the real-life experiences of Ceylan's nephew, Akın Aksu,[3] who not only co-wrote the script along with the director and his wife Ebru Ceylan, but also appeared in a supporting role as a young imam, *The Wild Pear Tree* follows Sinan, a teaching graduate and aspiring writer who is seeking funding for the publication of his first book, which he describes as 'a quirky, autofiction meta-novel'. The film recounts Sinan's encounters with various locals including, among others, the town mayor; a sand quarry owner 'with interest in books' as told by the mayor; a moderately famous local writer; two young imams; Hatice (Hazar Ergüçlü), a former love interest who, to Sinan's surprise is now betrothed to a wealthy, older jeweller; and Hatice's jilted, embittered ex-boyfriend Rıza (Ahmet Rıfat Sungar), Sinan's former school friend and rival. Sinan is a disaffected youth depressed by the prospect of spending the rest of his life in his small hometown, which, as he tells a friend over the phone, he would gladly 'nuke' if he had the chance. Sinan is one of those Ceylan characters who 'migrate from the small town to the big city (*Distant*) or return to their rural roots (*Clouds of May*) . . . but wherever they may happen to be, wherever they chance to find themselves, they are dissatisfied, disenchanted, disillusioned, dislocated, desirous only of being where they are not' (Diken, Gilloch and Hammond 2018: 4).

Like Saffet (M. Emin Toprak), the restless young man deeply frustrated with provincial life who appears in both *The Small Town* and *Clouds of May*, and Yusuf in *Distant* (also played by Toprak), Sinan harbours dreams of escaping to the city. During his brief exchange with Hatice, he claims he has 'no intention of rotting away in this town', clearly echoing Saffet/Yusuf. Thus, *The Wild Pear Tree* seems to be a logical progression from those earlier films, where 'the province signifies not a particular locality . . . but a mode of feeling. It is about sensing that life is elsewhere' (Suner 2010: 83). Sinan is also afflicted with this peculiar mode of feeling, which the Turkish literary critic Nurdan Gürbilek calls 'the boredom of provincial life' (2005: 55–6). As he wanders around town trying to raise money to publish his book, Sinan ponders what to do with the rest of his life. In a country with a soaring number of unemployed university graduates with teaching degrees, Sinan has little in the way of job prospects.[4] The only viable alternative to teaching seems to be joining the riot police like a fellow graduate who now makes his living 'bashing the skulls of leftist demonstrators', as he braggingly tells Sinan. For the penniless would-be writer, the future looks grim.

OF FATHERS, SONS AND 'SOLITARY, MISSHAPEN' TREES 155

Sinan is especially disheartened by the prospect of becoming a provincial schoolteacher like his father, who is counting the days until his retirement. The once respectable İdris has fallen in the public regard, after accumulating a huge debt from gambling on horse racing. The family home has already been sold to pay his debts, condemning the family to a cramped apartment in an impoverished part of town. They are in such a monetary crisis that they cannot even afford to pay the utility bills, which eventually results in the power being cut off. To make ends meet, Sinan's mother Asuman (Bennu Yıldırımlar) works as a babysitter. The economic and social emasculation of İdris is underscored repeatedly in the film as he complains bitterly that he no longer has any say in the family's financial matters, which have effectively been taken over by Asuman, who has confiscated his bankcard lest he gamble away his wages. Hence, it is his mother rather than his father who gives Sinan money to travel to the nearby town of Çanakkale to take the Public Personnel Selection Examination along with hundreds of thousands of candidate teachers all over Turkey in the hope of securing a teaching position in a government school. Never does İdris seem more stripped of dignity and self-respect than when he accompanies Sinan to the bus terminal with the sole aim of begging him for money.

İdris's persecution by creditors is another cause for concern for Sinan from the minute he sets foot back in town. A local jeweller claims that İdris owes him money that he has failed to repay, despite repeated entreaties. Such incriminating remarks are a constant source of embarrassment for Sinan, who, nevertheless, refrains from speaking ill of his father in public, even though he always treats him with open contempt and has only harsh words for him: 'You are dragging us into your swamp! How can you be so relaxed while we bear the brunt', Sinan snaps at his father when he finds him at the local betting parlour. Although he never actually catches him in the act, he is convinced that his father is secretly indulging his gambling habit.

Sinan is not satisfied until he succeeds in convincing his mother Asuman, too, that İdris has not quit gambling despite his claims to the contrary. In fact, he does everything he can to discredit his father in his mother's eyes, going as far as claiming that Asuman should not have married İdris in the first place. However, his attempts to turn Asuman against İdris prove futile. To Sinan's chagrin, Asuman remains devoted to her husband despite all his vices. Nor does she allow Sinan to speak ill of İdris, insisting that he should treat his father with respect. Sinan's resentment at hearing Asuman speak fondly of İdris reveals the Oedipal dynamics at work in his relationship with his mother, who makes up the third pole of the triangle. His feeling of rivalry with his father for the attention of his mother is particularly evident when he presents his mother the self-published book, bearing the inscription: 'I owe you everything and everything is only for you'. Watching his mother shed tears of joy over his son's achievement, Sinan wallows in self-satisfaction and pride, confident that he has triumphed over his father at last. This aspect of Sinan's relationship with his mother, however, is not explored further in the film, as Ceylan's films are invariably structured around male characters with female characters relegated to the fringes of the story, and Asuman's function in the film is limited to accentuating the Oedipal struggle between the father and the son.

What irritates Sinan the most is that, notwithstanding the suffering he has caused his family, İdris persists in his happy-go-lucky attitude, refusing to reform his ways, let alone acknowledge his addiction. As Ceylan puts it, 'Sinan feels very humiliated by his father's gambling, and his carefree attitude to life. He has debts he apparently doesn't care about, he always seems happy: the unbearable lightness of being' (cited in Andrew 2018: 48). İdris's elderly father, who lives in a nearby village, also berates İdris for his irresponsible ways, denouncing his long-lasting endeavour to dig a well on his property as a futile and frivolous undertaking. Despite derision and scorn from the family and the villagers, İdris persists in working on the well, hoping to discover water to turn the barren land green. In one memorable scene, grandfather, father and son, who have teamed up to remove a huge boulder from the bottom of the well, are framed in a three shot which shows them in the act of hauling a rope with all their might as if they are participating in some strange, patrimonial ritual. Their efforts come to naught, however, when the boulder falls back inside the well because İdris has failed to fasten it properly. As Ebiri underlines, '. . . everything Sinan's father touches seems to collapse: He has somehow never won anything in all these years of gambling, and owes money left and right. The well he's trying to dig on their property is clearly doomed to failure. Thus, Sinan . . . is embarrassed by what he perceives as his father's irresponsibility and lack of dignity, his odd, lackadaisical view of the world' (2018).

İdris's carefree attitude towards life is also manifested when he plays a practical joke on Sinan's younger sister by offering her a packet of chewing gum that gives a shock and chuckles at her reaction. This episode, which depicts İdris as an irresponsible, immature man given to childish antics, epitomises what Sinan finds so embarrassing about his father. Viewed from a sociohistorical perspective, the characterisation of İdris as a puerile man-child recalls an observation by the prominent Turkish writer, Oğuz Atay (1934–77) that 'we are a childlike nation who has failed to grow up' (1987: 26). Taking her cue from Atay, Gürbilek defines puerility as a characteristic of the Turkish national identity that can be traced to Turkey's underdevelopment in relation to the technologically, economically and politically developed modern countries of the West that it has been adulating as a model since the establishment of the Republic in 1923. In comparison to these Western powers, Turkey occupies the position of a humiliated child, claims Gürbilek (2012a: 55). This view of Turkey as one of the 'child nations of the East' resonates with the binary oppositions that underpin Orientalism, according to which 'the Oriental is irrational, depraved (fallen), childlike, "different"; thus the European is rational, virtuous, mature, "normal"' (Said 2003: 40). Gürbilek maintains that after being redefined as a virtue and associated with naivety, innocence and a natural simplicity untainted with the corrupting influence of the adult world, hence, being childlike was transformed in the Turkish national imagination into a source of national pride rather than humiliation (Gürbilek 2012b: 42). In this context, Gürbilek views popular Turkish films of the 1960s and the early 1970s which feature child stars known by the names of Ayşe'cik, Ömer'cik and Sezer'cik (the 'cik' as a diminutive when referring to a child) – *Ayşecik* (1960), *Ömercik, Babasının Oğlu/Ömercik, the Son of His Dad* (1969) and *Sezercik, Yavrum Benim/Sezercik, My Baby* (1971) – as allegories of a nation that identifies itself with the image of an upright, resilient child who succeeds against all odds, childish innocence triumphing against evil. Such films reflect a romantic view of childhood, glorifying childish virtue and innocence. Gürbilek interprets the popularity of these films among adults as attempts to come to terms with their social impotence as well as Turkey's impotent, childlike status in the face of the modern West through identification with the child heroes (2012b: 41-2). Thus, the portrayal of İdris as a humiliated man-child not only serves to endow the socially and economically impotent İdris with a romantic aura, but also evokes debates about Turkish national identity in terms of the conflict between the childlike, immature East and the adult, mature West, thus endowing the film with what Fredric Jameson calls an 'allegorical resonance'. In his well-known and highly contested article 'Third-World Literature in the Era of Multinational Capitalism', Jameson argues that all 'third-world texts, even those which are seemingly private and invested with a properly libidinal dynamic – necessarily project a political dimension in the form of national allegory' (1986: 71, 69).

LONGING FOR THE FATHER

İdris is not the only father depicted as an ineffectual and humiliated figure in *The Wild Pear Tree*. Sinan's slightly senile maternal grandfather, a retired imam, is faced with the threat of humiliation when asked to recite the call to prayer to fill in for a younger imam. Indeed, Sinan's grandmother is extremely worried lest he bungle the prayer and become an object of ridicule in the village. Eyüp (Yavuz Bingöl) in *Three Monkeys* who accepts a hefty sum of money to confess to a crime committed by his boss Servet (Ercan Kesal) and fails to take the appropriate action when he realises his wife had an affair with Servet during his imprisonment, is the epitome of a downtrodden father stripped of paternal authority. Eyüp's failure to openly confront either his wife or Servet about the betrayal eventually leads to the murder of Servet, as confessed by his son İsmail (Ahmet Rıfat Sungar), to compensate for his father's inaction, although it could easily be committed by Eyüp, whose impotent rage is finally reaching a boiling point. The motif of the humiliated father also appears in *The Small Town* as the family reminisce the deceased prodigal son, the 'good-for-nothing' to the point that Saffet, the young man dreaming of escape to the city from his suffocating small town, finally retorts: 'Why am I the only one in the family who is supposed to bear the shame of my father?' In *Clouds of May*, Muzaffer's father Emin (Mehmet Emin Ceylan) is also portrayed as an impotent, ineffectual figure. He is engaged in a losing fight with the authorities to prevent the confiscation of the small plot of woodland that he has cultivated even though it is apparent from the start that his attempt to save the woodland is a hopeless quest, much like İdris's efforts to dig a well in *The Wild Pear Tree*. For years Emin anxiously awaits the arrival of the land surveyors, but when they do finally arrive, he is not there to defend his case and prevent his trees from being marked for cutting.

The characterisation of fathers in Ceylan's films contrasts sharply with the feared Oedipal father of Freudian theory, the father who threatens his son with castration. Freud cultivated the idea of the strong, castrating father even though the real fathers he encountered in his clinical practice were often weak and ineffectual figures. Verhaeghe claims that 'to close the gap between clinical reality and his theory, Freud invented the myth of the primal father' (2000: 133). According to Freud's mythic account, the tyrannical, castrating primal father was murdered by his sons, who were, then, so riddled with guilt that they capitulated to the dead father's law and set up the two fundamental taboos against patricide and incest. Hence, 'the dead father became stronger than the living one had been' and was elevated to the position of symbolic authority (Freud 2001a: 143). The dead father was given conceptual status by Jacques Lacan, who coined the term the *Name-of-the-Father*, or the symbolic father, to refer to 'the *dead* father, the father, who, after his death, returns as his Name, that is, as the embodiment of the symbolic Law/Prohibition' (Žižek 2000: 316). Thus, Lacan establishes a distinction between the real, biological father and his symbolic function, also called the paternal function, which consists in imposing the Law – the primordial Law being the prohibition against incest. As Lacan puts it, 'it is in the *name of the father* that we must recognize the support of the symbolic function which, from the dawn of history, has identified his person with the figure of the law' (2001a: 50). The symbolic father, who encapsulates an amalgamation of prohibitive, legislative and protective functions, not only facilitates the child's entry into the Symbolic order, which is the realm of culture and language,[5] but also initiates the formation of two psychic agencies: 'the superego', the agency of repression and 'the ego ideal', the identificatory model that the ego strives to emulate. 'Though there always remains a distance between the actual flesh-and-blood father and the symbolic father, the actual father stands in for the latter, attempting to embody symbolic authority' (McGowan 2004: 41).

The Wild Pear Tree presents us with a family constellation where the father fails to embody symbolic authority, thus offering no effective way of guaranteeing the paternal function. Throughout the film, Sinan laments his father's failure to live up to the standards of a traditional authority figure. When his mother defends İdris as a gentle and loving man who has never laid a hand on Sinan, he replies that he would rather his father gave him a beating than continually lie about his gambling habit. Sinan's desire for strong paternal authority resonates with what Freud calls 'the longing for the father', an archetypal need that Freud traces back to the child's feeling of helplessness in the early phases of life: 'I cannot think of any need in childhood as strong as the need for a father's protection' (2001b: 72). Lacan, too, stresses 'this need for the real, creative and powerful father', asserting that when the real father fails to live up to his symbolic function, the stage is set for psychopathologies ranging from neuroses to psychoses and perversions (1991: 60). One of the best-known cinematic representations of the longing for the father is to be found in Nicholas Ray's *Rebel Without a Cause* (1955), which centres on a troubled youth, Jim Stark (James Dean), whose rebellious attitude stems from his resentment towards his humiliated father, a henpecked man dominated by his wife and thus unable to provide his son with a clear role model embodying phallic masculinity. In *Rebel Without a Cause*, 'there is also a "palpable desire" for paternal authority', so Sinan is not fundamentally unlike Jim, whose ultimate desire is to 'put the emasculated father back into a position of authority' (Lebeau 1995: 84).

Refracted through the lens of Turkish history and politics, the representation of the father–son relationship in *The Wild Pear Tree* acquires nation-specific implications, especially considering that the desire for paternal authority and the longing for a strong father are themes that have a long history in the Turkish cultural imagination, dating back to the dissolution of the Ottoman Empire, which deprived the nation of its traditional father figure, the Ottoman sultan, who wielded absolute power over his subjects. The 'Oriental Father', or the 'Oriental Emperor/Shah/Sultan/Father figure' was 'unforgiving, authoritarian and not bound by his own law' much like the primal father of Freudian theory (Somay 2014: 56, 54) although his power was already in decline a century before the empire's disintegration, when the nineteenth-century reform movement ushered in a wave of Westernisation and modernisation in all areas of life. Islamic societies that are in the initial stages of Westernisation – like the nineteenth-century Ottoman Empire – are afflicted with an intense longing for a just ruler embodying the symbolic father, claims the sociologist Şerif Mardin (2008: 87). Turkish literary critic Jale Parla identifies longing for the father as a key theme in the early Turkish novels written during the nineteenth century such as Recaizade Ekrem's *Araba Sevdası/Passion For the Carriage* (1898) and Namık Kemal's *İntibah/Awakening* (1876) which carry the fatherless child motif recurrently as an allegory for a nation treading on a precarious ground between tradition and modernity without the guidance and protection of a father figure (2004: 16). In *The Psychopolitics of the Oriental Father*, Somay explains how, after the establishment of the Turkish Republic, Mustafa Kemal, the founder of modern Turkey who was given the honorary name of Atatürk – the father of Turks – became established as the all-powerful, authoritarian father at a time when the nation was in desperate 'need of powerful father imagos' (2014: 141). As a rule, the representation of the father in Turkish cultural discourses oscillates between these two extremes; in other words, as Arslan points out in her analysis of the popular Turkish films of the 1970s, the father is represented as either too powerful or too deficient, 'he appears as either a lack or an excessive presence'. In the films analysed by Arslan, including *Çaresizler/The Hopeless Ones* (1973), *Cemil* (1975) and *Kılıç Bey/Mr Kılıç* (1978) – all of which feature the popular action star Cüneyt Arkın – regardless of whether the father is depicted as a deficient or an all-powerful figure, the father–son relationship functions as a metaphorical site onto which socio-political anxieties are displaced. (2005: 10–11). This is also true of *The Wild Pear Tree*, where not only Sinan's father İdris, but all figures of authority – including the town mayor, the wealthy sand quarry owner and the older writer that Sinan encounters in the bookstore – are depicted as deficient figures, none of whom offer Sinan any help. As a result, the whole film is permeated with the loss of faith in authority figures and, by implication, Turkish politicians who fail to offer a solution to the predicaments of the unemployed penniless youth like Sinan from the lower classes. Thus, the film can be said to reflect the mounting discontent with the current political situation in Turkey under President Erdoğan, who has been in power since 2002. During his rule, Erdoğan has consolidated more power, transforming Turkey into a one-man regime. The Gezi Park protests that broke out in June 2013 in Istanbul and later spread to other cities before they were violently crushed by the police, were a revolt against the increasingly authoritarian nature of his regime. The protestors were mostly young people who were fed up with Erdoğan's 'constantly meddling with their lifestyles', telling them what to do and what not to do like an all-controlling father (Somay 2014: 187). Turkey's economic deterioration in the past few years that has led to increasing unemployment and hopelessness about the future among the youth has further intensified the general discontent. Hence, it can be argued that *The Wild Pear Tree* is one of Ceylan's most socially aware films to date since it portrays Turkey as a country that fails to provide a bright future for its 'sons'.

FROM AGGRESSION TO IDENTIFICATION

'Normally, the conquest of the Oedipal realization', Lacan claims, 'is carried out by way of an aggressive relationship. In other words, it's by way of an imaginary conflict that symbolic integration takes place' (Lacan 1997: 212). Accordingly, although it never threatens to break into open violence, the relation between Sinan and İdris is suffused with hostility and aggression which reaches its peak when some of the money that Sinan has been saving to publish his book is stolen from the pocket of his coat hanging by the door in the hallway. Sinan immediately suspects his father of stealing the money to finance his gambling addiction, although the culprit could easily be Sinan's sister, or one of the movers who, just before the incident, knocked on the family's door to ask them to lend a hand with the furniture they were carrying upstairs. This incident serves to cast aspersions on İdris, giving rise to the suspicion that the father who is supposed to be the guarantor of the Law is a contemptible thief. Ceylan's engineering of the visual effects creates a sense of mystery as the camera lingers over the frosted glass door that obstructs the view, thus concealing the identity of the thief from the spectators as well, which could be interpreted as a deliberate attempt to ensure that İdris comes across as an opaque and enigmatic character whose exact nature is difficult to pinpoint: We cannot decide whether he is a despicable rogue, or a well-intentioned loser invested with a pathetic charm.

Although Sinan is convinced of İdris's guilt, he cannot bring himself to accuse his father openly, choosing instead to retaliate by selling İdris's beloved dog behind his back, which enables him to scrape together enough money to publish his book. The loss of his dog is a great blow to İdris, who, Asuman claims, cherished the dog even more than the family members, regarding it as the only creature in the entire world that loved him unconditionally and nonjudgmentally. Hence, Sinan's selling the dog amounts to no less than a deliberate act of filial betrayal, if not a form of metaphorical castration in the sense that Sinan deprives İdris of the most prized object of his affection. When Asuman tells Sinan about İdris's inconsolable grief over the loss of his dog, which causes him to weep at night, Sinan's reaction is a combination of both guilt and joy at having caused his father so much pain. This reaction evokes what Freud calls 'the primordial ambivalence of feeling towards the father' (2001b: 132), an ambivalence stemming from the interplay between fear and admiration, love and hate that colours the son's relationship to the father.

Sinan's ambivalent feelings toward his father are also manifested in a key episode that hints at his patricidal impulse. When, from a distance, Sinan sees İdris lying prostrate underneath the wild pear tree with a piece of rope dangling from an overhanging branch (Figure 1), he mistakenly assumes that his father has committed suicide. His initial reaction is to flee in guilt and fear, as if he is the one responsible for his father's death – an indication of his Oedipal guilt stemming from the assumption that his death wish against his father has come true. When he retraces his steps, he realises that his father is not dead; he has merely fallen asleep under the tree. Another key episode towards the end of the film reveals that Sinan's death wish against his father is reciprocated by

İdris's death wish against his son. This time we see Sinan's dead body dangling from a rope inside the well, leading us to assume that Sinan has committed suicide by hanging. Before long, however, the camera cuts to İdris who has just awakened from a nap; thus, Sinan's suicide is revealed to be İdris's dream, but 'in every dream an instinctual wish [is] represented as fulfilled' (Freud 2001c: 18). Taken together, the two correlative scenes bear witness to the fact that Oedipal relations are marked not just by patricidal, but also filicidal impulses: indeed, as Zepf *et al.* remark, Sophocles' *Oedipus Rex* is as much a tragedy about filicide as it is about patricide since what sets the drama in motion is not actually Oedipus's wish to eliminate his father, but Laius's wish to eliminate his son (2017: 28–31).

Patricide and filicide are archetypal themes that date back to ancient myths and recur across the literatures and cinemas of diverse cultures, establishing intermedial links between the two art forms. From Andre Bazin's essay 'In Defence of Mixed Cinema' through T. Jefferson Kline's book *Screening the Text: Intertextuality and the New Wave French Cinema* to contemporary theories of cinematic intermediality that explore the ways in which cinema 'can initiate fusions and dialogues between the distinct arts' (Pethö 2020: xiii), cinema's interconnectedness with literature has attracted much attention. A noteworthy example of intermediality is the resemblance between *The Wild Pear Tree* and the Turkish Nobel laureate Orhan Pamuk's 2016 novel *Kırmızı Saçlı Kadın/The Red-Haired Woman*, which also deals with the themes of father–son relationships, patricide and filicide and even includes the motif of well-digging. Pamuk's novel tells a story of patricide where the main character, Cem, who was abandoned by his father during childhood and later apprenticed to a well-digger before building a successful career as a geological engineer, eventually dies at the hands of his illegitimate son, of whose existence he was unaware until shortly before his death. *Oedipus Rex* and the Eastern classic tale about a father, Rostam, who unwittingly murders his son, Sohrab, recounted in the Persian poet Ferdowsi's *Shahnameh* are invoked throughout the novel as literary reference points for patricide and filicide, respectively. Cem has spent years pondering upon the two tales, which he believes possess the key to the enigma of fathers and sons: 'There were in fact surprising parallels between Oedipus's life and Sohrab's. But there was one fundamental difference, too: Oedipus murdered his father while Sohrab was murdered by his father' (Pamuk 2017: 141). This fundamental difference between the tales from the East and the West recall Somay's claim that 'Oriental cosmogonies and theogonies *do not* have patricide as their central metaphor', while the preoccupation with filicide appears to be universal (2014: 52–4).

As *The Wild Pear Tree* nears its end, a marked change develops in the way Sinan views his father, who rises in his son's estimation – and by implication the spectator's – until he is elevated to the status of an identificatory ideal. Notwithstanding his harsh condemnation of İdris, Sinan has always felt a certain ambivalence towards him. He has always defended İdris in public as mentioned earlier, at times justifying his gambling habit as a 'rebellion against the absurdity of life' as during a discussion with a conservative young imam. Like the spectator, Sinan cannot exactly decide whether İdris is a fraud, or a misfit branded as a loser because he does not conform to social norms. These two contradictory views of the father correspond to a devalued paternal imago and an idealised paternal imago, respectively. The paternal imago, or what Lacan calls 'the imaginary father', is 'the composite of all the imaginary constructs that the subject builds up in fantasy around the figure of the father ... The imaginary father can be construed as an ideal father, or the opposite' (Evans 1996: 63). For Sinan, the imago of the father as a contemptible gambler simultaneously coexists with the idealised imago of the father as a nonconformist whose gambling habit is a way of rebelling against dominant values and established norms. Sinan's mother Asuman plays a decisive role in the transformation of İdris from an object of contempt into an emulative ideal by reinforcing the idealised imago of İdris:

> He had such an incredible way with words. When everyone else was talking about money, he spoke of the smell of the earth, of lambs and the colour of the fields ... If we were to turn back the clock, and I was allowed to have a choice again, knowing what I know now, I'm sure I would do the same thing. I mean, I would marry your dad again.

Thus, Asuman elevates İdris to the status of a romantic idealist who does not attach any significance to wealth or social status. Asuman's declaration that, if she were given a second chance, she would have married İdris anyway posits İdris as the unshakable focus of the mother's desire, thus reinforcing İdris's position as the possessor of the 'phallus'. In Lacanian terminology, phallus does not refer to the biological organ, but to an unknown, 'imaginary object' that the child assumes satisfies the mother's desire (Lacan 2001b: 241); it is imaginary in the sense that it exists in fantasy rather than in reality.[6] When the child sees that his mother's desire is directed towards the father, he becomes convinced that the father possesses the phallus: 'The father ... represents the vehicle, the holder of the phallus. The father, as father, has the phallus' (Lacan 1997: 319). This realisation paves the way for the son's identification with the father in the hope that one day he, too, will have the phallus like his father.[7]

TAKING UP THE FATHER'S TASK

Having completed his military service – which is glossed over by a long take showing Sinan walking through a snow-covered terrain in slow motion with gun in hand – Sinan returns home to find that after retirement his father has retreated to the village. On the way to the village, Sinan is haunted by the apparition of a dog that closely resembles his father's – an apparent token of his filial betrayal and the ensuing Oedipal guilt. Failing to find İdris in the rat-infested, run-down shack where he has taken residence, Sinan takes advantage of his father's absence to rummage through İdris's wallet and is virtually moved to tears when he comes across a newspaper clipping about the publication of his book. He is even more astonished to learn that İdris has read his book, something that neither his mother nor his sister has bothered to do. So, İdris turns out to be the only family member – indeed the only person on earth – to appreciate Sinan's achievement and provide him with the recognition that he seeks, which helps redeem İdris in Sinan's eyes and reinstitute him within the familial matrix as a good father rather than a fraud. The crux of the film comes towards the very end when father and son sit side by side, engaged in an intimate conversation for the first time. It is then that we learn it was originally İdris who provided inspiration for Sinan's book, also entitled *The Wild Pear Tree*, by drawing his attention to a wild pear tree across from the school when Sinan was a primary school student in his father's class:

> Sinan: Did you read 'The Wild Pear Tree' chapter? I got that from what you told us at primary school.
> İdris: I'm glad to have been of some use.
> . . .
> Sinan: There was a wild pear tree opposite the school. You showed it to us.
> İdris: There's one here.
> Sinan: You know, sometimes things I see in you, in myself and even in granddad remind me of a wild pear tree. I don't know. We're all misfits, solitary, misshapen.
> İdris: Everyone has their own temperament. The thing is being able to accept it and like it.

In this key scene, Sinan associates his father, his (paternal) grandfather and himself with the gnarled and misshapen wild pear tree: they are all misfits who stand in stark contrast to the 'small-minded, bigoted' townspeople whom, early in the film, Sinan had likened to 'peas in a pod'. Consequently, the wild pear tree emerges as the symbol of a vital essence that is transmitted from father to son. This vital essence incarnated in the wild pear tree is the idealised paternal imago that is construed as a heroic rebel who refuses to be a 'pea in the pod' by rejecting established values of a small town. 'At the moment of the dissolution of the Oedipus complex', Lacan claims, 'something happens which we call *introjection*', for it is by means of the introjection, or internalisation, of the paternal imago that the son's identification with the father is achieved (1991: 168). Consequently, the paternal imago is internaliszed as the ego ideal, which will determine the son's orientation within the Symbolic order by providing him with a model to emulate. As Lacan underscores, the Oedipus complex involves 'the transmission of the ego ideal . . . from the father to the son', which is why particular tendencies and attributes tend to run in certain families (1995: 199). Sinan's identification with his father coincides with his realisation that he will never manage to escape from the constraints of the provincial life in which he is trapped. Not even one copy of Sinan's self-published book has been sold; his dreams of attaining social recognition, literary success and material wealth are hopelessly out of reach. At this point, Sinan is aware of his affinity with his father, who also had high hopes in his youth which he failed to fulfil due to socioeconomic restrictions. İdris abandons his last hope when he quits working on the well and accepts defeat: 'The villagers were right. I didn't find water', he tells Sinan with a rueful smile.

The closing shot of the film, a point of view shot that represents the optical vantage point of İdris, finds Sinan digging the well, which signifies taking up his father's unfinished task. Thus, the film ends on a note stressing that Sinan will follow in the footsteps of his father by adopting his utopian dream of turning the barren land green, which is, however, a doomed undertaking from the start. The sound of Sinan's pickaxe striking the rocks at the bottom of the well continues to echo even after the screen fades to black and the end credits begin to roll. This is far from a 'happy ending', for it suggests that Sinan has ultimately resigned himself to the narrow, provincial life that he once desperately hoped to escape. Like a wild pear tree, he will remain firmly rooted in the soil of his provincial homeland, heir to a patrimonial legacy of failure, disillusionment and thwarted hopes.

NOTES

1. An earlier version of this chapter was published in *CINEJ Cinema Journal*, Vol 8, No 2 (2020) as 'Wild Pear Trees, Patrimonial Legacies: Father-Son Relationship in Nuri Bilge Ceylan's *The Wild Pear Tree*' and it was thoroughly revised, updated and expanded for this volume with the kind permission of the editor, Murat Akser.
2. All translations from the Turkish sources, including English titles of films/novels not distributed internationally are mine.
3. Akın Aksu's debut novel *Bir Taşra Köpeği/A Provincial Dog*, which includes material that provided inspiration for *The Wild Pear Tree* was published in January 2019.
4. In 2021, the number of unemployed university graduates with a teaching degree awaiting appointment was around half a million. https://bianet.org/english/labor/256438-half-a-million-teachers-await-appointment-ministry-to-appoint-15-thousand (last accessed 19 January 2022)
5. The Symbolic order is one of the three registers of experience postulated by Lacan along with the Imaginary – the realm of imagination and deceptive images – and the Real, which lies beyond symbolisation. The Name-of-the-Father initiates the child's passage from the Imaginary to the Symbolic by intervening into the dual relationship between mother and child.

6. The definition given here is that of the imaginary phallus. The symbolic phallus, on the other hand, is defined as the signifier of lack, which, according to Lacan, is what causes desire.
7. This is the Oedipal scenario for the male child. The Oedipal scenario for the female child and her relation to the phallus is a different matter.

CITED WORKS

Akbulut, Hasan (2005), *Nuri Bilge Ceylan Sinemasını Okumak*. Istanbul: Bağlam.
Andrew, Geoff (2018), 'Return of the Native'. *Sight & Sound*, 28:12, 46–9.
Arslan, Umut Tümay (2005), *Bu Kabuslar Neden Cemil?* Istanbul: Metis.
Atay, Oğuz (1987), *Günlük*. Istanbul: İletişim.
Bowlby, Rachel (2007), *Freudian Mythologies: Greek Tragedy and Modern Identities*. Oxford: Oxford University Press.
Diken, Bülent; Graeme Gilloch and Craig A. Hammond (2018), *The Cinema of Nuri Bilge Ceylan: The Global Vision of a Turkish Filmmaker*. London: I.B. Tauris.
Ebiri, Bilge (2018), 'The Wild Pear Tree: Nuri Bilge Ceylan Gets Personal', *The Village Voice*, https://www.villagevoice.com/2018/05/21/the-wild-pear-tree-nuri-bilge ceylan-gets-personal/ (last accessed 19 January 2022).
Evans, Dylan (1996), *An Introductory Dictionary of Lacanian Psychoanalysis*. London and New York: Routledge.
Freud, Sigmund (2001a), 'Totem and Taboo', in J. Strachey (ed.), *The Standard Edition of the Complete Psychological Works of Sigmund Freud Vol. 13, 1913–1914*, London: Vintage, 1–162.
Freud, Sigmund (2001b), 'Civilization and Its Discontents', in J. Strachey (ed.), *The Standard Edition of the Complete Psychological Works of Sigmund Freud* Vol 21, 1927–1931, London: Vintage, 64–145.
Freud, Sigmund (2001c), 'New Introductory Lectures on Psychoanalysis', in J. Strachey (ed.), *The Standard Edition of the Complete Psychological Works of Sigmund Freud Vol. 22, 1932–1936*. London: Vintage, 5–182.
Gürbilek, Nurdan (2012a), 'Azgelişmiş Babalar', in *Kötü Çocuk Türk*. 4th ed. Istanbul: Metis, 52–65.
___ (2012b). 'Acıların Çocuğu', in *Kötü Çocuk Türk*. 4th ed. Istanbul: Metis, 37–51.
___ (2005), 'Taşra Sıkıntısı' in *Yer Değiştiren Gölge*. Istanbul: Metis, 47–74.
Jameson, Fredric (1986), 'Third-World Literature in the Era of Multinational Capitalism', *Social Text*, 15, 65–88.
Lacan, Jacques (2001a), 'The Function and Field of Speech and Language in Psychoanalysis' in *Ecrits: A Selection*, London and New York: Routledge, 23–86.
Lacan, Jacques (2001b), 'The Subversion of the Subject and the Dialectic of Desire in the Freudian Unconscious', in *Ecrits: A Selection*, London and New York: Routledge, 223–49.
___ (1997), *The Seminar of Jacques Lacan, Book 3: The Psychoses 1955-1956*. New York and London: W.W. Norton & Company.
___ (1995), 'The Oedipus Complex', in F. Peraldi (ed.), *Polysexuality*, New York: Semiotext(e). 190–200.
___ (1991), *The Seminar of Jacques Lacan, Book 1: Freud's Paper's On Technique 1953-1954*. New York and London: W.W. Norton & Company.
Lebeau, Vicky (1995), *Lost Angels: Psychoanalysis and Cinema*. London and New York: Routledge.
Mardin, Şerif (2008), *Jön Türklerin Siyasi Fikirleri 1895–1908*. Istanbul: İletişim.
McGowan, Todd (2004), *The End of Dissatisfaction?* Albany, NY: State University of New York Press.

Pamuk, Orhan (2017), *The Red-Haired Woman*. London: Faber and Faber.
Parla, Jale (2004), *Babalar ve Oğullar*. Istanbul: İletişim.
Pethö, Ágnes (2020), *Cinema and Intermediality*. Newcastle upon Tyne: Cambridge Scholars Publishing.
Raup, Jordan (2016), '*Winter Sleep* and *Once Upon a Time in Anatolia* Director Nuri Bilge Ceylan Reveals Next Feature', *The Film Stage*, https://thefilmstage.com/winter-sleep-and-once-upon-a-time-in-anatolia-director-nuri-bilge-ceylan-reveals-next-feature/ (last accessed 19 January 2022).
Said, Edward, W. (2003), *Orientalism*. London: Penguin Books.
Somay, Bülent (2014), *The Psychopolitics of the Oriental Father*. London: Palgrave Macmillan.
Suner, Asuman (2010), *New Turkish Cinema*. London: I.B. Tauris.
Verhaeghe, Paul (2000), 'The Collapse of the Function of the Father and Its Effect on Gender Roles' in R. Salecl (ed.), *Sexuation*. Durham and London: Duke University Press, 131–54.
Zepf, Siegfried and Florian Daniel Zepf; Burkhard Ullrich and Dietmar Seel (2017), *Oedipus and the Oedipus Complex: A Revision*. London: Karnac.
Žižek, Slavoj (2000), *The Ticklish Subject*. London and New York: Verso.

CHAPTER TEN

'Gender Trouble' and the Crises of Masculinities in the Films of Nuri Bilge Ceylan[1]

Gönül Dönmez-Colin

'Wherever there is trouble, there is a woman behind it', declares the commissar in Nuri Bilge Ceylan's award-winning *Bir Zamanlar Anadolu'da/ Once Upon a Time in Anatolia* (2011). The 'trouble' is the woman who wears a red scarf to the morgue. A close-up shot lingers on her high-heeled shoes. She is sister to Hester, the hero of the American classic, *The Scarlet Letter* (Hawthorne 1850) who embroiders with lively colours the letter 'A' for adultery she is condemned to wear on her chest. Hacer in *Üç Maymun/Three Monkeys* (2008) whose infidelity also results in murder feels neither shame nor guilt as she offers her body in her red negligee and her newly discovered sexuality to her husband just released from prison. Serap in *İklimler/Climates* (2006) indulges in shame-and-guilt-free sex with İsa while both are involved with others. Hatice in *Ahlat Ağacı/The Wild Pear Tree* (2018), betrothed to an older man for material comfort plays the vampire with an ex-admirer.

Men are prone to shame or guilt, from little Ali in *Kasaba/The Small Town* (1997) tormented by nightmares for overturning the turtle, to Mahmut in *Uzak/Distant* (2002) agonising over the semen spot on the bedsheet, to İsa in *Climates* suffering a sleepless night before abandoning Bahar one more time to Eyüp and İsmail in *Three Monkeys* visited by the ghost of the drowned son/ brother to Kenan in *Anatolia* shuddering from the enormity of his crime when faced with the angelic beauty of a village virgin.[2] Even Aydın in *Kış Uykusu/ Winter Sleep* (2014) and Sinan in *The Wild Pear Tree*, despite all self-centrism, face their conscience on occasion.

THE WOMAN HAS NO NAME[3]

In Ceylan's male-centred films, women are barely visible – an ignored voice on the answering machine (mother and sister in *Distant*); a face on a fading photograph (ex-wives in both *Distant* and *Anatolia*) or simply dead (the prosecutor's wife in *Anatolia*) – vessels to nourish the male narratives with their absence/presence. When diegetically present, their appearance is limited to the traditional roles of wife, mistress, sister and mother, staple derivative attributes since the early days of cinema (Haskell 1973/1987, Johnston 1973/1991; Mulvey 1975; Rosen 1973; Smelik 1998). Just as in classical cinema, which Claire Johnston analysed for stereotyping from a semiotic point of view drawing on Roland Barthes' notion of 'myth', the sign 'woman' is 'a structure, code or convention', representing the ideological meaning that 'woman' has for men, meaning nothing in relation to herself and negatively represented as 'not-man', being absent as 'woman' from the text of the film (Johnston 1991: 25, 26 quoted in Smelik 1998).

Women are rarely identified with a name. If they have a name, this could be symbolic like Bahar (meaning spring) or Serap (mirage) as in *Climates*. Bahar becomes Nihal in *Winter Sleep*, a young slender lover or a sapling removed from its roots to be planted elsewhere. Some names are Biblical, such as Hacer (Hagar) in *Three Monkeys*.[4]

Women depend on men for a living. Nihal has never worked in her life, having been married to the older Aydın with a substantial inheritance. Aydın's sister Necla, once a translator, lives on the same income. Mother Asuman in *The Wild Pair Tree* was married at sixteen; a similar fate awaits her daughter, more interested in television soaps than homework, while the village beauty Hatice has chosen a marriage of convenience over an independent life with personal choices. When women are employed, they are willing to drop all professional activity for love (Bahar in *Climates*), the job the script assigns to them is ill-fitted to their screen image (Hacer in *Three Monkeys*), or their involvement in the wheel of the economy is hardly significant ('babysitting others' children at forty' laments Asuman in *The Wild Pear Tree*).[5]

If women speak, their mono/dialogues are hysterical tirades that advantage the male protagonist (Nihal in *Winter Sleep*). As Silverman argues, 'sexual difference is the effect of dominant cinema's sound regime as well as its visual regime, and that the female voice is as relentlessly held to normative representations and functions as is the female body', the textual model holding 'the female voice and body insistently to the interior of the diegesis, while relegating the male subject to a position of apparent discursive exteriority by identifying him with mastering speech, vision, or hearing' (1988: ix).[6]

Presented as mothers, women are souls, not bodies (Samini 2016). When women become bodies (Hacer in *Three Monkeys*; Gülnaz in *Anatolia*), mayhem occurs. The 'mother-duality (phallic/angelic)' of the Freudian theory that E. Ann Kaplan underscores in *Psychoanalysis & Cinema* (1990: 130) comes to full force with these abject mothers, when juxtaposed with the 'angelic' mother Fatma (played by Ceylan's mother) in *The Small Town, Mayıs Sıkıntısı/Clouds of May* (1999) and *Climates* embodying the '. . ."positive" mother-pole in her self-denying nurturing' (Ibid.). Dominant narratives consider aggressive assertiveness as vital asset to successful manhood, imagined as the realisation of a distinct domination inherent in the male body while women endowed by nature with moral compassion, self-control and emotional sensitivity are expected to maintain order by transmitting these virtues to the man. As Forter quotes E. Anthony Rotundo (1993), 'Men's sphere depleted virtue, women's sphere renewed it' (2011: 2). In *Climates*, İsa's violent sex episode is cut to a visit to his mother who mends his clothes dutifully while advising him to settle down and have children.

The childless woman – Mahmut's ex-wife in *Distant*, Serap and Bahar in *Climates*, the doctor's estranged wife in *Anatolia* and Necla and Nihal in *Winter Sleep* – is another form of threat by defining the male body as a subordinated social entity unable to measure up to hegemonic ideals (even if childlessness is imposed by the male).

MASCULINITIES IN CRISIS

Distant, which established Ceylan as an auteur is the third segment of what I consider a tetralogy that also includes *The Small Town*, *Clouds of May* and *Climates* (Dönmez-Colin 2014). Continuing the earlier themes of home, identity, belonging and internal exile, the film juxtaposes two characters: commercial photographer, Mahmut (Muzaffer Özdemir) and his provincial cousin Yusuf (Mehmet Emin Toprak). Distant to his cousin, who reminds him of the roots he had severed while building a new identity in the city, Mahmut is also distant to his work, having surrendered to material gain rather than following artistic dreams, to the women in his life and to any form of commitment.[7]

Women exist mostly in the presence of Mahmut and other males in the film. A blurred image in a red blouse removing her black stockings is cut to a reverse shot of her gaze watching a weary man watching her and sighing deeply before approaching. She (Nazan Kırılmış/Kesal) cries silently in the toilet after sex off camera (an implied gaze) and then leaves the building in haste while the Anatolian superintendent shames her with his male gaze. The 'shamed' woman's hand reaches for her coat buttons self-consciously. '[A]t the moment of shaming, it is the man who sees himself seeing and the woman who sees herself being seen' (Pajaczkowska and Ward 2008: 10).

A third man also observes women. Yusuf, the unemployed unskilled cousin harasses women visually and even tactually (extending his knee on the tram) but, like Mahmut trying to say goodbye to his ex-wife while trapped inside the toilet, is unable to communicate with them. Diken, Gilloch and Hammond claim that as the camera follows the aloof Yusuf trailing the women he encounters, 'it is actually these women in the film that lead the viewer around the city', with Yusuf as the 'intermediary' (2018:157). I would argue that this does not elevate the women's status from the invisible extensions to embellish the male narrative, but rather confirms the traditional clichés of women as guides or muses. As undeveloped non-entities, neither the young neighbour (Ebru Yapıcı/Ceylan), nor the woman in the bookshop resemble the *flaneurs* of Ceylan's mentor Michelangelo Antonioni, who 'provide desperate proof of the alienation of the city' particularly in the trilogy – *L'avventura/The Adventure*, (1960), *La notte/The Night* (1961) and *L'eclisse/The Eclipse* (1962) – in which 'the female protagonist wanders through the often lunar landscapes of empty cities searching, wide-eyed and nervous, for the spiritual or emotional elements which modern life no longer provides', women 'removed from their surroundings, especially inhabited spaces that remain dominated by men' (Orban 2001).

'*Distant* constitutes both a melancholy cinematic study of metropolitan isolation and a darkly comic portrayal of masculinity as empathetic absence and communicative constipation, adding thereby the seductive but frozen urban environment as an inhospitable landscape of loneliness' assert Diken, Gilloch and Hammond (2018: 57). Referring to Dönmez-Colin's observations on gender and sexuality in the cinema of Turkey (2008), they underline that '*Distant* is also a sardonic study of the pathetic failings of masculinity and male relationship exemplified by the petty trials of Mahmut and Yusuf' (2018: 155). The film interrogates 'notions of masculinity' according to Çağlayan, 'the damaged masculinity inscribed in the images of the film's twin protagonists is configured through the characters' relationship to the city, particularly in the ways in which they operate through urban spaces like silent stalkers' (2020: 1). The male leads are 'lonely wanderers, whose desire for women is unmatched by their voiceless disposition and their inability to use language, which are

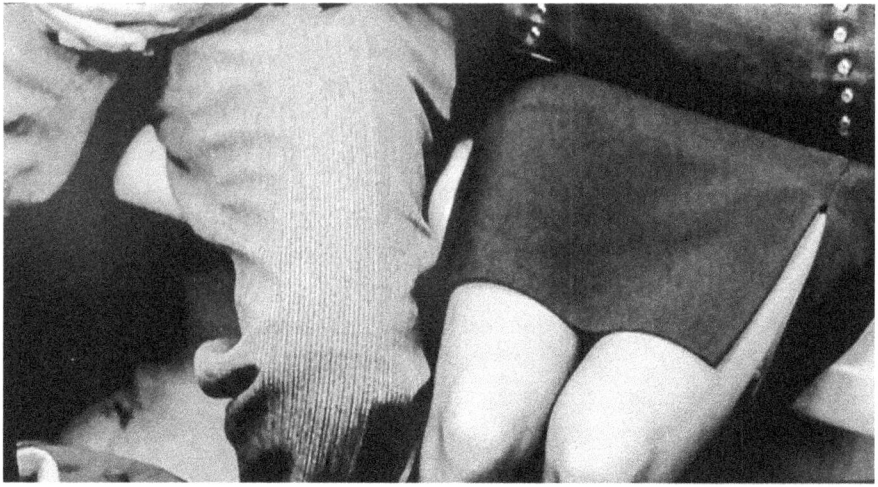

Figure 10.1 Yusuf harassing women on the tram. (Source: screenshot from *Distant* 2002.)

classic symbols of castration'. The 'similarity that binds them together' is 'impotence'. As opposed to the traditional definition of masculinity by 'action, determination and power', these men are characterised by 'immobility, shyness and failure, which are articulated through spatial arrangements'. Another similarity is the way they 'watch, stare at and objectify women' (Ibid: 3). Referring to literature in the Turkish context that considers the crises of masculinity in the post-1990 films and the 'deconstruction' of traditional masculinity as a symptom of wider social change and as the result of a 'collective experience of existential crisis and loss of power' (Ulusay 2004: 144–62); Erkılıç 2011:231–42), Çağlayan confirms the assumption that the absence of speech in the films of Ceylan and some of his contemporaries symbolises 'the difficulty and impossibility of articulating the historical crisis', which evokes 'sociopolitical issues like cultural amnesia, hidden violence, discrimination, prejudice, and crisis of identity' (Yücel 2009: 12–21 as quoted by Çağlayan 2020).

Anatolian migrants' 'helplessness and castration in the urban centers' as Arslan points out (2011) is nothing new to the cinema of Turkey although the cultural incompatibility between the urban and rural, the focus of the commercial Yeşilçam cinema, has developed into more complex issues of crisis of national and gender identities in the post-1990 films that lean on non-professional actors and a different sense of humour, according to Çağlayan. A good example is the scene in which Yusuf, in his black leather jacket with uplifted collar and dark sunglasses, posing in front of an expensive car to impress a young woman being humiliated by the alarm beep – a 'conventional narrative trope . . . parodying the virility of its characters and the masculine narcissistic need to receive attention, and on a broader level suggests the artificiality of hyper-masculinity' (2020: 5).

In *Climates*, homecoming and escape from home, the main concern of Ceylan's previous films, merges into the possibility of a home and the challenges of establishing roots and belonging to someone. A clumsy man approaching middle age, İsa (Nuri Bilge Ceylan) stumbles amidst the Roman ruins in a Woody Allen or Hong Sang-soo style self-parody, forewarning the audience of the demise of the relationship, which comes full circle when he falls again as he climbs the İshakpaşa Palace in Eastern Turkey. In both instances, the subjective camera angles reinforce the diminutiveness of his human figure against the colossal dimensions of the eternal monuments, exposing human fragility and vulnerability like the shots of Aydın against the landscape of Cappadocia in *Winter Sleep*.[8]

Bahar (Ebru Ceylan) is the ideal woman coveted by the patriarchal male: young, beautiful, silent and submissive. While her college professor lover gazes at the Roman ruins, she, the artistic director of a television series, gazes only at him. Ready to die rather than to live without her man, she covers his eyes during a motorcycle ride after his decision to end the relationship. When he comes back and repents, she drops all responsibilities to run back to him. On the other hand, Serap (Nazan Kırılmış/Kesal), the woman İsa meets for occasional sex,

'GENDER TROUBLE' AND THE CRISES OF MASCULINITIES 173

Figure 10.2 Yusuf in a 'conventional narrative trope' pose to attract the females. (Source: screenshot from *Distant* 2002.)

is detached from emotional ties. Bahar is soul; Serap is body, to use Samini's terms (2016). Bahar and İsa exchange brief moments of tenderness; Serap and İsa indulge in steamy sex. The two women correspond to the two essential women in Mahmut's life in *Distant*. The ex-wife Nazan (who he appreciates more from distance) is gentle and forgiving like Bahar, the woman men like to marry. On her way to immigrate to Canada with her new husband, she assures Mahmut that she is not blaming him for her abortion and subsequent sterility. The unnamed woman who visits Mahmut in the dark is a sex partner, and just like Serap is involved with another man (both are played by the same actor).

İsa assesses his limits in patronising women. During a dinner in Kaş, he scolds Bahar in front of his friends for refusing to wear a jacket despite her assertion that she is not cold, his possessiveness recalling the middle-aged director in Hong Sang-soo's *Claire's Camera* (2017) lecturing a young woman he had slept with once when drunk not to wear shorts and exhibit her legs as if she is for sale. Aydın uses the same possessive tone in *Winter Sleep*, treating his wife like a child, addressing her with diminutives of fondness during a serious argument (*iki gözüm*/apple of my eye, or *güzelim*/my beauty) and confiscating the ledger for her charity work, which he is certain she cannot manage. The sex that stimulates İsa is a mock-rape spectacle with the male rendering the woman immobile and powerless under his weight.

Male bravura in homosocial spaces, the conversations of İsa with his male colleague in the office, the tennis court or the sauna in the absence of women are indicative of the male standpoint in gender relations in Turkey, which crosses borders to Iran recalling the office bragging episode in Kiarostami's pre-revolution feature, *Gozareh/The Report* (1977) as well as several films of Hong Sang-soo. İsa is aware that the colleague would not break an engagement because his fiancée points a finger at him, but he plays along like Musa in *Yazgı/Fate* (Demirkubuz, 2001) who accepts to collaborate with his neighbour in the planned violence just for male camaraderie against a woman he has never met.[9] Men understand each other, as revealed during the dinner episode in Kaş. While the lady of the house remains in the kitchen most of the time and Bahar sulks in her corner, the two males communicate through facial expressions regarding İsa's anguish perpetuated by the behaviour of the immature and moody Bahar.

Asuman Suner underscores that Ceylan blocks identification in his films by building unsympathetic characters and the most unsympathetic males resemble himself – Mahmut in *Distant*, Muzaffer in *Clouds of May* and İsa in *Climates* 'which adds a further self-reflexive ambiguity' (2010). I would not confirm that these characters resemble Ceylan apart from certain autobiographical elements admitted by the filmmaker, but I would add Servet, the politician/boss in *Three Monkeys*, the pretentious prosecutor in *Anatolia*, the bourgeois/intellectual Aydın in *Winter Sleep* and the young smug Sinan in *The Wild Pear Tree* to update the list of 'unsympathetic males', a strategy also employed by Kiarostami, particularly in *The Report* and *Tam-e Gilas/Taste of Cherry* (1997). 'This blocking of identification related to the muted performances Iranian directors draw from their actors [is] a dedramatization that creates space for the intensification of images' (Chaudhuri and Finn 2003: 50–1 as quoted by Suner). Suner infers that, according to the authors, in Deleuzian terms, the failure of the character identification breaks the sensory-motor chain and somewhat releases our senses so that we become more receptive to the optic and sound situations as in Ceylan's films (2010: 93).[10]

According to the local critic Fatih Özgüven, İsa is settled in the city but not at ease with the 'climate' of the city. His behaviour during the Serap episode carries the obvious signs of a provincial man savouring a clandestine affair in the city and, like Mahmut's habit of spreading a towel before intercourse in *Distant*, carries the 'smell' of the country. Hence, *Climates* continues the story of the male character who 'lives his climates' between the city and the country (2006). Zahit Atam argues that at the centre of Ceylan's cinema is the clash of the East and the West and *Climates* could be examined from the perspective of this dualism. Ceylan is an Eastern man from the rural milieu who received his higher education in Istanbul at an elite university with Western standards, he reasons. Just like Dostoevsky and Chekhov, the nineteenth-century Russian writers that he admires, he has experienced the dualism of the East and the West, which is discernible in the character of İsa, an Eastern man also formed by Western ideas and ideals. İsa may advocate liberal points of view but he finds himself in the jungle of Eastern values if emotionally challenged. His values are Western, but his responses are Eastern, such as his possessiveness and his display of the privileges endowed upon him as an Eastern male, which explains İsa's discontent and desire for repossession when hearing about Bahar's productive life without him, and disappointment when she refuses him and retreat when she yields (2011: 151–202).

I would argue that İsa's character is more nuanced. The heavy fog or the snowflakes that block his vision and visibility through most of his time in Ağrı until he buys his return ticket reveal deeper turmoil than his façade.[11] Serap is the antithesis of Bahar who demands commitment and love. İsa cheats on gentle and loving Bahar with Serap who indulges in his violent sex fantasies. Serap is İsa's Doppelgänger. He returns to Bahar when he hears she is doing well since their separation. An independent woman with a life and aspirations of her own is more challenging. In a hasty move triggered by his fear of losing her, he woos her in the car with promises of a domestic life. When she comes back to him with nothing learned from the so-called period of independence, dropping her job to run to the arms of love, a long night of deliberation awaits İsa, a deliberation with himself, his character and Bahar's. Serap could be a mirage as the meaning indicates etymologically in Turkish. The ideal woman for İsa is Bahar and Serap in one, for Mahmut in *Distant*, Nazan, his ex-wife and the unnamed lover, and for the men in *Anatolia*, the virginal village girl and the unrelenting adulteress, the double faces of Eve. İsa makes a choice of integrity to his essence against the stifling traditions and obligations and leaves like Mohammad in Kiarostami's *The Report*.[12]

WOMEN AS TROUBLE FOR MEN[13]

Three Monkeys is a film about three men whose masculine hegemony is threatened by a higher hegemony (boss, father, state) and a woman who is caught in the web. Servet (Ercan Kesal), the businessman/politician devoid of any charm, loses the elections; Eyüp (Yavuz Bingöl), an Anatolian migrant serving as the personal driver to Servet, is demasculinised by his inability to improve the living standards of his family, and İbrahim (Ahmet Rıfat Sungar), the unskilled and unemployed son, has failed the university entrance examinations, much to the disappointment of his mother.

The fantasy object for the three men is Eyüp's wife, Hacer (Hatice Aslan). These men 'dislodged from the narratives and subject positions which make up the dominant fiction' (Silverman 1992) exploit her to re-enter the dominant fiction.[14] Servet seduces Hacer to regain his masculinity, damaged by losing the elections; Eyüp confesses to Servet's crime for a considerable cash sum to become a better provider for Hacer (without consulting her) and İbrahim uses Hacer to ask money from Servet to start a business to please his mother, inadvertently initiating her affair with Servet.

Critics and audiences alike were puzzled about Hacer's fatal attraction to a man like Servet, neither attractive nor kind. Some argued that Ceylan presented Hacer as a sex object, although the camera refrains from fragmenting her body and circumvents voyeuristic sex scenes. When İbrahim gazes through the keyhole, only his eye appears on the screen, the audience gazing at the son gazing at his mother in bed with a man who is not his father. Physical violence against Hacer is depicted in half-shadows to avoid inviting audience identification (Özdemir 2009). Yet, all three men abuse Hacer, verbally and physically. Servet first seduces her, then drops her when her obsession threatens his family life; İbrahim slaps her for her adultery (significantly to the sound of *ezan*, the call for prayer from the minaret) although he does not mind using Servet's money.[15] Eyüp, back from prison, becomes aware of Hacer's infidelity and abuses her during a violent bedroom scene. Hacer's affair with Servet begins and ends with degradation. Sitting uncomfortably in his office as an uninvited guest, she hears Servet scold the secretary for admitting 'no matter who'. Then, her phone, which she cannot locate among the jumble in her bag, chimes a silly love song, 'You, too, love but not be loved in return' while Servet does not hide his impatience. When she is abandoned, she falls on her knees to beg for love.

Chakravarty states that the erotic is associated with transgressive sexual desires and acts as they both seem to violate the social order while 'affirming its norms and procedures', but if we focus on the 'interplay of taboo and transgression that implicates the central female character in erotic experience, with violence unleashed against herself and others', the woman hence 'feels in her own body the conflicts over the prohibitions that the society of men has instituted and seeks to enforce' (2003: 82–3). This could explain the tragedy of Hacer, despite gaps in the script regarding the development of her character that block audience imaginary from fully understanding her sexual awakening. She is unable to harmonise her newly discovered body with her soul and free herself from serfdom to men (offering her body in a red negligée to her husband just released from prison, falling on her knees in front of Servet, removing her nail polish when Servet dies). 'But the texts undercut their own potential for a truly erotic sense of the revaluation of the past' according to Chakravarty.

For the aim of the filmmakers is to reject or rethink particular configurations of history, as far as the women are sexually inscribed in these scenarios, and symbolically annihilated for their sexual disobedience, the films reinstitute the same social order that is condemned in the first place. This is the double bind of these reflexive texts: to exorcise the past and yet to hold on to it; to represent sexual desire and yet to know it as entrapment; to celebrate the female figure and yet to exploit it within the terms of the classical grammar of film narrative (Ibid.)

Ceylan has claimed during interviews that Hacer, in her feeling of powerlessness, is attracted to what she sees as a symbol of power, and the film is a commentary on class differences, globally. Agreeing with Ceylan's statement, I would add that the 'double bind' Chakravarty identifies in 'reflexive texts' is the issue in Ceylan's view of women as manifest here, their sexuality and men's relation to women's sexuality.

Once Upon a Time in Anatolia depicts a society of lying, cheating, swearing and bullying men. A pompous prosecutor (Taner Birsel) imagines he resembles Clark Gable, disregards his adultery and blames his wife for her suicide ('People do it to punish the other', he claims, 'women can be very cruel'). A detached doctor (Muhammet Uzuner) can love a woman only from distance, recalling Mahmut's nostalgia for his ex-wife in *Distant*. A murder suspect does not remember where he buried the corpse but experiences catharsis through the gaze of a virgin beauty. A commissar is lost between power games and a nagging wife; a policeman is married to a woman from a village he hates; a commander competes for authority and a mukhtar and a morgue attendant are ready to exploit every opportunity to their benefit.

Two women appear diegetically, one is silent and the other hardly audible. The mukhtar's daughter (Cansu Demirci) mesmerises all men while serving tea in the light of a kerosene lamp. Men stare at her, and she stares back; she is like a mirror that reflects their soul. She is the light that briefly illuminates the darkness, a mirage in the desert, serving tea to quenched men; the ideal woman – young, pure, beautiful and 'silent'. Is her silence 'a trope for her disempowerment' to quote Marguerite Duras from her book *Nathalie Granger* (1972), or Kaplan, 'a political resistance to male domination through the power of silence; since the realm of the symbolic is able to express only male concerns and ways of being, women must find ways to communicate outside of, beyond, the male sphere' (1983: 9)? As her screen space is limited to advancing the male narratives, she remains as much of an enigma as most women characters in Ceylan's films.

Gülnaz, who arrives at the morgue with a red scarf to identify her husband's body, sheds a tear. For the dead husband, the lover to be jailed, the orphaned son, or herself, a woman who has lost two men simultaneously, losing male protection? She is another enigma, although she shares one common element with Hacer. They are both mothers; once they were souls (Samini 2016), then they became bodies disrupting the social order. They have 'crossed to the other side' to use the expression of Amin, the son in Kiarostami's *Dah/Ten* (2002) referring to his mother's divorce. Ceylan's camera plays with classic fetishist femme fatale fantasies to identify the 'adulteress' as it lingers on Gülnaz's high heels in the corridor of the morgue evoking images from earlier films – Serap in *Climates* challenging İsa to action with her spiky shoes, 'Gelsene!' ('Come over!') and Hacer in *Three Monkeys*, throwing her heels in the air after returning from Servet's office as İsmail watches with suspicion and guilt. Castrating females of film noir delighting in their sins.

Anatolia ends with the image of Gülnaz through the gaze of the doctor, one of the male protagonists who has just altered the official records to advantage the murderer. She is holding the hand of her son. In the eyes of the doctor, whose childless marriage terminated most likely due to his lack of commitment to parenthood (Mahmut in *Distant*), she has regained her mother identity, a soul without a body.

'I RISE IN FLAMES' CRIED THE HERO[16]

Narratives of consumed love do not exist in Ceylan's films, evoking most films of one of his mentors, Antonioni. Starting with *Koza/Cocoon* (1995), a short film without dialogue, the distance between women and men only widens. The Chekhovian *Winter Sleep* delves into the darkness of the human soul through a character trapped in its labyrinths. Aydın (Haluk Bilginer), a former theatre actor and a landlord in the feudal tradition of the *ağa* system (a common figure in the Yeşilçam tradition) lives off the labour of the others and the dichotomy in these identities determines his actions and reactions.

Aydın's character is drawn with generous nuances from the moment he appears on screen with his bourgeois coat. He knows who he is, and he constantly interrogates himself. Although his righteousness does not draw empathy, he is a strong character rounded with human weaknesses (jealousy for the youth of the schoolteacher; fear of losing control over his territory and his possessions including his wife). Among the three main characters, he is the only one resembling a human being, a tragic hero, an Othello, as the name of the hotel suggests.

Aydın's sister, Necla (Demet Akbağ) who disappears before the final act, functions as his alter ego, needling him from her position in the half-shadow. The dialogues between the two siblings sound like self-reflexive dialogues between Aydın and his conscience, cross-examinations of his actions and decisions regarding his life and work. When his sister is absent, he resorts to interior monologue. Necla is a typical bourgeois woman, a well-travelled, well-educated parasite, condescending to the less advantaged, complaining about a glass broken in the dishwasher and thinking of deducting the expense from the maid's salary ('I bought it at Çukurcuma', she specifies, referring to the antique shops in the gentrified bohemian bourgeois neighbourhood of Istanbul). While Necla reminds Aydın of his failures ('perhaps it was our fault for lionising you'), his young wife Nihal (Melisa Sözen) avoids him, trying to fill her empty life with charity work without understanding the first rule of charity: respect for the other. Her guilty conscience is appeased by organising wine-and-dine gatherings with other charitable souls. Her hysterical cry when the drunken İbrahim throws the hefty sum of money she offers him into the fire exposes her character better than the earlier tirade with her husband, which ends in childish hysterical sobs. Inside the poor man's house, not only does she not dare to stare at anyone but her gaze flounders seeking a direction to focus.

The two women live inside the walls they have erected for themselves. They have speaking parts and they speak volumes, to each other as well, and not only about men. Their presence is often duplicated by precisely arranged mirrors. Yet, their characters are not more developed than their predecessors and certainly less than Aydın who keeps asking his sidekick about their whereabouts, or spies on them. Other women -the housekeeper or the tenant's wife- simply serve men.

Aydın is a man educated in the Republican ideals of modernity, progress and intellectualism (Aydın means intellectual, but also enlightened in Turkish.) He is out of touch with the realities of rural poverty, expecting the peasants to be as enlightened as him without taking any interest in improving their situation except criticising the lack of aestheticism in the Anatolian towns in a local newspaper hardly anyone reads. He believes in gender equality, while maintaining prejudices about gender. He humiliates his wife and his sister with calculated cynicism. His stand evokes what Tekeli calls 'state feminism' of the Kemalist revolution that recognised women as modern citizens with equal rights but failed in the practice of implementing equality in the private space (1995: 12).

Yet Aydın is the most positive character in the film, a romantic who sheds a tear in the cemetery after his sister's reproach that he never visits his parents' grave. He evolves during the course of the film. The stone thrown at his car window by the son of his tenant İbrahim, who he has embarrassed in front of his family by sending the bailiff to confiscate the television for unpaid rent; the indictments of his sister who belittles his precious hobby, the ostentatious column in the local newspaper, *Bozkırın Sesi/ The Voice of the Steppe*; the confrontation with his wife who calls him a selfish misanthrope and threatens to leave him, and the presence of a younger man with common interests with his wife are serious threats to his masculine hegemony, which he feels is crumbling. The evening at his only friend Suavi's house is cathartic. Three men of different generations, the aged widower Suavi, the young schoolteacher Levent and the middle-aged Aydın serving as spatio-temporal tropes breach decorum in the homosocial space. With much alcohol, masculinities are stripped exposing human beings with faults and weaknesses. Aydın, not used to drinking, vomits violently. The next morning, the three men go hunting – a male game that can reinstate masculine identity. Aydın kills a rabbit and when he enters through the door of his property holding his trophy to Nihal watching him from the window above, he is ready to offer himself to his wife as an equal partner, declaring his love and even asking for forgiveness and begging her not to leave. This is what we learn through his interior monologue. Whether he actually pronounces these words to Nihal and whether he is sincere about them are left to speculation. He is an ex-actor. However, his relieved face as he finally sits down to type the title of his ambitious project, 'The History of Turkish Theatre' suggests that his catharsis has been completed. A new chapter will begin in Aydın's life.

MALE SUBJECTIVITY AND TRANSGENERATIONAL VULNERABILITY

The Wild Pear Tree is about transgenerational crisis of male subjectivity. Sinan (Aydın Doğu Demirkol) is an unemployed aspiring writer, sour, arrogant and Oedipal, a Raskolnikov who sells his father's cherished dog to publish a book to ease his coming into subjecthood. His father İdris (Murat Cemcir) is a character Sinan does not know to love or hate but comes to understand and appreciate. The paternal grandfather, Recep, is more stubborn and self-centred than the sum of the two.

The four women in the film – mother, sister, grandmother and Hatice (Hazar Ergüçlü), the object of sexual interest, are extensions of Sinan. Hatice appears briefly in one of the most beautifully composed episodes in the film, a fairy-tale primal forest with the ethereal light accentuating her rather folkloric peasant outfit juxtaposed by a fiery red blouse (red blouse of the clandestine lover of Mahmut, the red negligée of Hacer, the red scarf of Gülnaz).[17] She is the village beauty, the Helen of Troy all men desire (The Trojan horse built for a movie set stands tall at the town square). Hatice left her education because she was 'bored'. She yearns for other lives elsewhere, 'there are beautiful things in life, crowded streets, nice meals, ships that sail, balmy nights, loves, intoxications. Everything is so near, but so far'. But she does not think of acting upon her yearnings. One moment, she is the peasant girl fetching water with the traditional *yazma* covering her hair (a *clin-d'oeil* to the fountain eroticism tradition of Yeşilçam?) recounting her future marriage to the jeweller, the next moment, she is the femme fatale, drawing blood from Sinan's lips as if to punish him for his masculine lack.

Asuman (Bennu Yıldırımlar) as Sinan's mother revives Fatma Ceylan (Ceylan's mother) as she has appeared in Ceylan's earlier films, a simple woman, who tolerates her husband's oddities and loves her son without understanding him. Asuman fell in love with İdris and eloped when she was a teenager because he spoke well and was different; while the others discussed money, he noticed nature, the grass and the fields, an asset once now becoming an annoyance as years pass. All was well when he brought home the pay cheque, but things turned sour when he started gambling ('Women hero-worship and then blame men for failure', states Aydın in the previous film). She is proud of her son publishing a book to revive her fallen status among the neighbours (women wait for a man to exonerate them), but she will never read it. When Sinan leaves for the army, she stocks his books away provoking the father's sly remark that she does not like things that are not useful.[18] The third female, the sister, is disrespectful to the men in the house, spending most of her time watching television with her mother. The maternal grandmother (Özay Fetch), the wife of the imam, is the eyes, ears and brain of her ageing husband, but hardly significant in the narrative.

All women are passive in the film; they complain but do not act, perpetuating the tradition by their passivity. They exist in the shadows of men as wives, mothers, sisters or fiancées and make no effort to break the vicious circle. Their presence only contributes to the flow of the male narratives.

The Wild Pear Tree is open to Oedipal interpretations as much as *Three Monkeys* and both films have been decoded along these terms. The wish to kill the father and possess the mother takes several forms. After the son experiences the emotion of losing his father when he finds him lying still under the tree with a rope hanging over him, and the father dreams of his son hanging himself in the well, the denouement brings three generations of men – grandfather, father and son – under one roof, men without women, beside a well that does not have water: the missing element.

'Each of us is constituted politically in part by virtue of the social vulnerability of our bodies- as a site of desire and physical vulnerability at once assertive and exposed', Butler underlines, 'Loss and vulnerability seem to follow from our being socially constituted bodies, attached to others, at risk of losing those attachments, exposed to others, at risk of violence by virtue of that exposure' (2004: 20). *Climates* begins as crystals drop in close-up on the beautiful face of Bahar, and ends with Bahar's tears in addition to two instances of violent sobbing – the motorcycle episode in Kaş and the minibus episode in Ağrı. Except for Hacer in *Three Monkeys*, women bursting into tears – silent drops or hysterical outbursts – is a common sight in Ceylan's cinema, from the unnamed lover weeping in the toilet in *Distant* to the young wife Nihal in *Winter Sleep* throwing herself on the bed sobbing hysterically, indicating defencelessness, powerlessness or immaturity, a staple image in the commercial Yeşilçam melodramas, although the weeping women of Ceylan hardly create real melodrama. As characters distanced from the viewer, their tears barely induce empathy. The vulnerability of the women in Ceylan's films, that aspect which 'connects all human beings socially and politically' as Butler highlights, our 'shared vulnerability' that makes us 'physically dependent on one another, physically vulnerable to one another' (Ibid: 27) is as underdeveloped as their overall characters. On the other hand, vulnerability of the male characters appears as a regular signifier from Mahmut trapping his foot on the sticky band he sets up for the mouse in *Distant*; İsa's repeated tumbling in *Climates*; the machismo-match dialogues in both *Climates* and *Anatolia*; Hidayet, the sidekick of Aydın doing a Chaplinesque skidding number on ice at the train station; the unwelcome guest imam sitting in Aydın's eerie office wearing woman's slippers offered by the house-keeper; the drunk schoolteacher making a fool of himself in front of his socially superior elders and Aydın looking pathetic during the rabbit hunt with one sock missing are some of the prominent examples.

Ceylan presents a society on the threshold of modernity suffering from the erosion of traditional cultural values. His texts are open-ended and polysemic and include 'intertextual slippages' (Fiske 1987). Their discursive proficiency creates polysemic audiences. In terms of the presentations of women, however, his point of view remains traditional and does not necessarily reflect the women of Turkey today. In a society where hard earned social and cultural values of the Republic have been eroding, sanctioned and encouraged by authoritarian governments that favour cutting forests and destroying the cultural heritage to make room for shopping malls and gated communities, Hatices of this world may choose ageing jewellers over young and penniless admirers. On the other hand, women who fight the system exist, women who take active roles in their destiny, not only in the metropolises but also in remote corners of the country. They have yet to appear in the films of Nuri Bilge Ceylan, contemporary Turkey's most accomplished filmmaker.

NOTES

1. Sections of this chapter were originally published under the title 'His Films: Abbas Kiarostami and Nuri Bilge Ceylan' in Gönül Dönmez-Colin (2019) and thoroughly revised, updated and expanded for this volume with kind permission from Joe Whiting, the editor at Routledge.
2. In *Three Monkeys*, the spectre of the son drowned under undisclosed circumstances appears to the two males but not Hacer (absent signifier). Ceylan explained during an interview that he wanted the dead son to appear to those who felt a sense of guilt and 'women, instead of accepting guilt are often capable of transferring it to someone else' (Yücel 2008: 22–30).

3. A feminist novel by journalist/activist Duygu Asena (1946-2006), *Kadının Adı Yok / Woman Has No Name* (1987) was published during the second feminist wave in Turkey and translated into several languages. After becoming a best-seller, it was banned for obscenity. In 1988, Atıf Yılmaz Batıbeki turned it into an eponymous film (Dönmez-Colin 2004, 2014).
 4. Men also have their share of symbolic/Biblical names. See: Ayhan Eralp, 'Kış Uykusu Filminde Karakter İsimlerinin Çağırdığı Manalar', *Tüş ve Düşünce Dergisi*, 84–90. http://www.nuribilgeceylan.com/movies/wintersleep/press-tusvedusunce.pdf (last accessed 21 Jan 2022)
 5. According to Turkish government statistics, women made up 29.2 per cent of the work force in 2021. The percentage was much higher for educated women. Ceylan's producer for several films, Zeynep Atakan, is a woman. His wife Ebru Ceylan is active in the film industry and has collaborated on the scripts of several of his films.
 6. For more on how 'higher senses' are associated with men and 'lower senses' to women, see, *Ways of Sensing: Understanding the Senses in Society* (Howes and Classen 2014).
 7. For more on Mahmut's character, see the first chapter of the volume by Dönmez-Colin.
 8. A common trope which evokes, among other films, Wong Kar-wai's *Fa yeung nin Wah/In the Mood For Love* (2000) when Chow visits the ruins of Angkor Wat in Cambodia.
 9. Zeki Demirkubuz, along with Ceylan, is one of the pioneers of a movement in the 1990s, the New Turkish Cinema which came to be recognised today as the New Cinema of Turkey.
10. Favouring distanciation over identification is also part of the aesthetics of slow cinema, which, according to Schrader 'push[es] the viewer away from the "experience", from immediate emotional involvement . . . Slow cinema is passive aggression par excellence' (Schrader 2018). Regarding Ceylan's films as slow cinema, see Çağlayan (2018).
11. Ceylan uses the trope of snowflakes that he had employed in his early films to the fullest in *Winter Sleep* to convey Aydın's state of mind.
12. Made during a period of marital turbulence in Kiarostami's life and political turbulence in Iran, the film follows four to five days in the life of a minor civil servant at the Ministry of Finance. A married man and father of a small child, Mohammad is a nihilist, indifferent to material nitty-gritty of life. Following a violent confrontation, his wife attempts suicide. He spends the night with her at the hospital. When the day breaks and she begins to recover, he leaves (Dönmez-Colin 2019).
13. According to Judith Butler, 'trouble' at times euphemises some 'fundamentally mysterious problem usually related to the alleged mystery of all things feminine' (1999).
14. Silverman defines 'dominant fiction' as 'fiction' underscoring the imaginary rather than the delusory nature of ideology, while 'dominant' isolating 'from the whole repertoire of a culture's images, sounds, and narrative elaborations those through which the conventional subject is psychically aligned with the symbolic order . . .', borrowing from Rancière who considers a society's ideological 'reality' as its 'dominant fiction', which represents a category for theorising hegemony, 'the privileged mode of representation by which the image of the social consensus is offered to the members of a social formation and within which they are asked to identify themselves' (Rancière 1977: 28 quoted in Silverman 1992: 30).
15. Sons are ambivalent to the affairs of mothers in the contemporary cinema of Turkey. İbrahim comes home unexpectedly, hears his mother laughing and puts his eye to the keyhole of her bedroom. Devastated by what he has seen, his eye catches the kitchen knife. In *Süt/Milk* (Semih Kaplanoğlu, 2007), Yusuf, carrying a large stone, trails his mother's lover near the lake with thoughts of murder. Distracted by a fish, he chooses to compete for her love by offering it to her. İsmail plays the three monkeys, but later slaps his mother (Dönmez-Colin 2014).

16. The subheading borrows from the Tennessee Williams play, 'I Rise in Flame, Cried the Phoenix' (1951).
17. Some studies guided by colour-in-context theories and the effects of red on impressions related to sexual intent, attractiveness, dominance and competence argue that a woman wearing red is considered more sexually receptive, to have greater sexual intent and even low sexual fidelity. She is also considered as self-objectifying regarding her body image (Johnson, Lennon and Rudd 2014). Such attributes have been the staple clichés of cinema since its inception. Ceylan's coding of red, however, could also be related to the colour's association with power and strength, a threat to man's vulnerability (See Dönmez-Colin 2010: 88).
18. Why did İdris marry her? Unlike Asuman's motivation for marrying him, which the script exploits cleverly to embellish the character sketch of İdris, his motivation, which could have served a similar purpose, is absent.

CITED WORKS

Arslan, Savaş (2011), *Cinema in Turkey: A New Critical History*. New York: Oxford University Press.
Atam, Zahit (2011), *Yakın Plan Yeni Türkiye Sineması: Dört Kurucu Yönetmen: Nuri Bilge Ceylan, Yeşim Ustaoğlu, Zeki Demirkubuz, Derviş Zaimoğlu*. Istanbul: Cadde.
Butler, Judith (2004), *Precarious Life: The Power of Mourning and Violence*. New York: Verso.
____ (1999) *Gender Trouble: Feminism and the Subversion of Identity*. London and New York: Routledge.
Çağlayan, Emre (2020), 'Stalkers of Istanbul: Silence, Urban Space and Damaged Masculinity in Nuri Bilge Ceylan's *Distant*, *Quarterly Review of Film and Video*, 39:2, 323–40.
Çağlayan, Emre (2018), *Poetics of Slow Cinema: Nostalgia, Absurdism, Boredom*. Basingstoke: Palgrave Macmillan.
Chakravarty, Sumita S. (2003), 'The Erotics of History: Gender and Transgression in the New Asian Cinemas', in Antony R. Guneratne and Wimal Dissanayake (eds), *Rethinking Third Cinema*. New York and London: Routledge, 79–99.
Diken, Bülent, Graeme Gilloch and Craig Hammond (2018), *The Cinema of Nuri Bilge Ceylan: The Global Vision of a Turkish Filmmaker*. London and New York: I.B. Tauris.
Dönmez-Colin, Gönül (2019), *Women in the Cinemas of Iran and Turkey: as Images and as Image-makers*. London and New York: Routledge.
____ (2014), *The Routledge Dictionary of Turkish Cinema*. London and New York: Routledge.
____ (2010), 'Women in Turkish Cinema: Their Presence and Absence as Images and as Image-makers', *Cinema in Muslim Societies*, Ali Nobil Ahmad (ed.), *Third Text*, 24/1, London and New York: Routledge, 91–105.
____ (2008), *Turkish Cinema: Identity, Distance and Belonging*. London: Reaktion Books.
____ (2004), *Women, Islam and Cinema*. London: Reaktion Books.
Fiske, John (1987), *Television Culture: Popular Pleasures and Politics*. London: Methuen.
Forter, Greg (2011), *Melancholy Manhood: Gender, Race, and the Inability to Mourn in American Literary Modernism*. Cambridge: Cambridge University Press.
Haskell, Molly (1973/1987), *From Reverence to Rape: The Treatment of Women in the Movies*. Chicago and London: The University of Chicago Press, 1987 (revised edition; orig. 1973).
Howes, David and Constance Classen (2014), *Ways of Sensing: Understanding the Senses in Society*. London and New York: Routledge.
Johnson, Kim, Sharron J. Lennon and Nancy Rudd (2014), 'Dress, body and self: research in the social psychology of dress', *Fashion and Textiles*, 1: 20.

Johnston, Claire, (1973/1991), 'Women's Cinema as Counter-Cinema', *Notes on Women's Cinema*. SEFT, Glasgow: Screen Reprint, 24–31.
Kaplan, E. Ann (1990), *Psychoanalysis & Cinema*. London: Routledge.
Mulvey, Laura (1975), 'Visual Pleasure and Narrative Cinema', Screen 16/3, Autumn, 6–18.
Orban, Clara (2001), 'Antonioni's Women, Lost in the City'. *Modern Language Studies.* 31.2, 11–27.
Özdemir, Ece (2009), 'Üç Maymunda Kadın Temsili', *Sekans Dergisi, Sinema Yazıları Seçkisi*. http://www.nbcfilm.com/3maymun/press-sekansece.php (last accessed 16 December 2018 – no longer available)
Özgüven, Fatih (2006), 'Hava serin, iklim aynı', *Radikal*. http://www.radikal.com.tr/haber.php?haberno=202686 (last accessed 28 May 2022).
Pajaczkowska, Claire and Ivan Ward (eds) (2008), *Shame and Sexuality: Psychoanalysis and Visual Culture*. London and New York: Routledge.
Rancière, Jacques (1977), 'Interview: The Image of Brotherhood', trans. Kari Hanet, *Edinburgh Magazine*, 2: 28.
Rosen, M. (1973), *Popcorn Venus: Women, Movies and the American Dream*. New York: Avon.
Rotundo, Anthony (1993), *American Manhood: Transformations in Masculinity from the Revolution to the Modern Era*. New York: Basic Books.
Samini, Naghmeh (2016), 'Feminine Body, Feminine Mind; The Body of Woman in Iranian Woman Directors' Films', Lecture at Stanford Iranian Studies Program, January 13, 2015, published 28 September 2016. www.youtube.com/watch?v=rSBQWxBetMw (last accessed 9 June 2022).
Schrader, Paul (2018), *Transcendental Style in Film: Ozu, Bresson, Dreyer. Oakland:* University of California Press.
Silverman, Kaja (1992), *Male Subjectivity at the Margins*. New York and London: Routledge.
Smelik, Anneke (1998), *And the Mirror Cracked: Feminist Cinema and Film Theory*. London: Macmillan.
Suner, Asuman (2010), *The New Turkish Cinema: Belonging, Identity and Memory*. London and New York: I.B. Tauris.
Tekeli, Şirin (1995), *Women in Modern Turkish Society*. London: Zed Books.

CHAPTER ELEVEN

Auteurism, Recognition and Reception: Ceylan as a Global Auteur

Özgür Yaren

Auteur theory and the very concept of the auteur have long lost their pertinence in the academia. Film studies scholarship today focuses more on reception and spectatorship and tends to conceive of films, whether labelled as artworks or popular cultural products, more as the products of social and political context than the individual 'craftsmanship' of the directors/producers. Nevertheless, auteurs, as well as the term itself, seem to endure paradigmatic theoretical shifts. Having accomplished becoming simultaneously a transnational filmmaker and a part of the national film canon, despite the different and sometimes conflicting requirements of each role, Nuri Bilge Ceylan personifies what auteur – or global auteur – means today. To understand how Ceylan has secured his position in the complex and precarious map of competing value systems, we need to explore contemporary auteurism and the tensions between different modes of artistic recognition in global and national contexts.

For *Cahiers du Cinema*'s young critics of the late 1950s, and Andrew Sarris, who transposed the French term to Anglo-Saxon film criticism in the early 1960s, auteur was a rank reserved exclusively for those offbeat filmmakers who assumedly contended to create genuine, individual work despite the forbidding unifying codes of studios and genre conventions. These bona fide filmmakers were striving for greater authority and control over their films. Decades after auteur theory lost its relevance, the term auteur could no longer maintain its original meaning, only to find a new one that encompasses a remarkably larger group of filmmakers, and in most cases producer-directors. Unlike many of their counterparts who worked in the heyday of the Hollywood studios and sought a way to deliver individual artistic expression while on the studio payroll, new auteurs are independent – in the sense of precariousness – and unavoidably multitasking filmmakers. They write, direct and produce (seeking funds and making co-production deals through their own companies, which are dedicated to producing their films only), thus nominally have full control over every level of production, thanks to their artisanal production mode. The *politique des auteurs* in this new global environment is also quite different from the young film critic Truffaut's brawling days when a generation of director-to-be critics was contesting the established field of art cinema, its production mode, the film industry, the evaluation circles and the dominant politics of evaluation. The *Cahier*'s auteurism was launched as part of a battle plan for reforming the French film industry to allow control of filmmaking by the worker (Staiger 1985: 12). Above that, they were rebelling against *le cinéma de papa* and its outdated aesthetic qualities.

This setting is in deep contrast with the global age, where 'auteurism has been completely institutionalised in film archives, mass media, festival circuits, academic curriculum and even commercial theatres, to the extent that paradoxically it no longer triggers noteworthy polemics once a director has been recognised and granted authorship' (Jeong 2016: 4). This dramatic drift is a sign that although the term auteur is still in use, its shape and scale have changed drastically. Therefore, it makes sense to designate today's auteur filmmakers as 'global auteurs' since their status is granted by a global network, unanimously within the chain of hierarchy, from major European film festivals (none more so than Cannes) to lesser international film festivals around the globe.

However, the totality of the global age's established art field, its aesthetic references (in short, modernist European cinema) and its mechanisms of validation and recognition could be limiting in terms of artistic expression. Hence, the redefined, extended idea of the auteur is far from being independent, let alone 'offbeat'. In other words, the determining power of the framework of festivals and the global market paradoxically limit the auteur's freedom, even as they grant authorial brand to filmmakers. This brings back the constituent problem of the auteur as an idealised artist, struggling to have maximum control over their works and to claim their individual means of expression against all industrial and structural constraints. For many critics, the dependency of the art house filmmakers (particularly in non-western cultures) on the global market and the film festivals forces them to adjust to the expectations of such and to provide an 'exoticism either in the form of gritty realism or picturesque squalor' (Elsaesser 2016: 26) or a political statement aligned with global, neoliberal values. This obligation however has many filmmakers facing a dilemma since the domestic audience is very susceptible to 'self-exoticizing visual gestures' (Chow 1995: 171), judging them as a lack of authenticity. Prominent Turkish film critic Onat Kutlar once famously told a panel that he and his close circle of critics hastily baptised rural stories of late 1970s Yeşilçam as 'Young Cinema' while these films looked like 'kilim' (handwoven Turkish rugs) (Kuzu 2021). Kutlar's pun, likening the word 'film' to 'kilim' ('film' is generally pronounced as 'filim' in Turkish), wittily sums up what Chow calls self-exoticism (1995: 171). In addition, filmmakers from illiberal countries such as Iran, China and Turkey have a political dilemma which Elsaesser defines as serving at least two masters, or 'double occupancy': 'a government exerting censorship, versus the international film festival whose director expects dissidence and resistance' (2016: 26–7).

If we name the complex mechanisms which define hierarchical boundaries within a cultural field and validate a particular cultural form by elevating it to the status of 'art' as 'cultural legitimation' (Baumann 2001), this double occupancy is a clear token of the tension between its different modes in global and national contexts. French sociologist Pierre Bourdieu suggests that cultural legitimation has three primary forms: a 'specific' legitimacy which is maintained by other cultural producers, a 'bourgeois' legitimacy, granted by agents and institutions of the dominant class and a 'popular' legitimacy based on public acclaim (1993: 50–1). Bearing in mind that Bourdieu's theory of social fields, which explains the institutions, the processes of evaluation and mechanisms of legitimation and recognition, was developed strictly in and for the French national context, one can cautiously try to use it to understand the working principles of different contexts (Mangez and Liénard 2015: 184). That is what Allen and Lincoln (2004) did when they successfully adopted the forms of cultural legitimation to the field of film and introduced three main types of recognition: professional, critical and popular. Accordingly, film festivals and awards are specific institutions where the professional recognition of a film and a filmmaker is bestowed by other artists and filmmakers. Critics and film scholars are discernibly the main agents for the critical recognition of films. Audience attendance and box office figures as reliable statistical indicators represent popular recognition, and thus the legitimacy of films as cultural products (2004: 879–80).

The most common tension within the film field obviously stems from the distinction between commercial cinema and art cinema, where diverse types of recognition typically contradict each other. As it would be difficult for a commercial film to gain critical recognition, an art house film attracting popular recognition is equally rare. Moreover, the three types of recognition mentioned earlier rarely an overlap. Nevertheless, there is an ongoing trend challenging the hierarchies in the cultural field, blurring the distinction between highbrow and lowbrow cultural products. Wider cultural trends influence and complicate the film field by altering established classifications (Yaren and Hazır 2020). Mutual hybridisation of mainstream and art house films (Andrews 2013: xi; Drake 2008) and growingly eclectic, broadening cultural repertoires of audiences further complicate classical distinctions within the film field (Barnett and Allen 2000: 145). The tension between different modes of artistic recognition in global and national contexts is particularly important in the case of global auteurs.

AUTEURISM, RECOGNITION AND RECEPTION 189

Since it is hard to please separate sets of expectations at once and virtually impossible in certain national contexts when discrepancies are too distinct to reconcile, filmmakers with an art house agenda tend to choose one over the other, usually preferring international festival audiences to domestic filmgoers. Three Turkish filmmakers who began their careers in the 1990s, Zeki Demirkubuz, Yeşim Ustaoğlu and Nuri Bilge Ceylan, have demonstrated different strategies for coping with this problem. Demirkubuz has opted for a domestic audience later in his career and ceased to seek international acclaim for his homespun dramas. Ustaoğlu has gone in the opposite direction by targeting national and international festival audiences to tackle political themes and the questions of history, identity and patriarchy in Turkey. Ceylan, however, has succeeded to be an exception not only in Turkey, but among art house filmmakers of the same generation globally in terms of vanquishing the constraints of the word auteur, holding control of his films and exhibiting defiance if not contravening global and domestic expectations regarding his works.

RECOGNITION

Ceylan's film career initially affirmed the distinction and the artistic hierarchy with clearly defined boundaries: an art house filmmaker committed to the European art cinema tradition who has targeted festival audiences over domestic popular audiences (Erdem 1997). He found some ground at Cannes with his debut short film *Koza/Cocoon* (1995). His early feature films, *Kasaba/The Small Town* (1997), *Mayıs Sıkıntısı/Clouds of May* (1999) and *Uzak/Distant* (2002) were entirely independent, low-budget national productions. They were loosely interconnected by strong autobiographical elements, and shared a common style with certain aesthetic strategies that would later come to be associated with Ceylan as an auteur. The minimalist, slow, image-oriented stylistic preferences were on a par with or even obligated by this production mode.

Distant was the last of Ceylan's early films that were the output of a certain amateur artisanal production mode (Çağlayan 2018: 215). Before the professionalism and division of labour steps in, this mode of production allows the director to hold full control of his work, not for creative preferences alone – for being a resolute filmmaker, not wanting to surrender control of any aspects – but due to financial constraints as well. In the 2000s, there were still no producers in Turkey willing to invest in art-house films, nor were there banks ready to lend money to film producers, which resulted in some directors establishing their own production companies to apply for national and international film support funds (Zıraman 2018: 78). 'When I interviewed Nuri Bilge Ceylan in Cannes last year, the Turkish director was personable but clearly tired', wrote Jonathan Romney in *Sight & Sound*, 'having spent the previous few days selling his film (that is, selling not as in talking up his work on the interview circuit, but as in being his own sales agent). Ceylan is about as hands-on as a filmmaker can be, financing his own features, photographing them himself, casting friends and family, drawing inspiration from his life' (Romney 2004: 20).

The international recognition of *Distant* drastically changed Ceylan's production mode and film style as well as his career as a filmmaker. The film won the Grand Jury and the Best Actor prizes (shared by Muzaffer Özdemir and Mehmet Emin Toprak, who lost his life in a road accident soon after the completion of the film) at the 2003 Cannes Film Festival, and this marked a turning point for Ceylan: marking him exclusively as a Cannes director. All his films from then on premiered at Cannes, where he has continued to receive major awards, as well as becoming a jury member. The recognition of *Distant* provided by Cannes gave Ceylan stupendous critical recognition in leading newspapers and journals from Europe, North America and Asia, of which many examples are proudly presented on the film's press page on the web. The initial success at Cannes was followed by more awards within the global festival network from New Delhi, Manila, Mexico City, Beirut, Singapore and several other film festivals, making *Distant* a showcase in demonstrating how film festival circuits work today. The *New York Times* critic Elvis Mitchell admitted *Distant* did not initially catch his attention and only after a second viewing that he would appreciate 'the minimalist scale of the Turkish comedy-melodrama, which received the Grand Jury prize at this year's Cannes International Film Festival (admittedly, not always an indicator of worthiness)' (2003). Mitchell's initial reluctance towards an unanimously praised work of art here is linked with his scepticism of Cannes as a viable institute of evaluation in a world where film festivals are not a European privilege but are spread all over the world. However, the multitude of dots on film festival maps did not much change the fact that 'very few of the world's many festivals, with Cannes (and France) are still the decisive place for authenticating internationally recognised auteurs' (Elsaesser 2016: 24).

After the successful international recognition of *Distant*, which sold some sixty-thousand tickets in Turkey, but found an audience roughly three times larger in France,[1] Ceylan changed production mode by leaving his previously minimalistic artisanal mode and venturing financially into the European film universe. He started to collaborate with the producer Zeynep Özbatur Atakan and found European co-producers. Despite these efforts, his domestic reception remained limited to art-house audiences. *İklimler/The Climates* (2006), which received the FIPRESCI (The International Federation of Film Critics) prize at Cannes with overwhelming critical acclaim, was the peak of this divide, establishing Ceylan as a clear-cut international festival auteur who does not address the domestic audience, very much like Abbas Kiarostami (Zeydabadi-Nejad 2007: 391), Apichatpong Weerasethakul (Barrington 2014) or Hou Hsiao-hsien (Wei 2008: 274). *The Climates*' humble domestic box office revenues were challenged in North America, surpassed in the UK, and quadrupled in France.[2] Ceylan was gaining an iconographic significance so far that his authorial brand made it into the Coen Brothers' short film *World Cinema*, part of an anthology called *Chacun son cinema/To Each His Own Cinema* (2017), commissioned by the Cannes Film Festival to celebrate its 60th anniversary. The film features a Midwestern cowboy hesitantly watching *The Climates* in a desolate film theatre in the middle of nowhere and finding something in it for himself. Availability in a remote Midwest American town and intelligibility by simple folk signifies the global outreach of cinema (and Cannes) as well as marking Ceylan as a growing global auteur.

The divide between domestic and international audiences dissolved only after Ceylan secured his position in the European art house film production habitat, thanks to the prestige he obtained at Cannes and other film festivals. A complex collaboration with multiple national and international co-producers (French Pyramide, Italian BIM, and Turkish Imaj) facilitated access to public funds (French *Centre national du cinema*, Council of Europe's Eurimages and Turkish Ministry of Culture in this case) and distribution deals, which in turn enabled higher budget projects. This shift in the mode of production had an apparent impact on Ceylan's style. With a budget of 1.8 million euros (Lemercier 2008), he could now venture into more complex stories that were not entirely shy of genre cinema, and he could collaborate with professional actors and celebrities who could appeal to both international and domestic audiences. In addition to bearing Ceylan's powerful authorial mark, *Üç Maymun/Three Monkeys* (2008) was familiar to the domestic audience with its family drama narrative and the leading actor Yavuz Bingöl, a famous folk singer. Not only did Ceylan receive the Best Director prize at the Cannes Film Festival (2008) and two dozen awards that followed it, but the film also attracted a greater audience in the domestic market than in the rest of the world.[3]

Some critics attributed this unexpected domestic attention to Ceylan's acceptance speech at Cannes, in which he dedicated the award to his 'lonely and beautiful country' that he loves passionately. According to Suner, this statement was later incorporated into the nationalist discourse (2011: 24), and hence fervently commended by the mainstream media which is heavily under the influence of the present Recep Tayyip Erdoğan's government with 'native and national' credentials. Ceylan's statement and its public reception was particularly striking when compared to the case of Orhan Pamuk, who had been awarded the Nobel Prize for Literature two years prior to Ceylan's major international success. Being the first of its kind in the history of Turkey, Pamuk's achievement was then commonly linked with his earlier interview in a Swiss magazine, where he had stated 'a million Armenians and 30,000 Kurds were killed in this country and I'm the only one who dares to talk about it.'[4] After that interview a feverish campaign branded Pamuk a traitor, which led to official charges against him for 'public denigration of Turkish identity' and forced him to exile. For nationalist torchbearers, Pamuk's Nobel Prize did not come for his literary genuineness but for selling out his country. Predictably, Pamuk's conviction in the political field has permeated literary discussions and inflated claims that Pamuk's prose is stilted and halting, his knowledge of Turkish culture flawed, and the biggest of all literary crimes in a national context, that he targets foreign rather than domestic readers.

The dramatic contrast between the receptions of Pamuk and Ceylan demonstrates the tension between national and international expectations. International recognition can be discordant with the national context in societies where the field of culture and art is not autonomous – that is, not run by its own rules – but heavily under the influence of the political field. Accordingly, domestic critics may argue that works of art may be mistakenly appraised in international circles of evaluation despite their inability to represent society and despite their flaws that only natives can spot. Ascribing a certain level of naïveté to international audiences usually accompanies the unjust assumption that the artist has ulterior, malevolent motives and animosity towards their country. Writing on the films of Jafar Panahi, Mohsen Makhmalbaf and Abbas Kiarostami, internationally renowned Iranian filmmakers who fail to reach a domestic audience, Zeydabadi-Nejad underlines the 'allegations . . . that they show "backwardness, poverty and negative images of Iranian society" which conform to the stereotype of the country, and that is why they are popular at festivals' (Zeydabadi-Nejad 2007: 391). Ceylan's acceptance speech has helped to extend his scope to encompass a general domestic audience by warding off nationalist scepticism over international recognition. Moreover, a widened scope can give a global auteur more autonomy from international expectations which would potentially limit his creativity.

Ceylan's following film, *Bir Zamanlar Anadolu'da/Once Upon a Time in Anatolia* (2011) was another turning point for him. Finally, he found a way to skilfully perform 'double occupancy' as a global auteur and a prominent filmmaker in the domestic market and appealed to festival goers and general audiences alike. *Anatolia* followed a similar path as *Three Monkeys*. It combined a refreshed execution of Ceylan's auteur style with a film-noir-like plot and a Western-like setting, while starring Yılmaz Erdoğan, a popular comedian/actor and one of the most successful commercial filmmakers in Turkey. Collaboration with several national production and post-production companies including the public *Turkish Radio & Television* (TRT) and inclusion of a European co-producer (from Bosnia Herzegovina) to fulfil the requirements for Eurimages (European Cinema support Fund of the Council of Europe) co-production support resulted in a relatively high budget film, which shared the jury's Grand Prix with the Dardennes brothers' *The Kid with a Bike* (2011) at

Cannes and, despite its two-hour thirty-seven-minute length, found a slightly larger audience in its native Turkey than in France.[5]

Ceylan's global auteur brand has provided him multiple co-production deals and easy access to all available major public funds both in Turkey and in Europe. His later films with higher budgets are rare exceptions to the independent/art house category. During a briefing after the screening of *Anatolia*, he did not hide his own astonishment at the rate of growing budgets with his every new film:

> Film crews getting more crowded with each new production worries me as well. At first, I was working with a crew of 5-6 people. My latest films have had exceedingly crowded crews. I wonder whether I write more daring scripts now. Is that what happens when you have a bigger budget? . . . Of course, night shootings forced us to have a bigger crew. We were setting up the film set like Las Vegas in the middle of the night. Long-haul trucks, trailers, vehicles . . . Naturally, it is not cheap. Imagine buying meals for all those people.[6]

Including the Eurimages fund of 330,000 euros, the budget of *Anatolia* did not exceed 1.9 million euros. The following film, *Kış Uykusu/Winter Sleep* (2014) would cost three million euros.[7] The public funds alone received for *Ahlat Ağacı/The Wild Pear Tree* (2018) from German Meidenboard, Eurimages[8] and the Turkish Ministry of Culture[9] amounted to one million euros in total. Ceylan's latest film *Kuru Otlar Üstüne/About Dry Grasses* in production during 2022, secured the same amount in Eurimages and Ministry of Culture funding.[10] Thus, his production budgets have surpassed the median average budget of a European theatrical fiction film, commercial or art house, which was roughly two million euros in 2017 (Kanzler 2019).

In *Winter Sleep*, Ceylan drastically altered his authorial mark and added new tools to his toolbox. Like other filmmakers of the contemporary cinema of Turkey such as Zeki Demirkubuz and Semih Kaplanoğlu, he has shown interest in nineteenth-century Russian literature earlier in his career which corresponds to the literary public's familiarity and fascination with the Russian writers of this époque. An irresolute national identity, a complex relationship with the Western modernity and the focus on the suffering of the intellectuals straddling redemptive ideals and despairing reality provide a common ground wide enough to deem nineteenth-century Russian literature relevant for contemporary Turkish readers and filmmakers. Yet *Winter Sleep* is not only inspired by or loosely adapted from stories of Chekhov but kicks off with the main plot point of *The Cherry Orchard* (1903) and adapts, almost line for line, several key scenes from Chekhov's short stories *Excellent People* (1886) and *The Wife* (1892) (Mathew 2019: 13). It was a risky strategy since Chekhov's conversations brought into this three hour sixteen-minute-long talk-heavy film were 'literary dialogues that compel a filmgoing audience to think in real time about what concepts like "non-resistance to evil" might mean, or how altruism might only benefit the person doing the giving' (Mathew 2019: 22). Despite these challenging aspects, *Winter Sleep*, set in Cappadocia with outstanding cinematography and popular actors, appealed to a wide range of audiences and gained critical, professional and popular recognition at the same time. The film received the Palme d'Or at Cannes, and it has reached 360,000 admissions in France alone, while its gross world box office receipts exceeded four million USD.[11]

The Wild Pear Tree was not as successful as Ceylan's earlier films outside of Turkey. It was the first Ceylan film that returned from Cannes empty handed. Its overall recognition at the world film festivals has also remained limited. It is tempting to attribute the lukewarm reception of *The Wild Pear Tree* in the film festival circuit to its preceding failure at Cannes considering the power of Cannes in determining the global reception of films. However, the critical and popular recognition of the film in Turkey was positive. It won all major categories at the Turkish Film Critics Association 2018 Awards and got a quarter of a million admissions in the domestic market.[12]

RECEPTION

Ceylan's filmography is marked by co-productions with European producers, European public funds and a perpetual professional recognition by Cannes and other film festivals. As of today, despite his increasing domestic popularity, Ceylan's overall box office gross has been bigger in France than in his native Turkey. His reception by critics and film scholars also confirms that Ceylan's works are considered 'in the context of classical European thought, literature and films' and are the products of a transnational imagination (Diken *et al.* 2020: 18).

This is not surprising considering how Ceylan has carefully kept referring to major auteurs of modernist art cinema (while leaning on nineteenth-century Russian literature and accommodating classical music into his film scores). For Jeung, rather than playful gestures, references to modern auteurs should be read as a marker of some significance, moral or otherwise, and for this reason, Ceylan's reverent nods seem like symptoms of global capitalism rather than a resistance to it (Jeung 2016: 11). Either way, the reasoning behind positioning Ceylan's work within the European cinema primarily relies on the dichotomy of Hollywood and European cinema and their differences in production mode and storytelling (Deslandes and Maixent 2011). Turkey's political approximation towards the EU in the first decade of the AKP government, which came to power in 2002, also enabled the reception of Ceylan as a European director. Ceylan's films were coming from the film culture of an aspiring European country. This film culture was operating in a European (non-Hollywood) manner with its two prominent production modes: commercial cinema in tandem with independent/art house. In Turkey, commercial cinema has never lost the muscle memory of Yeşilçam (the Turkish equivalent of Hollywood) which provided a robust domestic cinema with its own aesthetics, unique production mode and formulaic low-quality film production from the late 1950s to 1980. It is the continuation of this film culture in which Ceylan configured his style in opposition to a snappy, vivid commercial cinema, producing genre films, low-brow comedies, melodramas, historical fantasies (swords and shields) surpassing mighty Hollywood productions and producing the biggest domestic box office revenues in Europe. The same film culture also housed a stream of independent films which flourished in the late 1990s, avidly baptised with the generic title of 'New Turkish Cinema', and created consistency in modes of production, funding and exhibition, if not in terms of aesthetics (apart from the common denominators of modernist cinema: minimalism, slowness, subordination of plot).[13]

Ceylan was one of the pioneers of the 'New Turkish Cinema', along with Derviş Zaim, Yeşim Ustaoğlu and Zeki Demirkubuz. Certain aspects of his film style, which form the unique auteur trademark, have ironically served as a framework for several young filmmakers who have been influenced by the auteur to imitate his style. Over time, his legacy has become so prominent that film critic Cem Erciyes underscored Ceylan's 'overcoat' referring to the expression often misattributed to Dostoyevsky: 'We all come out from Gogol's *Overcoat*' (Erciyes 2015).

It is worth mentioning that the public funding sources Ceylan has helped to create and continued to influence have streamlined independent Turkish cinema. First the Eurimages funds (since 1990), then the Turkish Ministry of Culture's feature film support (since 2005) and the various support schemes and awards offered by the film festivals, proved to be the lifeblood of a flourishing independent cinema in Turkey. It is also noteworthy that the appetite for supporting films with artistic merit came only after the international recognition of Ceylan and other filmmakers and the consequent soaring of the legitimacy of the field of cinema.

As Ceylan's production mode has changed, his style has also evolved from minimalist, universal and humanist narratives to complex and multi-layered stories, gradually making room for social commentary in the Turkish context. However, he has preserved the aspects of the film language that have been associated with him since the beginning. This consistent auteur quality, providing a contemplative spectator experience forms a fertile hypertextual ground for exploration and interpretation as it has changed the reception of his films. The critiques of his early films demonstrated a relative uniformity of themes to describe Ceylan films. *The Small Town* for instance was described by veteran film critic Atilla Dorsay as a simple and amateur film, 'in a good sense' (Dorsay 1997). For other critics, it was slow (Özgentürk 1998), documentary-like (Çapan 1997), unable to escape from monotony and boredom (Villalba 2014) and certainly not for everyone (Arslan 1997). Almost all the critics appraised the film for the ingredients which it did not contain: a tight story, spectacular effects and Hollywood pace, very much like consumers in search of natural products, reading labels marketing the excluded contents (gluten-free, paraben-free, silicon-free). These attributions did not change with his subsequent films. They were 'simple' (Lieb, 2009), 'slow' (Deslandes and Maixent 2012: 89) and 'boring' (Foundas 2014). Curiously, these remarks were not as disheartening as they sound. On the contrary, they were employed as a sign of a deep appreciation, a hard-won status to enjoy and a reminder of certain requirements and acquired taste. Then many critics would exert themselves to demonstrate how the slow rhythm serves the formalism, allowing the spectator to contemplate and thus place Ceylan next to major auteurs. Slow paced films with long, contemplative takes, stagnant countryside, idyllic mise-en-scene, and strong atmospheric effects were his authorial marks. Tufts of grass, tulle curtains or hair blowing in the wind, subtly implying a visual translation of the inner world of the characters were cinematographic and narrative qualities of Ceylan, who shared them with other auteurs such as Kiarostami, Hou Hsiao-hsien and Béla Tarr.

With *Anatolia*, critiques have begun to employ a richer variety of themes and interpretations. While comments on Ceylan's cinematographic and narrative qualities have remained, they began to be accompanied by thematic interpretations, or scrutinised for symbolism, allegories and hidden meanings. Various interpretations have suggested that *Anatolia* had several layers of philosophical and political meanings: The close-up of the murder suspect's face was reminiscent of a Byzantine religious icon (Kickasola 2016: 1); the film represented 'the difficulty of uncovering meaning and truth in a psychoanalytic process of coming to "know thyself"' (Dudai 2019: 1); it presented 'a pseudo journey after the knowledge (of death), where the things which are imperceptible for the ones who are imprisoned in the power of the knowledge appears momentarily' (Aytaç 2011: 30).

Ceylan's wry style and his self-absorbed, calculating characters who err, doubt and fail to communicate have led the critics to recognise universal themes about the flaws of the human nature, although Turkish critics have been finding national allegories in his later works. *Winter Sleep* and *The Wild Pear Tree* demonstrate an allegorical quality, particularly in terms of the configuration of the characters and the conflicts. In that sense, they resemble other films of the decade such as Emin Alper's *Tepenin Ardı/Beyond the Hill* (2012), Tolga Karaçelik's *Sarmaşık/Ivy*, (2015) and Berkun Oya's widely discussed TV series *Bir Başkadır/Ethos* (2020), which have provided allegorical stories taking place in familiar locales (a farm, a freighter) and presenting characters that belong to certain segments or ethnic groups of Turkish society. Although Ceylan's films are not as committed to their allegorical configuration as these latter titles, they are also eagerly recognised as an attempt for social commentary on contemporary Turkish society and its major fault lines.

Winter Sleep is embraced as 'an allegory of Turkey' (Liktor 2014) and 'a semi-political parable on contemporary Turkey' (Özgüven 2014). The critics see the cynical protagonist Aydın (whose name conveniently means 'intellectual' in Turkish) as a leftist intellectual who has been alienated from his own people after the 1980s (Kaya 2014), 'an affluent and pretentious republican bohemian' (Özgüven 2014), whose 'elitist and secular' attitude becomes evident in the way he patronises the local imam (Günerbüyük 2014). These allegorical readings rely on the now exhausted centre–periphery theory (Mardin 1973), which reads the modernisation of Turkey as a conflict between the secular elites of the Republic and the disfranchised traditional/religious lower classes.

While Ceylan's *The Wild Pear Tree* is not subjected to an all-out allegorical reading by the domestic critics, it has been praised for its precision in diagnosing the political tensions and maladies of 'The New Turkey' (Özgüven 2018; Baran 2018) – once a bold slogan of the two decades long rule of the Erdoğan government, reminiscent of the Philippines' notorious dictator Marcos's 'New Society'. The slogan was meant to demonstrate the economic and democratic progress of the country while hinting that the 'peripheral forces' have toppled oppressive elites of the secular republic to take over the power. Increasing disillusionment brought a new and ironic usage of the phrase 'New Turkey' corresponding to the decadence of the institutions and the parliamentary democracy, corruption, and clientelism. Local critics, whether or not they articulate the exact phrase, consider *The Wild Pear Tree* as a keen commentary on contemporary Turkish society (Özkaracalar 2018; Aydemir 2018; Açar 2018), an emphasis which has been largely absent in the international critiques of the film, which have concentrated on the universal themes – father–son conflict, returning home, an amateur writer's vain efforts for literary recognition – although a few have recognised the social commentary in such scenes as the telephone conversation between Sinan and his policeman friend about employment options, providing 'glimpses of a wider and more riven society' (Lane 2019).

This new aspect of Ceylan's films, a keen concern about the different segments of society, particularly evident in *Winter Sleep* and *The Wild Pear Tree*, has appealed to the Islamist/conservative intellectuals who could relate to his work on a political basis. *Winter Sleep*'s Aydın as a cartoon figure of the republican intellectual, alienated from his own people's culture and religion, led them to conclude that Ceylan's understanding of Turkish society corresponded to theirs (Karmaskalı 2020: 19). *The Wild Pear Tree*'s imams, who discuss theological and philosophical topics such as free will at length may not be novelty, reminding us of characters from the works of Bresson, Chekhov or Dostoyevsky, but they are novelty for Turkish cinema and palatable for the conservative audiences. Considering the Islamist government's declaration of war on 'cultural hegemony' and the widening cultural cleavage, Ceylan's ability to appeal to different segments of audience becomes significant.

CONCLUSION

The tensions in the film field regarding taste and legitimacy limit the overlap of diverse types of recognition. The components of the complex mechanism establishing which film should be elevated to the status of art, which will be affirmed as valuable, significant, banal or trivial, do not work in tandem. Festival awards and critics' standing ovations may not necessarily lead to the countenance of the audience. Furthermore, global and national contexts (particularly in the case of non-Western societies) create another fault line crossing these forms of recognition. Simultaneously holding the roles of global auteur and national cinema figure is a delicate task given the tension between clashing expectations for a universalist humanist storyteller and a national figure whose films are under pressure of being read as either national allegories or political manifestations.

Affirming these tensions, Ceylan initially gained success in the global festival circles but failed at the box office. As a successful Cannes director his reputation overflowed the confines of the film festivals and reached a wider audience as in France, where he gained considerable box office success. In recent years, his domestic popularity has improved as well, while he beat the odds to become part of the national cultural canon despite the highly polarised and politicised cultural field of contemporary Turkey. Social commentary in his latest films, an aspect generally missed by the foreign media, resulted in augmenting the positive reaction of the local audiences. Casting well-known actors also played a role in attracting larger audiences who would otherwise hesitate to leave the mainstream for an art-house film.

Attracting various parties could be possible with an exceptional autonomy, which is a luxury only true global auteurs can enjoy. Ceylan's reputation has led to a diversification of resources and funds, both global and national, which in turn has saved him from dependency on the specific expectations of the global festival directors or national film fund managers. He has successfully used his autonomy to build a very personal variation of a modernist and minimalist cinema, which is open ended, multi-layered, ambiguous and apolitical at first sight. Overcoming the contemporary constraints of the autonomy of the filmmaker, Ceylan has succeeded in becoming an auteur in the original sense of the term, while coping with the requirements of the global film industry.

This is a success story, but while Ceylan – if we eavesdrop on the rumours in filmmaking circles – unwillingly influences the younger generation of filmmakers with his distinct auteur style, he would hardly make a practical model for future auteurs, for many reasons. As populism and a new surge of authoritarianism is on the rise, nation states are consolidating themselves against global and neoliberal trends. In a post-Covid world, borders are restricted, even international travel is severely limited. The gap between the global and the national widens. The film industry and its global community is not safe from these overwhelming affairs. It is harder now than at any time to be approved as a global auteur who can simultaneously link their works with an overarching tradition of modernist cinema while building an authentic auteur brand. It is equally difficult to be part of the national film canon by gaining unanimous recognition, taking a moral stance and being critical without catching heat from political power, which can sever public funds. It takes a juggler's precision.

Table 11.1 Admissions in France and Turkey[14]

Title/Year	Admissions FRANCE	Admissions TURKEY
Clouds of May (1999)	11,746	24,006
Distant (2002)	153,092	63,845
Climates (2006)	132,738	35,345
Three Monkeys (2008)	47,307	127,668
Once Upon a Time in Anatolia (2011)	137,720	161,181
Winter Sleep (2014)	360,000	304,782
The Wild Pear Tree (2018)	125,400	246,766

NOTES

1. See Table: Admissions in France & Turkey.
2. Figures are provided by *IMDbPro* https://pro.imdb.com/signup/index.html?u=https%3A%2F%2Fpro.imdb.com%2F (last accessed 1 August 2021).
3. Figures are provided by *IMDbPro* https://pro.imdb.com/signup/index.html?u=https%3A%2F%2Fpro.imdb.com%2F (last accessed 1 August 2021).
4. See https://www.theguardian.com/world/2005/oct/23/books.turkey (last accessed 1 October 2021).
5. See Table: Admissions in France & Turkey.
6. Translation by the author. See 'Nuri Bilge Ceylan ile 90 dakika' https://www.ntv.com.tr/turkiye/nuri-bilge-ceylan-ile-90-dakika,4MGzhIzsmoKYVVtyk7sd9A (last accessed 1 October 2021).

7. See https://www.nytimes.com/2014/12/23/movies/winter-sleep-a-nuri-bilge-ceylan-take-on-turkish-life.html (last accessed 1 October 2021).
8. See https://www.crew-united.com/fr/Le-Poirier-sauvage__223199.html#!&tabctl_15249142_activeTab=1189721449 (last accessed 1 October 2021).
9. See https://boxofficeturkiye.com/haber/sinema-destekleme-kurulu-yeni-donemde-destek-alacak-filmleri-acikladi--2546 (last accessed 1 October 2021).
10. See https://www.dailysabah.com/arts/cinema/eurimages-fund-supports-turkish-director-nuri-bilge-ceylans-latest-movie (last accessed 1 October 2021).
11. See Table: Admissions in France & Turkey.
12. See Table: Admissions in France & Turkey.
13. Since the 2000s, the term 'Turkish Cinema' has evolved to 'Cinema of Turkey' to recognise the increasing contributions of the diverse nations and minorities of the country. (editor's note).
14. Figures are provided by *Allocine*, https://www.allocine.fr/article/fichearticle_gen_carticle=18636358.html and *Box Office Türkiye* https://boxofficeturkiye.com/ (last accessed 1 August 2021). Figures for *Winter Sleep* and *The Wild Pear Tree* are provided by Memento Distribution (Request for information regarding Nuri Bilge Ceylan films, e-mail, 2021).

CITED WORKS

Açar, Mehmet (2018), 'Bir memleket filmi', *Habertürk*. 3 June. https://www.haberturk.com/yazarlar/mehmet-acar/1998073-bir-memleket-filmi (last accessed 1 August 2021).
Allen, Michael Patrick and A. E. Lincoln (2004), 'Critical discourse and the cultural consecration of American films', *Social Forces* 82. 3: 871–94.
Andrews, David (2013), *Theorizing Art Cinemas: Foreign, Cult, Avant-Garde, and Beyond*. Austin: University of Texas Press.
Arslan, Tunca (1997), 'Kasaba: Puslu manzaralar', *Radikal*. 2 December. https://www.nuribilgeceylan.com/movies/kasaba/press_radikaltuncaarslan.php (last accessed 1 August 2021).
Aydemir, Şenay (2018), 'Ahlat Ağacı: Kör kuyularda . . .', *Gazete Duvar*, 1 June. https://www.gazeteduvar.com.tr/yazarlar/2018/06/01/ahlat-agaci-kor-kuyularda (last accessed 1 August 2021).
Aytaç, Senem (2011), 'Bir Zamanlar Anadolu'da Hakikat Kırıntıları', *Altyazı*, 110: 28–31.
Baran, Tanju (2018), 'Babalar ve Oğullar ve Rüyalar: Ahlat Ağacı', *Tersninja.com*. 3 June. http://www.tersninja.com/ahlatagaci (last accessed 1 August 2021).
Barnett, Michael L. and Michael Patrick Allen (2000), 'Social class, cultural repertoires, and popular culture: The case of film', *Sociological Forum* 15, 1:145–63.
Barrington, Matthew (2014), 'The Ethnographic Every day in the Cinema of Apichatpong Weerasethakul', *Cinea* 2. https://cinea.be/the-ethnographic-everyday-the-cinema-apichatpong-weerasethakul/ (last accessed 1 August 2021).
Baumann, Shyon (2001), 'Intellectualization and art world development: Film in the United States', *American Sociological Review* 66, 3: 404–26.
Bourdieu, Pierre (1993), *The Field of Cultural Production: Essays on Art and Literature*. New York: Columbia University Press.
Chow, Rey (1995), *Primitive Passions*. New York: Columbia University Press.
Çağlayan, Emre (2018), *Poetics of Slow Cinema: Nostalgia, Absurdism, Boredom*. Cham: Springer International Publishing.
Çapan, Sungu (1997), 'Hayat üstüne farklı bir film', *Cumhuriyet*. 5 December. https://www.nuribilgeceylan.com/movies/kasaba/press_cumhuriyetsungu.php (last accessed 1 August 2021).

Deslandes, Ghislain and Jocelyn Maixent (2012), 'Turkish Auteur Cinema and European Identity: Economic Influences on Aesthetic Issues', *Journal of European Popular Culture* 2, 1: 81–98.
Diken, Bülent, Graeme Gilloch and Craig Hammond (2020), *Nuri Bilge Ceylan Sineması: Türkiyeli Bir Sinemacının Küresel Hayal Gücü*, trans. Ahmet Nuvit Bingöl. Istanbul: Metis.
Dorsay, Atilla (1997), 'Yalnız şövalyenin yalın "amatör" filmi', *Yeni Yüzyıl Gazetesi*, 5 December. https://www.nuribilgeceylan.com/movies/kasaba/press_yeniyuzyilatilla.php (last accessed 1 August 2021).
Drake, P. (2008), 'Distribution and marketing in contemporary Hollywood', in McDonald, P. and Wasko, J. (eds), *The Contemporary Hollywood Film Industry*. Hoboken, NJ: Wiley-Blackwell, 63–82.
Dudai, Orit (2019), 'The Impossible Possible Narrative: The Quest for Truth in *Bir Zamanlar Anadolu'da/Once Upon a Time in Anatolia* (Nuri Bilge Ceylan, 2011)', *Studies in European Cinema*, November 7, 1–16.
Elsaesser, Thomas (2016), 'The Global Author: Control, Creative Constraints, and Performative Self-Contradiction', in S. Jeong and J. Szaniawski (eds), *The Global Auteur: The Politics of Authorship in 21st Century Cinema*. Bloomsbury Publishing USA. 21–42.
Erdem, Mehmet (1997), 'Nuri Bilge Ceylan ile Söyleşi: Piyasa Acımasız ve Demirden Yasalarla İşliyor!', *Antrakt Sinema Gazetesi*, 59 December, 19–25. http://www.nuribilgeceylan.com/movies/kasaba/press.php?mid=9 (last accessed 1 August 2021).
Erciyes, Cem (2015), 'Nuri Bilge'nin parkası ve Emin Alper', *Radikal*, 30 July. http://www.radikal.com.tr/yazarlar/cem-erciyes/nuri-bilgenin-parkasi-ve-emin-alper-1406183/ (last accessed 1 August 2021).
Foundas, Scott (2014), 'Nuri Bilge Ceylan on "Winter Sleep" and Learning to Love Boring Movies', *Variety.com*. http://variety.com/2014/film/features/nuri-bilge-ceylan-on-winter-sleep-and- learning-to-love-boring-movies-1201346563/ (last accessed 1 August 2021).
Günerbüyük, Çağdaş (2014), 'Uyanmak Başka Bahara', *Evrensel*, 13 June. https://www.evrensel.net/yazi/71559/uyanmak-baska-bahara (last accessed 1 August 2021).
Jeong, Seung-hoon and Jeremi Szaniawski, eds. (2016), 'Introduction', *The Global Auteur: The Politics of Authorship in 21st Century Cinema*. Bloomsbury Publishing USA, 1–18.
Kanzler Martin (2019), *Fiction film financing in Europe: A sample analysis of films released in 2017*, European Audiovisual Observatory, Strasbourg.
Karmaskalı, İsmail (2020), 'Soyu Kesik bir Cins Yönetmen: Yücel Çakmaklı', *Türkiye Notları* 2, 12: 15–20.
Kaya, Evrim (2014), 'Kış Uykusu', *Arka Pencere* 242, 13–19 June. 6–8.
Kickasola, Joseph (2016), 'Tracking the Fallen Apple: Ineffability, Religious Tropes, and Existential Despair in Nuri Bilge Ceylan's Once Upon a Time in Anatolia', *Journal of Religion & Film* 20, 1(13): 1–36.
Kuzu, Hüseyin (2021), 'Nedir Bu Sinemamızın "Türk Sineması Tarihi" Yazımından Çektiği?'http://www.kameraarkasi.org/makaleler/makaleler/nedirbusinemamizinturksinemasiyazimindancektigi.html (last accessed 1 August 2021).
Lane, Anthony (2019), 'The Beige Noir of "Serenity"', *The New Yorker*, 25 January. https://www.newyorker.com/magazine/2019/02/04/the-beige-noir-of-serenity (last accessed 1 August 2021).
Lemercier, Fabien (2008), 'Thunderrolls in Three Monkeys', *Cineuropa*,16 May. https://cineuropa.org/en/newsdetail/84228/ (last accessed 1 August 2021).
Lieb, Marie-Anne (2009), 'Le « huitième climat » ou l'ailleurs contemplatif dans le cinéma de Nuri Bilge Ceylan', *Double jeu*, 6: 55–62. http://journals.openedition.org/doublejeu/1409 (last accessed 1 August 2021).
Liktor, Coşkun (2014), 'Bir Türkiye Alegorisi Olarak "Kış Uykusu"', *Altyazı*, 25 August. https://altyazi.net/yazilar/elestiriler/bir-turkiye-alegorisi-olarak-kis-uykusu/ (last accessed 1 August 2021).

Mangez, Eric and Georges Liénard (2015), 'The field of power and the relative autonomy of social fields: the case of Belgium', in Mathieu Hilgers and Eric Mangez (eds), *Bourdieu's Theory of Social Fields: Concepts and Applications*. London and New York: Routledge, 183–98.

Mardin, Şerif (1973), 'Center-Periphery Relations: A Key to Turkish Politics?', *Daedalus* 102, 1: 169–90.

Mathew, Shaj (2019), 'Traveling Realisms, Shared Modernities, Eternal Moods: The Uses of Anton Chekhov in Nuri Bilge Ceylan's Winter Sleep', *Adaptation* 12, 1: 12–26.

Mitchell, Elvis (2003), 'Not Exactly Felix and Oscar, but an Odd Couple All the Same', *The New York Times*, 15 October. https://www.nytimes.com/2003/10/15/movies/film-festival-reviews-not-exactly-felix-and-oscar-but-an-odd-couple-all-the-same.html (last accessed 1 August 2021).

Özgentürk, Işıl (1998), 'Kasaba', *Cumhuriyet*, 1 November. https://www.nuribilgeceylan.com/movies/kasaba/press_cmhrytozgntrk.php (last accessed 1 August 2021).

Özgüven, Fatih (2014), 'Kış Uykusu: Her Şey Ölünce', *Radikal*, 12 June. http://www.radikal.com.tr/yazarlar/fatih-ozguven/kis-uykusu-her-sey-olunce-1196717/ (last accessed 1 August 2021).

Özgüven, Fatih (2018), 'Mayıs Sıkıntısı'na Dönüş', *Ekranella*. http://www.ekranella.com/ozel/mayis-sikintisi-na-donus (last accessed 1 August 2021).

Özkaracalar, Kaya (2018), 'Ahlat Ağacı: N.B. Ceylan'ın Memleketinden İnsan Manzaraları', *İleri* 2 June. https://ilerihaber.org/yazar/ahlat-agaci-nb-ceylanin-memleketinden-insan-manzaralari-86062.html (last accessed 1 August 2021).

Öztürk, S. Ruken (2007), 'Uzak/Distant' in Gönül Dönmez-Colin (ed), *The Cinema of North Africa and the Middle East*. London: Wallflower, 247–356.

Romney, Jonathan (2004), 'A Silky Sadness', *Sight & Sound*. 14, 6: 20–3.

Suner, Asuman (2011), 'A Lonely and Beautiful Country: Reflecting upon the State of Oblivion in Turkey through Nuri Bilge Ceylan's Three Monkeys', *Inter-Asia Cultural Studies* 12, 1: 13–27.

Staiger, Janet (1985), 'The Politics of Film Canons', *Cinema Journal*, 24, 3: 4–23.

Villalba, Nacho (2014), 'Nuri Bilge Ceylan . . . a examen', *Cinemaltido*, 12 October. https://www.cinemaldito.com/nuri-bilge-ceylan-a-examen/ (last accessed 1 August 2021).

Wei, Ti (2008), 'How did Hou Hsiao-Hsien change Taiwan cinema? A critical reassessment', *Inter-Asia Cultural Studies*, 9:2, 271–9.

Yaren Özgür, Irmak Karademir Hazır (2020), 'Critics, politics and cultural legitimation: An exploratory analysis of the Turkish film field', *European Journal of Cultural Studies*, 23, 4:611–29.

Zeydabadi-Nejad, S. (2007), 'Iranian Intellectuals and Contact with the West: The Case of Iranian Cinema', *British Journal of Middle Eastern Studies*, 34, 3: 375–98.

Zıraman, Zehra Cerrahoğlu (2019), 'European Co-productions and film style: Nuri Bilge Ceylan', *Studies in European Cinema* 16, 1: 73–89.

Index

absence(s), 4, 12, 20, 33; *see also* individual films
 aesthetics of, 92–4
 architectural landmarks, 76
 dialogue/speech, 115, 123, 135, 172
 frames of, 90, 91
 and presence(s), 8, 85, 99, 169
 and space, 12, 79, 85, 86, 87, 89, 92, 93; *see also* space
 women, 87, 93, 169, 174, 182n
Agamben, Giorgio, 112–13, 136
Ahlat Ağacı/The Wild Pear Tree (2018), 2, 3, 4, 5, 6, 9, 10, 11, 13, 20, 24, 25, 52, 69, 71, 124, 136–7, 174, 193, 194, 196
 boredom, 154
 humiliated father, 153–7
 identity crisis, crisis, 147–9
 intermediality, 162
 longing for the father, 159–60; *see also* Freud
 masculinities in in crisis, 154–65, 180
 Oedipus complex, 164–5
 patricide and filicide, 153, 161–2
 politics of, 20, 159–60
 women, 168, 169, 180–1

alienation, 4, 20, 108, 110, 136, 171
 Kış Uykusu/Winter Sleep, 107
 Koza/Cocoon, 19
 Üç Maymun/Three Monkeys, 81
Anderson, Benedict
 imagined community, 42
Antonioni, Michelangelo, 12, 40, 63, 88–9, 171, 178
 'incommunicability trilogy', 54, 86, 89
 prediegetic/postdiegetic, 89, 100
 presence of architecture, 63; *see also* Bruno
auteur(ism), 186–99
autonomous camera, 28–9

Balázs, Béla,
 close-up, 51, 56–61
 İklimler/The Climates, 62
Barthes, Roland
 Camera Lucida: Reflections on Photography (1981), 97
 narrative, 41
 notion of 'myth', 169
 photographic image, 98
Baudrillard, Jean,
 simulacrum, 3
Bazin André, 29, 162
 realism, 60, 69

Benjamin, Walter, 110
  experience, 39
  memory, voluntary and involuntary, 39–40
Bergson, Henry
  pure memory, 39
  recollection-images, 8
Bir Zamanlar Anadolu'da/Once Upon a Time in Anatolia (2011), 2–3, 4, 84–7, 92–100, 111–14
  absence, 92–100, 107, 110
  boredom, 110, 111
  Chekhov, 105
  identity, 87, 178
  masculinities in crisis, 177
  politics, 113
  spectral present, 85, 98–9, 100
  women, 93, 168, 177–8
Blanchot, Maurice,
  'everyday escapes', 42
boredom, 33, 135, 149, 196; *see also* individual films
Bourdieu, Pierre, 2, 15n
  cultural legitimation, 188
Brazilian Cinema Novo/New Wave, 24, 33
Bruno, Giuliana
  motion and emotion in cinema, 61
  presence of architecture in cinema, 63; *see also* Antonioni
Butler, Judith, 13, 181–2

Cannes Film Festival, 187, 190
Ceylan, Nuri Bilge
  autobiographical elements/tone, 29, 37–8, 54–5, 86, 109, 142, 152, 174, 189
  Cannes, 1, 4, 14, 16n, 35n, 42, 49n, 75, 76, 86, 89, 119, 120, 122, 189, 190, 191, 193–4, 198
  cinematic influences of, 12, 13, 21, 86, 99, 199
  intermediality, 55, 60–5
  intertextuality, 10, 12, 174
  photography, 2, 12, 51, 54–55, 59–61, 63–5, 69, 97–9

  politics, 4, 14, 29, 70–2, 119–20
  reception, 13–14, 71–2, 86, 120, 186, 189–99
  recognition, 14, 86, 189–194
  self-reflexivity, 2, 15, 21, 37–8, 39, 135
  social and political context, 7, 12–13, 24, 46, 69–77, 88, 119–133, 136, 149, 156–7, 160, 172, 196–8
  subtractive aesthetics, 103, 106
  transnational filmmaker, 7, 19–20, 103–4, 186, 194
Chatman, Seymour
  on prediegetic/postdiegetic space, 89, 92; *see also* Antonioni
  separate reality, 90, 104
Chekhov, Anton, 13,103, 104, 108, 113, 116, 125, 136, 175, 198; *see also* individual films
  'The Cherry Orchard', 106, 193
  'Excellent People', 105, 106, 125, 193
  'Perpetuum Mobile', 105
  'The Wife', 105, 114, 115, 123, 193
Cioffi, Angelo
  on dimensions of political cinema, 130–1
class(es), 2, 20, 30, 42–4, 46, 68, 73, 86, 122, 125, 127, 137, 143, 146–7, 148, 160, 177, 188, 197
  affective register of, 43

Çağlayan, Emre, 13, 135, 171–2, 189; see also slow cinema

Davis, Glyn
  photographs as referents, 99; *see also* Laura Mulvey and Apichatpong Weerasethakul
Deleuze, Gilles
  'affection image(s)', 51, 57–60; *see also Üç Maymun/Three Monkeys*
  cinema 'of the seer', 71
  classical cinema/modern cinema, 46–7
  close-up as Entity, 58–60
  contested territory, 74
  de-territorialization/re-territorialization, 113

interactions, 148–9
movement image/time-image, 8, 25, 68–9, 71, 103, 110, 135
recollection images, 21
repetitions, 9, 105
speech acts, 148
Demirkubuz, Zeki, 1, 11, 174, 189, 193, 195
Derrida, Jacques, 48n, 85, 94, 97, 100,
  spectrality, 85, 97
Diaz, Lav Indigo, 12, 109, 111
dominant narratives, 20, 34, 169
Dostoyevsky, Fyodor, 11, 104, 111, 116
Dönmez-Colin, 34n, 52, 54, 80, 85, 135, 171
dramaturgical approach/theory, 137, 138

Epstein, Jean
  close-up, 56
  photogénie, 56
Erdoğan, Recep Tayyip, 120–1, 160, 191, 197
  authoritarianism, 120, 126, 133, 199
  Justice and Development Party (Adalet ve Kalkınma Partisi; AKP), 69, 70, 121, 122, 194
Eurimages, 191, 192, 193, 195

Farhadi, Asghar
  Jodaeiye Nader az Simin/A Separation (2011), 127
Foucault, Michel
  memory without recollection, 40
Freud, Sigmund
  on primal scene, 38–9
  on the longing for the father, 159–60
  on the primal father, 158

Gezi movement/protests, 75, 121, 122, 160
Güney (Pütün), Yılmaz, 6–7, 9, 33, 46, 129
Gürbilek, Nurdan, 107, 136, 149, 154, 156–7

Hong Sang-soo, 12, 172, 174
  Claire's Camera (2017), 173

identity, 2, 4, 13, 38, 70–1, 85–6, 104, 109, 135, 137, 170; *see also* individual films
  crisis of, 15n, 147–9, 172
  national, 154, 156–7, 192, 193
Italian neo-realism, 24

İklimler/The Climates (2006), 2, 4, 5, 6, 10, 21, 25, 37, 51–65, 86, 136, 170, 178, 181, 182, 191, 199
  absence, 60, 73, 79
  identity, 108
  Kuleshov effect, 56, 87, 98
  masculinities in crisis, 172–5, 176
  'moving portraits', 51, 59–62
  photography, painting and film, 51, 54–5, 59–60, 61, 65

Jameson, Fredric, 27
  'allegorical resonance', 157
Junior, Oliveira, 51, 59

Kasaba / The Small Town (1997), 4, 5, 8, 10, 26, 27, 29, 31, 32–3, 37–8, 52, 135, 136, 137, 152, 153, 154, 158, 168, 169, 170, 189, 195–6
  identity, 19, 21
Kış Uykusu/Winter Sleep (2014), 2, 3, 4, 5, 11, 20, 25, 72, 103–10, 114–16, 119–33, 136, 137, 138–44, 148, 152, 193, 199
  allegory/metaphor, 149, 196–7
  anomalous category, 144
  boredom, 115, 149, 154
  Chekhov, 11, 105–7, 114, 115, 123, 133, 178, 193
  cinempathy, 127; *see also* Sinnerbrink
  emotional allegiances, 132
  historical and political context of release, 120–4
  identity, 107, 180
  not resisting evil, 125–6
  politics, 122, 129–33
  subtitles, 123, 127–8
  women, 168, 169, 170, 172, 173, 178–9, 193

Kiarostami, Abbas, 8, 9, 12, 16n, 28, 72, 86, 109, 190, 192, 196
  Bad Mara Khahad Bord/The Wind Will Carry Us (1999), 9, 111
  Dah/Ten (2002), 178
  Gozareh/The Report (1977), 174–5, 183n
  Tam-e Gilas/Taste of Cherry (1997), 174
Koza/Cocoon (1995), 3, 5, 8, 9, 19, 24, 27, 39–40, 41, 51, 52, 54, 137, 178, 189
Kuru Otlar Üstüne/About Dry Grasses (2023), 21, 193

Lacan, Jacques, 153, 158, 159, 160–5
  imaginary father, 163
  introjection, 164
  Name-of-the-Father, 158
  paternal imago, 163–4
  phallus, 163
  symbolic order, 158, 165
Latour, Bruno, 103
  concept of the network, 104

male subjectivity, 180–2
Marks, Laura
  'intercorporeal relationship', 14
Márquez, Gabriel Garcia
  Cien años de soledad/One Hundred Years of Solitude (1967), 11, 16n, 26
Martel, Lucrecia, 12, 90
  La mujer sin cabeza/The Headless Woman (2008), 89–90
  on politics and cinema, 88
masculinity, 171–2, 176, 180
  performances, 137
  phallic, 171
Mayıs Sıkıntısı/Clouds of May (1999), 2, 4, 6, 9, 10, 16n, 19, 21, 24, 26–9, 31, 33, 34n, 38, 52, 69, 70, 71, 110, 137, 146, 152, 153, 154, 158, 174, 189, 199
  absence, 27, 60
  identity, 48n
  boredom, 26
  women, 169–70

Mead, George Herbert, 85, 94–7, 100
  specious present, 85, 95–7, 99
memory, 20, 21, 25, 37, 41, 47, 48n, 63, 78, 87, 88, 95, 100, 137, 149
  site (lieux de mémoire), 3
  voluntary /involuntary, 39, 59
  without recollection, 39–40; see also Foucault
modernity, 2, 13, 26, 62, 103, 104, 107, 108, 110, 116n, 121, 140, 160, 179, 182, 193
  belated, 149
modernisation, 140, 147, 149, 159, 197
Mohaghegh, Jason Bahbak, 73
  'eastern thought', 68,
  Iranian new wave poetic tradition, 71
  'the radical unspoken', 69, 71–2
Mulvey, Laura, 61, 69, 98, 169
  death drive, 76
  on use of still images, 99; see also Davis

Naficy, Hamid, 109
  An Accented Cinema, 37–8
narrative silences, 12, 71, 76
national allegories, 157, 196, 198
New German Cinema, 24
New Turkish Cinema/New Cinema of Turkey, 1, 14, 70–1, 108, 195

Orient, 113
Oriental, 156, 159, 162
Orientalism, 149, 156
  and Turkish national identity, 157
Ottoman Empire, 106, 159
Ozu Yasujirō, 5, 8, 12, 32, 86, 109

Özal, Turgut, 30

Palme d'Or, 1, 49n, 122, 194
Pamuk, Orhan, 14, 191–2
  Kırmızı Saçlı Kadın/The Red-Haired Woman (2016), 162
Panahi, Jafer, 28–9, 192
  Ayneh/The Mirror (1997), 28

Parajanov, Sergei
  Sayat Nova/The Colour of Pomegranates (1968), 10
paternal imago, 163; *see also* Lacan
  Ahlat Ağacı / The Wild Pear Tree, 164
patricide, 158, 162; *see also* filicide
  in *Oedipus Rex*, 162
  in *The Red-Haired Woman*, 162
performance(s), 48n, 55, 64, 123, 139, 147, 148, 174
  imitation, 140–4
  interiorised, 88
  of relationships, 137–42
  staged, 114, 137
Pethő, Ágnes, 63
  intermediality, 64–5, 64n,162
  presence of architecture in cinema, 63, *see also* Antonioni
point zero, 24, 32–4
political cinema, 46, 119–33
  in Turkey, 129, 133

Rancière, Jacques, 20, 34n, 64, 74, 76, 78, 79, 183n
  'politico-cinematic approach', 69
Russian realism, 106

Schultz, Corey,
  moving portraits, 51, 59–60
Shakespeare, William, 3, 103–5, 106, 107, 108, 115, 116, 123, 133, 139, 142
Sinnerbrink, Robert,
  cinempathy, 127; *see also Kış Uykusu / Winter Sleep*
slow cinema, 34, 40–1, 68, 110, 115, 129, 135, 183n
Soma, 120–1, 122
space
  absence, 79, 84, 86, 90, 92
  aesthetics, 30, 84, 88
  homosocial, 174, 180
  interstitial, 78
  paradoxical, 137
  prediegetic/postdiegetic, 89, 92, 100
  spectral, 76

'Third Space of enunciation' (Bhabha, 1994), 31
spectrality, 94–8; *see also* Derrida and titles of individual films
speech-act
  Uzak/Distant, 45
  Üç Maymun/Three Monkeys, 76, 80
Spivak, Gayatri Chakravoty, 49n, 71
subtitles, 123, 127

Tarkovsky, Andrei, 8–9, 12, 21, 24, 25, 31–2, 86
  Andrei Rublev (1966), 29
  Ivanovo detstvo/Ivan'sChildhood (1962), 10
  Stalker (1979), 8
  Zerkalo/Mirror (1975), 8
Tarr, Béla
  'geographies of indifference', 34
  Sátántangó (1994), 24
  slow cinema, 40, 196
temporality, 20, 21, 103–4
  Barthes, 97–8
  cinema portraits, 59–60
  cinema's, 59–61
  Kasaba/The Small Town, 21, 25
  Non-affirmative, 80
  theories, 85, 98
  Üç Maymun/Three Monkeys, 80
transfuge(s) [*de classe*], 2, 5, 15n, 20
transnational, 7–8, 103
  aesthetics of contemplation, 108–11
  approaches, 1; *see also* New Turkish Cinema
  cinema, 109–11
  indistinctions, *Bir Zamanlar Anadolu'da/Once Upon a Time in Anatolia* and
  Kış Uykusu/Winter Sleep, 103–16
  narrative(s), 2, 114,
Tsai Ming-Liang, 40, 109
  He Liu/The River (Taiwan, 1997), 10

Turkey
　authoritarianism, 120, 199
　authoritarian populism, 133, 199
　domestic politics, 121
　history, 14, 159, 189, 191
　political culture, 121, 123

Uzak/Distant (2002), 2, 4, 5, 6, 7, 8, 10, 11, 12, 14, 20, 21, 24, 25, 27, 29–32, 33, 37–47, 52, 137, 146, 153, 154
　absence, 171
　finitude, 40–1
　identity, 30–2, 49n, 170
　international recognition of, 189–90, 199
　masculinities in crisis, 170–2
　women, 19, 30, 31, 49n, 168, 169, 170–2, 173, 174, 175, 177, 178, 181–2

Üç Maymun/Three Monkeys (2008)
　absence, 7, 73, 76, 79, 86–92, 94–5, 99, 107
　affection-images, 57, 60; *see also* Deleuze
　identity, 87
　masculinities in crisis, 175–6
　non-affirmative time-image(s,) 73, 76, 77–81
　politics, 7, 69, 70, 73–7, 81
　sound and image, 73, 78

spectral present, 85, 98, 100
spectrality, 79–80
woman, 168, 176–7, 182n

Weerasethakul, Apichatpong, 109, 190
　still images, 99
Williams, Raymond, 43–4, 49n
　class difference, 43
　knowable community, 43
women, 169–170, 183n; *see also* individual films
　'double bind' 177
　childless, 170
　presentation of, 182
　status, 171
　weeping, 5, 181–2

Yeşilçam cinema, 7, 34, 152, 172, 187, 195
　melodramas, 6, 8, 33, 182
　Ahlat Ağacı/The Wild Pear Tree, 6, 180
　Kış Uykusu/Winter Sleep, 178
　Üç Maymun/Three Monkeys, 6, 7

Zhang Yimou
　Da hong deng long gao gua/Raise the Red Lantern (PRC, 1991), 10
Zhangke, Jia
　Ershisi cheng ji/24 City (2008), 59
　spectrality, 79–80

EU representative:
Easy Access System Europe
Mustamäe tee 50, 10621 Tallinn, Estonia
Gpsr.requests@easproject.com

www.ingramcontent.com/pod-product-compliance
Lightning Source LLC
Chambersburg PA
CBHW051123160426
43195CB00014B/2322